Q

2014

WARRIORS
OF THE SKY

WARRIORS OF THE SKY

Springbok Air Heroes In Combat

Peter Bagshawe

SUFFOLK COUNTY COUNCIL	
06748337	
Bertrams	17.03.06
940.5449	£19.99
712570	

Pen & Sword
AVIATION

First published in South Africa in 1990 by
Ashanti Publishing (Pty) Ltd

Published in Great Britian in this format in 2006 by
Pen & Sword Aviation
An imprint of
Pen & Sword Books Ltd
47 Church Street
Barnsley
South Yorkshire
S70 2AS

Copyright © Peter Bagshawe, 1990, 2006

ISBN 1 84415 337 1

Printed and bound in England
By CPI UK

Pen & Sword Books Ltd incorporates the Imprints of
Pen & Sword Aviation, Pen & Sword Maritime, Pen & Sword Military,
Wharncliffe Local history, Pen & Sword Select, Pen & Sword Military
Classics and Leo Cooper.

For a complete list of Pen & Sword titles please contact
PEN & SWORD BOOKS LIMITED
47 Church Street, Barnsley, South Yorkshire, S70 2AS, England
E-mail: enquiries@pen-and-sword.co.uk
Website: www.pen-and-sword.co.uk

Eric Ben Horton Impey,
killed over Warsaw, 16-17 August 1944

An Airman's Prayer

My God, this night I have to fly,
And ere I leave the ground,
I come with reverence to Thy Throne
Where perfect peace is found.

I thank Thee for the life I've had,
For home and all its love,
I thank Thee for the faith I have
That cometh from above.

Come with me now into the air,
Be with me as I fly,
Guide Thou each move that I shall make
Way up there - in the sky.

Be with me at the target, Lord,
When danger's at its height
Be with me as I drop my load
And on the homeward flight.

And should it be my time to die,
Be with me to the end,
Help me to die a Christian's death,
On Thee, God, I depend.

Then as I leave this mortal frame
From human ties set free,
Receive my soul, O God of love,
I humbly come to THEE.

All the stories in this book were edited by Peter Bagshawe except three of which he is the author.

Content:

Introduction

This book, with its stirring Foreword by the famous 'Laddie' Lucas, and its crowded battle reminiscences of so many distinguished Air Force men, will quicken the heart-beat of those of you 'who were there' and will fan the glow of pride you must feel in being a member of the Air Force family. The book is also sure to capture the imagination of those of you of later generations who are interested in Air Force lore.

A striking feature in these tales of brave men is the closeness of the SAAF to the RAF and the other Commonwealth Air Forces during World War II. Thousands of RAF personnel served in the Empire Air Training Scheme in South Africa. At the same time many members of the RAF, the RCAF, the RAAF and the RNZAF were seconded to SAAF squadrons in the field, and vice versa. In my squadron alone there were air crews and ground personnel from each of the other Commonwealth Air Forces. Conversely, large numbers of SAAF members, mainly air crew, served on secondment, particularly to the RAF, to say nothing of the many South Africans who enlisted directly in the 'Mother Air Force'.

A few years ago, in Australia, my wife and I ran into the Douglas Baders. We were staying in the same hotel. I had only met him twice before, on his rare visits to South Africa after the War. On this occasion he asked us to dine with him. The other guests were John Waddy and his wife, whom we then met for the first and only time. John had been a Group Captain in the RAAF and finished the War with a DSO and a DFC. He later turned to politics, and became a member of the New South Wales Cabinet. No sooner had we met, than John reeled off the names of a string of SAAF fighter pilots whom he had met in the Western Desert, and he added: 'You of the SAAF and we of the RAAF are as blood brothers'. That mirrored my own sentiments perfectly.

After World War II came the Korean War, when No. 2 Fighter Squadron of the SAAF forged new links, particularly with the United States Air Force. There was a time when the United States Air Force Group, in which 2 Squadron served, required that on ceremonial occasions the opening bars of our national anthem be played before the American anthem. This gesture was a mark of its admiration for the achievements of our Squadron.

These bonds with the RAF and the other Commonwealth Air Forces, and more latterly with the USAF, are part of the imperishable traditions of the SAAF.

Since those days further annals have been written in the history of our Air Force. In the Border War, the SAAF fought alone, against advanced versions of Soviet aircraft and weaponry, and against what was then the most sophisticated and powerful network of ground to air defences ever assembled beyond the borders of the Soviet Union. Once again the SAAF came out on top and wrote a further saga of courage, devotion to duty, skill and resourcefulness, which qualities are the hallmark of the Air Force.

I count it a very special privilege to have been invited, through this introduction, to pay tribute to the men and women of the SAAF, to the air crews, to the boffins, the technical specialists and ground crews, and to the superb leadership, indeed to all of you who have helped to weave the inspiring story of the SAAF, of which the chapters of this book are such a magnificent part.

C S Margo
Johannesburg
1990

Acknowledgements

My sincere thanks to all contributors to this exciting collection of wartime operational flying experiences and for sharing them with my readers. A special thank you to Charles Barry and A Q de Wet for their valuable assistance, and to the Director of SAAF Public Relations, Col L E Weyer, for his co-operation.

The introduction to this book by the Hon Mr Justice Cecil Margo is greatly appreciated. Apart from his exceptional achievements in the legal profession, Cecil was a distinguished pilot and leader in World War II. He commanded the celebrated 24 Squadron SAAF.

I am grateful to Laddie Lucas, the distinguished fighter leader, politician, businessman, sportsman and author, for his foreword. It was Laddie's expertise as editor of a number of books comprising the individual accomplishments of Allied airmen in World War II which influenced me to initiate this project embracing the adventures of South African airmen who played a dynamic role in three wars since 1939. The Border War contributors have shown beyond any doubt that they are equally as courageous and skilful as their predecessors and I salute them.

My thanks to Major-General Jimmy Durrant for his postscript. All South Africans who fought in World War II will remember Jimmy as a brilliant group leader. At the end of the war he was the youngest Major-General in the Allied forces and had Japan not surrendered, he was destined for higher command and greater achievement. He was the only SAAF officer to be awarded the CB.

Finally, I gratefully acknowledge the priceless role played by my wife Gill towards the production of this book, not only with her tireless work on the word processor, but also with her realistic criticism and suggestions.

Peter Bagshawe
Durban 1990.

ALLIED FORCE HEADQUARTERS

April, 1945

SPECIAL ORDER OF THE DAY

Soldiers, Sailors and Airmen of the Allied Forces in the Mediterranean Theatre

Final victory is near. The German Forces are now very groggy and only need one mighty punch to knock them out for good. The moment has now come for us to take the field for the last battle which will end the war in Europe. You know what our comrades in the West and in the East are doing on the battlefields. It is now our turn to play our decisive part. It will not be a walk-over; a mortally wounded beast can still be very dangerous. You must be prepared for a hard and bitter fight; but the end is quite certain — there is not the slightest shadow of doubt about that. You, who have won every battle you have fought, are going to win this last one.

Forward then into battle with confidence, faith and determination to see it through to the end. Godspeed and good luck to you all.

H. R. Alexander

Field-Marshal,
Supreme Allied Commander,
Mediterranean Theatre.

World War II Spitfire in Battle of Britain.

P B 'Laddie' Lucas CBE, DSO, DFC.

Foreword

A September evening in 1985 in Guildhall in the city of London. Some 700 members of the UK's famous Aircrew Association, their ladies and their guests, are at the end of a finely-appointed banquet... Spirits are running high as befits a splendid Royal Air Force occasion dominated by well-decorated 'veterans' of the air campaigns of World War II... All the old commands and theatres are represented... The collective experience is very wide... In the mellow afterglow of brandy and cigars the speeches are about to begin...

The master of ceremonies, in red tail-coat, stiff shirt, white tie and waistcoat, erect and suitably haughty, hammers the old striking block four times - decisively - with his gavel. The noise in the centuries-old hall which, forty-five years before had stood up defiantly to the Nazi onslaught, falls away. Chris Foxley-Norris - Air Chief Marshal Sir Christopher Foxley-Norris - still an upright, commanding figure, offers the customary toasts from the Chair. Then he invites the defence representatives of the various overseas embassies in London to stand in turn and identify themselves as their countries are called. Each is warmly applauded as memories of wartime endeavour flow back...

Now it is the turn of the South African defence staff's representative from the embassy in Trafalgar Square, an officer of the South African Air Force, to stand and take a bow. As he gets to his feet, the great gathering erupts as one into a full-throated roar of welcome... The applause takes moments to subside...

Sir Chris, with a Wykehamist's sense of propriety and good manners, pauses tellingly to give the meaning of this reaction adequate time to sink in. He knows as well as anyone else in the hall - and perhaps better - the significance of the welcome... Against the inconsistencies and paradoxes of modern international politics, it is the UK's salute to the example of the South African Air Force, to its unforgettable contribution to victory in the Desert, in Malta, Sicily and Italy and elsewhere forty-odd years before, and to the imperishable memory of the Republic's favourite sons who travelled individually to England in the late 1930s, joined the Royal Air Force, mostly on short-service commis-

'Sailor' Malan.

sions, and, when war came, achieved greatness... It is a transparent demonstration of true 'gut-feeling'...

Peter Bagshawe's collection of first-hand recollections and experiences confirms the substance behind Guildhall's echoes. Here, gathered in one volume, are the intimate reflections of members of a service whose contribution to victory over Nazi Germany matched anything that any of the Allied air forces could muster.

It is well for the record that Peter should have edited the work. As an Englishman, his own decorated service with the Royal Air Force in World War II, first during a long operational spell based in the U K and, later, in the Italian campaign flying Kittyhawks and P-51D Mustangs alongside his South African counterparts, gave him a solid and quite impartial base upon which to form personal judgements. In 239 Wing in Italy in 1944-45 and particularly during his command of 250 Squadron, he saw the SAAF (its groundcrews as well as its aircrews) as it really was - a dedicated, utterly dependable and rugged entity whose operators played it hard but who also brought to the daily task a spirited humour which set them apart.

The contributors to this collection who served in World War II, the Korean and Border wars, are numbered among the Service's elite; their reminiscences expose their quality. But for those who experienced such worth at first hand - as, indeed, I did in the Malta battle in 1942 even among ordinary squadron members - the evidence of these pages serves happily to refresh pristine memories which will never die.

Courage, precision and aggression were essential prerequisites of successful wartime flying. But there was another attribute which separated the outstanding leaders from the rest - judgement. The South African leaders in the Royal Air Force had it in abundance and this they shared with their SAAF counterparts. The names come tumbling down; Hannes Faure, Bert Rademan, Kalfie Martin, Doug Loftus, Piet Hugo, Sailor Malan, to cite but a few. All had their fair share of this priceless commodity, but none possessed it in more distinct measure than Sailor Malan whom many will argue was Fighter Command's most comprehensively accomplished squadron and wing leader in the first half of World War II.

I remember a story - a little-known tale - which Douglas Bader once told me when I was in the throes of writing a biography about the legless marvel. It exemplifies my point.

It was late summer of 1941. Douglas was then leading the Tangmere Wing and Sailor Malan the one at Biggin Hill.

They were, in fact the first two wing leaders to be appointed in March 1941, when the post of Wing Commander Flying was initially established in Fighter Command. The squadrons had gone over to the offensive and, in C-in-C Sholto Douglas's graphic phrase, were now 'leaning out over France'. The sweeps across the Channel, escorting small forces of medium bombers, were in full swing, the aim being to provoke the Luftwaffe squadrons in occupied Europe into battle.

Sailor's Biggin Wing, like Bader's at Tangmere, was in the thick of it. But by then, with all the earlier fighting over Dunkirk followed by the rigours of the Battle of Britain, tiredness was beginning to overtake some of the most active leaders. They had had a basinful. Sailor, with his rare judgement and sensitivity, recognised, that for him, exhaustion was very close.

I doubt whether there was another leader in Fighter Command at that time who would have had the prescience or the guts to do what he then did. With upwards of thirty victories and heaven knows how many operational hours standing to his credit - and with all the glamour of the publicity which then surrounded him - he sought, off his own bat, a private meeting with Leigh-Mallory. Face to face, he confided in his AOC the truth - that he felt worn out and must go off for a rest. Who else would have had the courage to admit it even if he knew it to be the case?

L-M, to his immense credit, instantly acknowledged the great South African's premise and took him off operations there and then. The next day he sent for Bader. 'Douglas,' he said, 'I want to tell you privately that Sailor feels he is overtired and must take a rest. He thinks that if he were to go on it could start to impair his leading.'

'Now, you have had the same stomachful of fighting as Sailor - Dunkirk, the Battle of Britain and now some five months of leading the Tangmere Wing on sweeps. Tell me honestly, do you feel you're getting to the end of the line?'

Bader's reaction was as predictable as it was typical. 'No sir,' he replied at once, 'I still feel fine with plenty of fight left. The Wing is going well with the squadrons working closely together and there's still much good shooting to be had over France. I'd like, if I may, to see the season out and then stand down in the autumn when the weather begins to change...'

Leigh-Mallory accepted the answer at its face value and let Douglas stay on.

A short while later, on 9 August 1941, Bader was shot down, his Spitfire VB being felled by Oberfeldwebel Max Mayer in a Messerschmitt 109F from one of the staffeln in Jagdgeschwader 26 based in the Pas-de-Calais. Nearly four years as a prisoner of war were to follow, three of them spent in Colditz. Was Leigh-Mallory right to allow himself to be swayed by Douglas's enthusiastic persuasion? It's anyone's guess.

What is undeniable in these exchanges is that Sailor Malan's mature judgement - and his manifest honesty - dictated, for him, the right course. No one could have been more aggressive than he and none more successful. But he had the sense and the mental discipline to balance natural 'press on' spirit against the limits of the human frame.

Come to think of it, wasn't this a characteristic of South African leadership? Read the stories which follow and see.

'Laddie' Lucas
South Kensington
London SW7
1990

Douglas Rogan

A Fair Share of Adventure

As a youth I always yearned for adventure. World War II brought me more than a fair share when three dramatic occasions were engraved in my memory.

Disaster While Tank Busting

Towards the end of November 1941, General Rommel planned to surround the Eighth Army in the Tobruk/Sidi Rezegh area. When his intention became obvious, the Desert Air Force was called upon to provide every available aircraft to help counter the threat.

During the late afternoon of the 23rd, I was strafing a column of tanks with 2 Squadron SAAF, when an enemy shell ripped through my Tomahawk's cockpit almost severing my right leg just below the knee and lacerating my right arm and left thigh.

While heading back towards friendly territory, blood was spurting profusely from the leg and in sheer desperation I thrust the parachute strap and buckle into the joint linking leg and body, a measure helping to stem the flow of blood.

My initial intention was to lob the aircraft down amongst our forward troops, but then it occurred to me that without timeous medical attention, the chance of survival would be minimal. Consequently there was no other alternative than to make for 2 Squadron's base at Maddalena.

My senses began to reel from the loss of blood and it appeared inevitable that my life would soon be terminated in a holocaust of flesh and burning metal as my Tomahawk ploughed into the ground. Suddenly I remembered the water bottle which pilots were obliged to carry in case of a forced landing. This item undoubtedly saved my life, for after pouring water over my head and down my parched throat, I was sufficiently refreshed to remain conscious until a safe landing was made at Maddalena.

There was no question of saving my leg and it was duly amputated. Our legendary sweep leader, Lawrie Wilmot, bade me farewell on my

Doug Rogan.

departure for South Africa promising to promote my return to operations, a promise firing my determination to fly again. If Douglas Bader could fly without any legs, I could do likewise with one, and so, within twelve months I became reasonably versatile on a wooden leg. Lawrie's promise was fulfilled, and on the anniversary of the day my leg was lost, I returned to operations in the Western Desert.

This time, I joined the celebrated 1 Squadron flying Spitfires, and was fortunate enough to take part in many glorious operations while helping the top scoring fighter squadron to clear the African, Maltese and Sicilian skies of enemy aircraft.

An Uninvited Passenger

During December 1942, I was involved in a scrap with some ME 109s over Marble Arch and my Spitfire was holed in several places. As a result of this damage, I was obliged to fly the aircraft to the repair base at Agedabia. Along the route lay Timini airfield where my brother was stationed with a bomber squadron, so I decided to break my flight and spend an evening with him.

Rain fell during the night and the taxi track was wet and slippery in the morning, making it advisable for someone to ride on my Spit's tailplane while taxiing, acting as ballast to prevent a nose over. On reaching the runway I observed the human ballast spring clear so opened the throttle and took off noticing with alarm when airborne, that the controls were not handling normally and the aircraft was flying tail heavy.

Glancing in the rearview mirror, I was horrified to observe an RAF mechanic clinging frantically to the tailplane. No doubt two men had decided to act as ballast and one of them had failed to hop off in time. I observed this phenomenon with a mixed sensation of utter disbelief, horror and fear. It was no hallucination or ghostly figure but a living human being; and the uninvited passenger had to be deposited safely back on the runway!

Reducing speed, I flew gently around the circuit with bated breath and the feeling of relief was overwhelming when the wheels of my Spitfire touched the runway with the mechanic in a state of rigor mortis but still clinging frantically to the tailplane.

Several stories have been written about this extraordinary occurrence. I have been quoted as saying that on looking in the rearview mirror, I saw the mechanic perched on the tailplane like a monkey on top of a pole, a terrified expression on his face, eyes closed and per-

Fred Cottingham's position on the Spitfire's tail.

3

spiration pouring down his cheeks. This was an exaggeration, because Yorkshireman Fred Cottingham was lying on his stomach, his backside facing the slipstream and that part of his anatomy certainly wasn't happy!

Fred jumped off the tailplane, staggered along to the cockpit where I was battling to extricate myself, and croaked 'Are you alright, sir?' 'Hell's teeth,' I replied with astonishment. 'What do you mean, am I alright? What about yourself?' 'Well sir, I'm OK. The slipstream kept me pinned down but I don't think I could have stayed there for more than a hundred miles!'

Several hours later shock set in and poor Fred was carted away to a casualty clearing station. I wasn't, however, allowed to leave Timini before signing a certificate to the effect that LAC Fred Cottingham RAF had flown on a Spitfire's tail!

The Demise of two Spitfires

No 1 Squadron returned to its home base one afternoon from an operation in the Agheila area to find a raging dust storm blotting out the airstrip. All we pilots could do was to land individually at safe intervals.

When my turn came to land, the dust was exceptionally thick and the visibility almost nil. After touching down safely and while battling to keep straight along the airstrip, I was confronted by another Spitfire immediately ahead. It all happened so quickly in the limited visibility, that avoiding action was impossible and my Spitfire literally climbed on top of the other becoming totally entangled.

Doug Rogan and Derrick Gilson escaped without a scratch.

Both aircraft were smoking and I battled to extricate myself from the cockpit, bent on assisting the pilot who I believed was in the mangled cockpit of the Spitfire beneath. Suddenly one of the pilots who had flown on the operation, Derrick Gilson, appeared through the dust and asked whether he could help me. 'Bloody hell,' I yelled at him in a highly exasperated manner, 'pull the pilot out of the other Spit. Both these aircraft will go up in flames at any moment.' 'But I'm the pilot from that aircraft,' stuttered Derrick. 'My Spit's left front wheel was stuck in the sand. I had jumped out of the cockpit and was endeavouring to free it when your Spit rudely whipped it out of my hands!'

Two lucky pilots celebrated their survival in the mess that evening, but the Spits were a total write off.

Tailpiece

Doug was known as South Africa's Douglas Bader. He shot down three enemy aircraft and was credited with two probables. He was decorated with the DSO for determination, courage and devotion to duty of the highest order. Sadly his two brothers, Mackenzie and Harold, who both fought with SAAF bomber squadrons, lost their lives on operations in the Desert and Italy respectively. Doug lives in Margate, Natal.

A downed ME 110 in the desert.

A Couple of Brilliant Leeches

As the observer in David Liddell's crew, I was fortunate enough to join 24 Squadron just in time for the battle of Gazala and the long retreat back to El Alamein. This must have been one of the busiest and most exciting periods of the entire war. Let it suffice to say that I flew my first six operations in twenty-four hours. At the time, the Luftwaffe literally dominated the Western Desert skies and however well our fighter pilots performed, their Tomahawks and Kittyhawks were no match for the ME 109s. Our fighter losses were severe, but so well did they escort our bombing raids that from Gazala onwards, not one Boston was lost to an enemy fighter.

To make the task of the fighter escort as easy as possible, it was essential that the bombers flew in tight formation presenting the fighters with minimum space to cover.

At the time, 24 Squadron had as its commanding officer the magnificent Bert Rademan, surely one of the greatest leaders of the war who led by example. His wingmen were the two best formation flyers in the squadron, Andy Jordan and Dirkie Nel. Naturally every pilot hoped for the honour of flying alongside the CO and so flew as tight as he knew how, but no one could really emulate the feats of these two. On one occasion Bert Rademan jokingly remarked that they were a pair of leeches who flew so tight that they made turning on to a target a hazard.

It so happened that before the end of my rather long tour, I led the squadron with both of them; Andy on daylight raids and Dirkie on night raids. While both were brilliant pilots, they were totally dissimilar characters. On the ground Dirkie was always active while Andy wandered around apparently in a daze. He was certainly one of the slowest moving people one could expect to meet but in the air it was a different matter. He lived for his flying and he was undoubtedly the most accurate pilot I flew with. A raid near El Alamein cost us two leading observers killed, which caused a reshuffling of crews; and that is how I came to fly with Andy, who was a deputy flight commander. The first raid we led was during the El

Peter Atkins.

Alamein battle. After the planning had been completed I handed over to Andy to carry out the briefing but he just handed the task back to me and said: 'You do it'.

On the way out to the aircraft I realised that he had paid no attention to the briefing. In his opinion it was his task to get the formation together and then it was up to me to do the rest. When underway, I felt a measure of panic. All good pilots can fly within a degree or two of the course given them but after flying for about ten minutes, my pair of compasses had not moved a fraction and I thought something must be wrong with them. I need not have worried, for that was the way Andy flew. In our raids together I never had to make a correction of course or, for that matter, a single correction during a bombing run. Such incredibly accurate flying was almost unbelievable.

Andy's real love was low flying. He was the only Desert Air Force pilot to capsize a Felucca when crossing the Nile! Before that second battle of El Alamein, two squadrons of American Mitchell bombers parked with 24 to learn the game. They were a great crowd, and when eventually leaving us, they sent a flight of three Mitchells to 'beat up' our mess flying so low that their 'props' raised dust from the runway. That was a challenge which could not be ignored and Andy's two 'beat

A Boston on a desert airstrip. This is a detail of the painting by Peter Wheeler used on the jacket of Peter Atkins's book *Buffoon in Flight*.

ups' in reply were spectacular to say the least. On the first he removed the top of their mess tent and on the second, forced an entire parade to lie flat on their faces! This caused quite a stink and 'beat ups' were then forbidden.

I had only one 'dicey' raid with Andy. On that occasion we were not leading the raid but only one of the 'boxes'. Just before coming airborne there was a considerable explosion and when asking what the hell it was, I received the nonchalant reply: 'Just the port tyre bursting. Not to worry!'

It was not a pleasant or particularly well-led raid and we got severely shot up. The observer in the aircraft on the port side was killed. On landing it was Andy at his superlative best. He whispered the Boston on to the ground at little over stalling speed and it touched down on the right wheel only. Due to the slow speed, the nose wheel came down almost immediately but Andy kept the port wheel in the air until the aircraft was travelling at little more than walking pace, whereupon the slowest ground loop followed with no more damage to the aircraft. It was a superb piece of flying but I was shocked in the mess that evening when the engineering officer, Ben Vorster, called me over and said, 'You were bloody lucky. Most of the flying surfaces on that aircraft were damaged and damn few pilots would have got it back in one piece!'

That was one of the last raids I flew on with Andy and when he became tour-expired I was at a loose end for a couple of weeks. Then Lew Feinberg, Dirkie's observer, was wounded on a raid and I took his place. At that stage of the game the Eighth Army was chasing Rommel but Montgomery was so slow moving that we were seldom close enough to the enemy to stage daylight raids, so all my raids with Dirkie were at night. Few were easy as the weather during that time of year was seldom good and the Boston's instruments were rudimentary for night 'ops'.

We enjoyed a couple of interesting and, from my point of view, hair-raising experiences. The first raid was on the major airfield of the region, Castel Benito, a few miles south of the port of Tripoli. Naturally, heavy flak from that port had to be avoided which meant that the run-up was made from a pinpoint which was further from the target than was desirable.

There was no difficulty in locating the target but just halfway through my bombing run, our Boston was coned by six searchlights. Needless to say no one had warned us of searchlights! I managed to

Bostons cross the enemy coast.

get the bombs away on what seemed a good aiming point, and then the most peculiar thing happened. I was slammed back into my seat and my flying helmet, none too well fitting, landed on my nose. After managing to claw it away, I saw to my amazement, four bombs falling towards us instead of away from us. By then the searchlights had been lost but the fall of those bombs puzzled me. It was not until debriefing that Dirkie admitted he had stall-turned the Boston as the bombs were released. Only a pilot with an almost cheeky disregard for danger would perform aerobatics over a target!

Just how we escaped with our lives from the second experience is difficult to say, but it was probably a combination of some superb flying on Dirkie's part, a quiet but brilliant commentary from our top gunner 'Andy' Anderson and a spot of luck on my part.

At the time Rommel was racing back to the Mareth line which was about the last place he could hope to hold the Eighth Army at bay. Our troops were out of touch with the retreating enemy and it was left to the Desert Air Force to harass the Afrika Korps.

This particular op was one on which any roadside German laagers could be found, bombed and strafed. No 24 Squadron was briefed to reconnoitre from Medenine back to the little settlement of Ben Gardane and then 12 Squadron was to take up the hunt back to Zuara.

It was a beautiful moonlight night and there was little trouble in finding targets for our bombs, but it was frustrating when one dropped in a large laager but failed to explode. Then it was Dirkie's turn. He came down to about 200 ft to strafe and there were so many targets that he was out of ammunition well before we reached Ben Gardane. When asking whether he should start climbing, I made the luckiest decision of my life and replied: 'No, wait until we reach Ben Gardane and I'll give you a course from there.' The little settlement was very easy to identify and we were cruising over it when a mass of heavy and light flak hit us from all directions.

Dirkie slammed open the throttles and brought the famous Boston P down almost to ground level, in fact, the telegraph wires were above us! Meanwhile Andy's calm voice was pinpointing the main trouble areas while I shivered as numerous shells shot over our aircraft bursting on the road ahead. I suppose the entire episode was over in about a couple of minutes but, believe me, it seemed half a lifetime!

Just how did it all happen? At briefing we had been told that there were no enemy troops within miles of Ben Gardane, which made it an ideal turning off point. The information on enemy troop movements came from Army Intelligence and, from past experience, information from that source should have been ignored. I often wonder how many aircraft were lost or, for that matter, how many ground troops were killed due to the hopelessly inept information of Army Intelligence.

Tailpiece

Peter Atkins was undoubtedly one of 24 Squadron's most able and respected navigator/bomb aimers and as leading observer, his immense skill, courage and dedication spearheaded numerous successful raids on the enemy for which he was awarded the DFC.

Bostons over Cairo

Whispering Death

I was flying a Wellington bomber across the Mediterranean from Malta to the Western Desert to join 222 Squadron RAF, when the rear gunner reported a night-fighter was approaching from the west. The atmosphere was electric for the 'Wimpy' stood little chance of survival with its limited armament. I was about to take violent evasive action when the radio operator, who had been peering out of the astrodome, shouted: 'It's not a bloody night-fighter but the morning star!' The relief was unbelievable; the message received in Malta was remembered, warning us that the morning star rose at a remarkably fast rate in the Middle East and could be mistaken for a night fighter.

This episode was my introduction to two hazardous tours of operations which lay ahead, the first with 221 Squadron RAF, one of the few units focusing its activities on attacking ships supplying essential requirements to the enemy forces in the desert war. Early in 1941, the monthly average tonnage of enemy supplies shipped to Libyan ports was 150 000 tons but thanks to the outstanding results achieved by air and sea action, this figure was reduced to 50 000 tons in October and 37 000 tons in November.

With the advance of Rommel's Afrika Korps towards Cairo, all British forces withdrew eastwards and 221 Squadron moved from LG 89 to Shallufa on the Suez Canal where it was re-formed and the pilots trained for night torpedo attacks. In January 1943 the re-equipped squadron flew to Luqa airfield in Malta to take part in night operations against enemy shipping.

I commanded one of the two flights of eight Wellingtons and within three weeks half our complement of aircraft had been lost, most of them shot down by night-fighters. Out of a total of 128 aircrew, 64 men went missing, most of them killed in action. Enemy radar picked us up from Sicily and night-fighters were vectored on to us. On one occasion two JU 88s closed in on either side of my Wellington and I was only able to shake them off by reducing height to 50 ft above the sea where no doubt they were scared to manoeuvre.

At the close of my first tour of operations in February 1943, I was

Don Tilley (left) and Gil Catton.

appointed as Chief Flying Instructor to the Middle East Torpedo Training School. In December the same year, the school decided to train Beaufighter pilots in the use of rockets, a weapon which, if used correctly, could achieve devastating results. It was this development which persuaded me to seek a second tour of operations. The RAF had agreed to hand over their 221 Beaufighter squadron to the SAAF, which consequently became 19 Squadron SAAF and I was appointed as the first CO. The Beaufighters were not equipped to use rockets so I was sent on a two weeks' fighter training course while the equipment was fitted.

The South African take-over contingent assembled at Benghazi. The former CO, Wingco Blackburn, asked whether he could move with the squadron and fly on its first operation before he departed for the United Kingdom. I granted his request, a decision proving to be one of the luckiest I'd ever made. The day after the squadron had landed at Biferno, its new base in Italy, the Wingco led that first operation, was shot down and spent the rest of the war as a POW.

The squadron's activities were directed entirely in support of the Yugoslav Partisans who regularly reported targets to Group Headquarters. After one month, our Beaufighters were fitted with rockets and our major targets consisted of German troop trains, oil storage tanks, barracks and shipping. We were encouraged by frequent messages from the Partisans congratulating us on results. I recall one message which read: 'Six trains destroyed, petrol dumps set on fire and still burning - Good show!'

Our attacks were carried out at tree-top height. A Beaufighter

The Chief of Staff congratulates Don Tilley while Gil Catton looks on.

could scarcely be heard approaching at low level and consequently it became known by our enemy as 'the whispering death'. Havoc was wreaked amongst trains which usually hauled one or two carriages bristling with anti-aircraft guns. We would silence these guns with our cannons and machine-guns and then attack the trains with rockets. It was not uncommon to see German troops piling out of carriages and diving for cover. Towards the end of the year, several Beaufighter squadrons combined on these attacks which were so effective that in the opinion of the Partisans, the withdrawal of the German troops from Yugoslavia was hastened.

Don Tilley joined 227 Squadron for his second tour of operations in July 1944, and remained when it became 19 Squadron SAAF. He was already a legendary South African, who on his first tour of operations had been labelled the most outstanding torpedo pilot in the Mediterranean. As a close friend, I always considered it a privilege to be associated with such an admirable character. He was the most like-able and endearing person anyone could hope to meet and certainly the bravest pilot. He possessed amazing courage when pressing home attacks against enemy targets, many of them extremely heavily defended. Daylight torpedo attacks were amongst the most hazardous operations ever undertaken by a pilot for he was obliged to fly towards an enemy vessel at low level right into the teeth of fierce anti-aircraft fire. 39 Squadron suffered terrible losses and Don was lucky to survive. The Press dubbed him 'Lucky Tilley'.

By the time his first tour of operations had expired, Don had made nine torpedo drops and was determined to equal the record of another RAF pilot with ten drops before calling it a day. Over a beer in Malta I had pleaded with him not to tempt fate, but my pleas fell on deaf ears and he dropped his tenth torpedo successfully. One of the most outstanding torpedo drops during his first tour, was on 21 February 1943. His torpedo hit and sank a 10 000 ton tanker off Sicily which cost the enemy 3 000 000 gallons of much needed fuel for the beleaguered desert forces.

In 19 Squadron Don continued to hit the headlines when taking part in several hair-raising operations. On 24 October 1944 he led eight Beaufighters in two sections of four to attack Kriz marshalling yards in Yugoslavia. Don's section attacked first, his rockets smashing into three trains. While making a fourth strafing run, one of his aircraft's engines was hit by flak, so he feathered it and made a forced landing in Partisan territory, but not before warning the second section led by myself, to attack an alternative target because the flak at Kriz was too heavy. The Partisans looked after him and three weeks later he returned to the squadron.

On 21 February 1945 Don was promoted to Lieutenant-Colonel and took command of 19 Squadron when my tour had expired. Shortly

A Wellington on patrol.

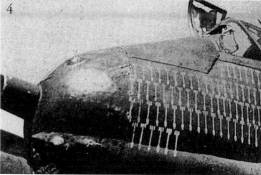

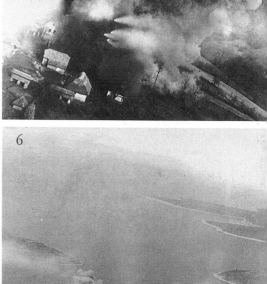

1. Beaufighters were fitted with nose-cameras which operated when guns and rockets were fired.

2. MTB blown up

3. A train destroyed.

4. Gil Catton's rocket sorties were recorded on his Beaufighter.

5. An army barracks destroyed.

6. Coastal defence guns rocketed at Lussino. The navy landed immediately afterwards - not a shot fired by the enemy.

7. Rockets fired at ship.

8. Liner sunk.

9. Power station attacked.

10. Oil tankers fired.

11. Occupied village under attack.

after this promotion he led the squadron on one of its most successful achievements, an air attack on the *Kuckuck*, a German minelayer in heavily defended Fiume harbour. He decided that surprise could best be obtained by approaching from inland and pouncing on the ship from behind a slope.

Four Beaufighters took part in the operation each carrying six 25 lb armour-piercing rockets and the attack took the enemy totally by surprise. All aircraft were safely out over the sea, noses down and throttles fully open by the time the harbour defences had woken up. Four of Don's rockets hit the *Kuckuck* below the water-line and the other two on the water-line amidships. A photo recce showed the minelayer on its side lying across the entrance to the harbour and almost totally submerged.

Don completed the war in command of 19 Squadron. His decorations included the DSO, DFC and bar, and in my opinion he should have received the VC.

Tailpiece

Gil Catton tells little about his own extraordinary exploits as a ship-buster and low level Beaufighter pilot, but he was painted with the same brush as his good friend Don Tilley. Gil was a brilliant leader who won the DSO, the DFC and was mentioned in dispatches. He lives in Houghton, Johannesburg.

Beauforts torpedo attack a convoy.

Night Ambush

It was the evening of 23 August 1981. The following day 'Operation Protea' was to become the greatest mechanised operation by South African ground forces since World War II.

As I left the briefing room at Ondangwa Air Force Base in northern South West Africa/Namibia, the sun had long since set and it was a dark, moonless night. Strolling briskly towards the flight dispersal, I thought to myself: 'This mission won't be too much of a hassle.' It involved flying into southern Angola and making radio contact with a special force carrying out a reconnaissance prior to our mechanised forces moving in to attack Swapo bases in the morning.

On reaching the flight dispersal, I collected my flying helmet and survival equipment jacket and then walked out to my Impala Mark II jet fighter. The ground crew were waiting for me and I chatted to them about the imminent operation, wanting to show them how much I appreciated their services and to make them feel part of the team. In spite of the fact that I did not expect to use weapons on this sortie, I nevertheless carefully checked that the twenty-four 68 mm rockets had been loaded into the four rocket pods and that the 30 mm cannons had been re-armed and were ready for use.

The Impala Mark II, in comparison with modern jet fighters, is relatively unsophisticated but proved itself in the Border war to be an effective ground attack aircraft as well as being a pleasure to fly. On strapping myself into the ejection seat, I started sweating profusely from the intense heat, even at that time of night, and this was intensified when I donned my helmet and oxygen mask.

While opening the throttle to full power on take-off, I experienced that uneasy feeling prior to an operation, even though I'd learnt from a tour of ops as a young pilot in Korea during 1952 and from many sorties across the Border, that pre-flight nerves are soon replaced by a sensation of excitement and anticipation as an operation gets underway.

Once airborne, I set course towards Angola. The cooling system became operative and I felt comfortable and at home in the Impala's cockpit. All exterior lights had been switched off prior to taxiing out

Dick Lewer in his Korean War Mustang.

to the runway and except for the dim glow from the instrument panel, I was surrounded by a sea of blackness.

Shortly after making radio contact with the Ground Forces Unit, I received a call from the controller at Oshakati, the forward headquarters of Western Air Command, asking me to proceed to a specific grid reference where a company of our forces had been ambushed and was facing a serious situation. In the cramped cockpit of a single-seater jet fighter at night, it is not advisable to start fiddling around with maps, so I called the radar operator at Ondangwa for a heading and distance to the grid reference. A few seconds later the radar operator's friendly voice came back with the required information.

On reaching the target area I made contact with the Company Commander who advised that his men were pinned down by a large, heavily armed Swapo force which was extremely close. A few flares were the only equipment available to mark the enemy position. I was instructed by the controller at Oshakati to make a pass over the area at full throttle and hopefully cause a distraction. No firing attacks were to be made due to the high risk of flying into the ground if a close support attack was attempted in the prevailing circumstances.

The Company Commander complied with my request to fire a flare towards the enemy territory and then I flew over it as requested. Apart from alerting Swapo that a jet aircraft was over their area, this action

Three decades later, Dick Lewer with his Border War Impala jet.

had no effect whatsoever and the attack on our forces continued unabated.

I advised Oshakati of this negative aspect and requested permission, at my own risk, to attack with rockets and cannon. As the situation was critical, permission was granted and I began to plan the attack and select the necessary switches on the armament panel.

As this operation was not the one for which I had been briefed, I was not aware of all the details which led to my involvement, but perhaps at this stage of my story, readers should know these facts.

A company comprising an elite force of Bushmen and South African soldiers had penetrated on foot, deep into southern Angola to act as a stopper group near the combined Swapo/Fapla fortress of Xangongo, formerly known as Villa Rocadis, which was to be one of the main targets of the mechanised forces which would move in the next day. Unfortunately the company's presence had been detected and it had walked into a heavily armed ambush resulting in three serious casualties. This had occurred after dark in terrain covered by thick bush and open pans known as *shonas*. No ground relief could reach the company before dawn the next morning.

My safest form of attack would have been to fire all the rockets in salvo, in other words, simultaneously, and then to pull out of the dive immediately after firing. Unfortunately this would have meant that only a small area of approximately 50 metres in diameter would be covered by the rockets causing minimal damage to the enemy. I decided therefore to set my rocket selector for each of the four pods on to single firing which meant that every time I pressed the button on the control column, only one set of rockets would be released.

I contacted the Company Commander and obtained confirmation that the enemy force lay to the east of his position. Accordingly I planned to attack from south to north to avoid hitting our own men and requested him to fire a flare towards the enemy position. The flare suddenly appeared, but in quite a different position to that anticipated. It would burn for only a short while so extreme manoeuvring was required to position myself quickly and correctly for an attack.

As the enemy was close to our forces, I decided to fire from as low an altitude as possible to ensure maximum accuracy and minimal risk to our own men. I released one set of rockets, lifted the aircraft's nose and gave a burst with the cannons, followed by another set of rockets and another burst of cannon fire, and so on. The Impala was travelling in a dive at about 400 knots and the only guide to the height above the ground was the standard altimeter and the knowledge that the ground height was approximately 3 600 ft above sea level.

On my first run, when my aircraft was at a critically low height, the flare burnt out and I pulled up with a sick feeling in the pit of my stomach that the aircraft had almost hit the ground.

The remains of a dozen SAAF aircraft gathered together in an open plot adjacent to government buildings in Xangongo, south Angola. All had either been shot down by enemy fire or destroyed in ground attacks during SADF cross-border raids.

By carrying out this hazardous type of attack, I covered virtually the entire target area with rocket and cannon fire. A disconcerting aspect was that on applying full throttle when pulling up, a long bright flame appeared from the tail pipe - the perfect target for a SAM 7 missile which I expected to hit the aircraft at any moment. I was to discover later that the enemy forces were so devastated by the attack that no missiles were launched. Another hazard was caused every time the cannons and rockets were fired when sparks shot in all directions, highlighting the Impala for enemy ground fire.

The Company Commander informed me over the radio that the attacks were right on target so I repeated them until my ammunition was expended and then I flew, partially disorientated, away from the target area until the gyros in my head had returned to normal. As far as I know, this was the first time a low level close support attack had been made in total darkness by a single-seater jet.

I returned to Ondangwa airfield with the adrenalin still pumping through my veins from the excitement of the attacks. To celebrate the occasion I flew low above the runway lights breaking left over the camp, no doubt disturbing everyone's dreams!

SAAF Impalas in formation.

Tailpiece

Dick received an official letter from one of the beleaguered company's officers on his return to Pretoria, which reads as follows:

'Thank you for your courageous action on the night of 23 August. Your assault on the Swapo position was totally successful and the enemy was crippled to such an extent that our force was able to withdraw to safety. The circumstances in which you carried out the attacks placed yourself and the aircraft in extreme danger.'

For his exceptional bravery, Dick was awarded the Honoris Crux (Silver). He was the first jet fighter pilot to win this coveted award. The citation stated that he had continued launching attacks against the enemy with little regard for his own safety and with an unparalleled consideration for his fellowmen.

He is also the only South African fighter pilot to have fought in both the Korean and the Border Wars. In the former war, the Americans decorated him with the DFC. In civilian life Dick is a professional land surveyor and he carried out all his Border operations as a volunteer Citizen Force pilot attached to a permanent force squadron. He lives in Bloemfontein.

From Death Unveiled
They Never Quailed

During the closing stages of the war in Italy, armed reconnaissance operations reaped rich rewards. Enemy rolling stock boxed up along the main escape routes to the north were destroyed in their hundreds by Allied aircraft. A similar situation developed in Yugoslavia where the enemy lines of communication were hammered mercilessly.

SAAF's 5 Squadron, equipped with long range P51 Mustangs, played its fair share in these operations and was called upon to display devotion to duty of the highest order. Targets consisted of road and rail traffic, marshalling yards and bridges which were heavily defended and the squadron suffered heavy losses.

In October 1944 the CO, Bob Morrison, was lost and in November his replacement, Tom MacMurray, and six other pilots were shot down. On 6 December the Squadron took off from Fano airstrip on the Italian east coast for an armed reconnaissance over Yugoslavia. Of the ten aircraft which became airborne on that ill-fated day, I was fortunate enough to be one of the pilots who survived to tell the tale.

Shortly after setting course, one of our aircraft aborted and about the same time, a RAAF squadron reported to 'Commander' control that the weather was adverse over Yugoslavia and it was returning to base. Our leader Bill Lombard, indicated to 'Commander' that he'd heard the message but intended to press on.

After a while the squadron flew into broken strato-cumulus cloud which gradually thickened and the leader put us into a single 'vic' formation of nine aircraft. I was positioned No 4 on the extreme right flank formating on Peter Macguire, flying No 3. As the weather closed in, Lombard indicated his intention to climb through the overcast.

On reaching 30 000 ft without breaking cloud, he decided to abort and return to base. In the turnabout, his instrument flying obviously deteriorated because suddenly the entire formation became ragged, a situation which was disastrous for the pilots on the flank.

A Q de Wet in Wonju, 1952.

I saw two aircraft on the port side disappear in a graveyard spiral and the next moment I could only see Peter Macguire's Mustang and realised that he had lost the formation. This turned out to be fortunate for both of us.

Peter was faced with the exacting task of changing from formation to instrument flying and at the same time he was obliged mentally to calculate a course for base to be followed until 'Commander' came within range and provided an accurate course.

The relief in knowing that the drama was almost over as far as we were concerned, as well as the fatigue resulting from the long hours of concentration when formating, must have caused momentary relaxation, for suddenly Macguire had disappeared and I was alone. Luck was on my side when a small opening appeared in the cloud through which I spotted Peter's aircraft to port allowing me to swing back into formation.

The opening had also provided a glimpse of the sea beneath, ensuring us that it would be safe to reduce height. In due course we broke cloud a couple of hundred feet above the water and a few minutes later were landing back at Fano, the only two aircraft of the ten which had set course that morning, to return safely to base.

It was learnt later that 'Ossie' Osler, still in a spin, had broken cloud in a Yugoslavian valley and while recovering, he pulled so much 'G' that the tops of his Mustang's mainplanes were rippled. After flying out

Mustangs of 5 Squadron return from an operation.

of Yugoslavia and across the Adriatic sea, he landed at the nearest airstrip in Italy with both fuel gauges registering zero, and in fact while taxiing, the engine fizzled out.

Geof Kilpin who had retained control of his aircraft after the formation broke up, calculated his position and set course for base. Over the Adriatic Sea he decided to let down through the murk, a move which almost ended in his watery death. As the cloud broke, he saw the sea immediately beneath, yanked back desperately on the stick, at the same time opening the throttle against the gate. The Mustang mushed and hit the water as it changed direction, and only the powerful Merlin engine pulled it out of the drink.

Geof climbed back to 10 000 ft and managed to make radio contact with 'Commander'. However, resulting from the adverse weather, a safe let-down or a rescue if he baled out over the sea could not be assured, so the only alternative was to fly on until his engine ran out of fuel, hopefully over land. When finally taking the plunge into the unknown, he landed in a Po Valley redoubt manned by elderly Austrian soldiers and spent the rest of war as a POW.

Toby Burnett lost control of his Mustang, presumably during the turnabout. He baled out and was rescued by the Partisans eventually returning to Italy but not to the squadron. Bill Lombard, George Begg, Tim Hart and 'Porkie' Hall were all killed. Porkie baled out but pulled the ripcord too late and his body was found close to the remains of his aircraft.

Road and bridge in an Alpine pass near Villanova hammered by 5 Squadron.

Peter Macguire returned safely from that ill-fated mission on 6 December but he was shot down and killed on 4 February 1945 during an attack on the Piave River bridge. Only the day before his tragic death he had shaved off his moustache to disprove the superstition prevailing in the squadron that any pilot who did this during an operational tour would be shot down. 'A load of bull,' Peter told us in the mess, the evening before he died. I was saddened by his loss and a few weeks later, Adjutant Japie Smuts and I visited his grave which was close to the bridge he'd attacked.

In addition to the six aircraft lost on 6 December 1944, three pilots went down over the remainder of the month and another six in January, four in February and eight in April 1945. During the latter months the CO 'Tank' Odendaal baled out over Yugoslavia and was rescued by the Partisans with whom he fought until the end of the war. On returning to the squadron he was awarded a bar to his DFC.

'Nobby' Clark, a brave, dedicated leader, succeeded 'Tank' as CO. He was awarded a well earned DFC early in April, and on the 29th of the same month, after his aircraft had been hit by flak twenty times in one day, a party was thrown at which Nobby declared that he had 'come of age' and was immune to flak! On his very next operation, just short of completing his second tour and only a day before the war ended, he was shot down and killed, his death causing great sorrow amongst his many friends and admirers.

Peter Macguire, the day before he was shot down.

I had served with 5 Squadron for exactly six months, and during this period thirty pilots had gone down including four commanding officers. Fortunately eight pilots had managed to bale out, Tank Odendaal and Tom MacMurray among them, although the latter lost a leg.

A fighter squadron comprised a complement of 18 pilots and 18 aircraft which meant that in six months, 5 squadron had suffered a 188 per cent casualty rate. Throughout its history the squadron had suffered heavy losses, especially between 1942 and 1943 when flying inferior aircraft against the formidable Luftwaffe's ME 109s; and although these adversities and losses had often shaken the pilots, their morale and aggressive fighting spirit were never broken. This is so well reflected in the following ode:

Pottie turned to spin and burn
Nobby and Morrison died
In battle flame on the fields of fame
with their comrades by their side.
From death unveiled they never quailed
But rose under strain, to fight again
As the ghosts of the 5th shout attack!

Nobby Clark, a 5 Squadron CO, who was killed one day before the ceasefire.

Tailpiece

A Q was a flying instructor for three and a half years during World War II and his valuable services were rewarded with an AFC. On operations in Italy he proved himself to be one of 5 Squadron's stalwarts during an extremely dramatic period and he was awarded the DFC for his courage and leadership. At the end of the war he was acting CO of the squadron. He also served in the Korean War, and retired from the SAAF as a Brigadier with the Southern Cross as an addition to his other decorations. He lives on his wine farm near Bonnievale, Cape.

L E 'Cookie' Leon

The Phantom Bridge

Northern Italy January 1945. The Royal Air Force 232 Wing was based at Falconara, just north of the Adriatic port of Ancona. The wing was part of the legendary Desert Air Force which had been welded together in the Egyptian desert during the early days of 1940 and 1941 making essential co-operation between army and airforce operations feasible and highly workable.

It was a remarkable composite force comprising units and personnel from all the Commonwealth Air Forces with a sprinkling of airmen from countries overrun by Nazi Germany. There were squadrons from the RAF, the South African, Australian, New Zealand, and United States Air Forces, and even a Polish squadron. Within these units, the mix of nationalities from all over the world helped to create the outstanding morale existing in the Desert Air Force. No 55 Squadron RAF, which I commanded, was typical of this mix introducing a diversity of ideas and outlook - but all put to a common cause. Our wing was made up of five squadrons; four equipped with Boston V aircraft and one Mosquito Squadron armed with four 20 mm cannons.

From the early beginnings in 1940-41, the Desert Air Force had fought its way along the North African coast to Tunis and the final defeat of the Axis forces at Cape Bon. The campaign in Sicily and the slow fight up the length of Italy followed, combatting not only the formidable German forces, but some of the worst terrain, and in winter, the most appalling weather imaginable.

The winter of 1945 was fierce with all of northern Italy covered in a deep mantle of snow which was particularly frustrating for our night intruder wing. Frequently the Po Valley, the main area of operations, was blanketed at night by thick ground mist. Just as frequently, if no ground mist, a low solid overcast often down to 400 ft above the ground, would make flying difficult and dangerous. Our main task was the interdiction of military traffic at night behind enemy lines by attacking roads, rail and sea traffic. This area stretched from the French Maritime Alps across the entire Po Valley up to Austria; a heavy responsibility for one wing with five squadrons. Only in 1945 did another wing

Three South Africans in the RAF (left to right) Bob Graham, Cookie Leon and Peter McMillen.

of three squadrons of night intruders join in the operations covering the area.

Difficult and often impossible night flying weather persisted week after week, but in February 1945 came a sudden, freak break. In the full moon period and for a whole week, the skies over northern Italy not only cleared, but produced weather which airmen referred to as CAVU - ceiling and visibility unlimited. On some occasions, when flying high enough over the Bologna area, the width of Italy could be seen from sea to sea and with the deep covering of snow and the full moon, visibility was exceptionally good.

These conditions motivated our night intruder squadrons to make a maximum effort and operations were flown at low altitude, generally at 1 000 ft or below; sometimes as low as 100 feet. The Bostons carried four 500 lb general purpose bombs and were armed with five heavy machine-guns firing forward and from a turret.

With the incredible bright and clear weather conditions, the Luftwaffe was quick to take advantage of the situation. We found ourselves having to cope with Messerschmitt 210 and 410 night-fighters and on some occasions even ME 109s. It was a disastrous week for 232 Wing with heavy losses but at least culminating in one very successful operation.

For some time our crews had reported a bridge across the River Po in the Pollesella area, over which traffic activity was heavy and the surrounding flak intense. As the bridge was not a healthy place to hang around, details were sketchy. Strangely enough, 'first-light' fighter-bombers could find no sign of the bridge and consequently there was a fair amount of scepticism at DAF intelligence. In fairness, however, this department requested a night reconnaissance photo flight from Benson in the U.K. A long range recce Spitfire took the photographs, landing at Falconara to have them developed and to refuel before returning to England. Sure enough, the light of the million candlepower flare showed the 'phantom' bridge clearly and distinctly in the recce photos including considerable traffic activity. Once again, the 'first-light' fighter-bomber leaders reported there was no sign of a bridge.

From the recce photos, the bridge was obviously of pontoon structure. With the considerable width and swift flow of the Po River and the formidable number of pontoon barges involved, the mystery was how the German engineers could erect and dismantle such a large and cumbersome structure to make it usable at night yet totally obscure during daylight hours. It had to be borne in mind that although the recce photographs were sharp and clear, they were taken from 25 000 ft, but the mystery of the 'phantom' bridge was soon to be solved.

The task of 'taking out' the bridge was given to 232 Wing and the Group Captain decided that all five squadrons would take part in the operation, each contributing two aircraft and synchronising different methods of attack. The Mosquito fighter bombers were to attack first, flying west to east along the river using their cannons against the pontoons in an attempt to persuade the enemy flak crews, comprising some fifty 20 mm and 40 mm guns, to keep their heads down and promote a less blistering path for the Bostons.

Bostons in the moonlight, preparing for an interdiction call.

NIGHT - in position for traffic

DAYLIGHT - each half of the bridge swung against the river banks and was hidden by branches of trees.

The Phantom Bridge, hidden by day, in operation at night.

This led to the first tragic misfortune of the night when the Wing Commander in the leading Mosquito, swept in at low level to strafe the north bank approaches to the bridge. The recce photos hadn't shown the twin towers which stood some 60 ft high and were heavily camouflaged with the branches of trees. The Mossie's port wing was sheered off when striking the structure, the aircraft flick-rolling and ending up as a fiercely burning wreck, just a couple of hundred yards downstream from the bridge.

These towers, situated on the north and south banks of the river, supported steel cables attached to the bridge sections which were swung across to meet in the centre of the river at nightfall. Just before dawn they were swung back to the river banks becoming hidden and unobserved during daylight hours. A brilliant field engineering scheme.

The four Boston squadrons carried out various types of attack: precision bombing from 1 000 ft, shallow dive bombing, low level bombing, and 55 Squadron's two aircraft led by myself dropped mines from 50 ft just upstream from the bridge. They were fused at minimum depth to ensure detonation just below the pontoons. Some of the bombs and a few of our mines were effective. The operation was a success and the bridge was 'taken out'.

This attack was the culminating operation of the seven nights of freak weather. The Wing paid a terrible price over this week, its five squadrons losing a total of 25 crews including two wing commanders and five squadron leaders; 232 Wing's worst loss during the entire war and 55 Squadron was the hardest hit. At the beginning of the week the squadron had 16 operationally fit crews, but by the end of the week only eight crews were left with both flight commanders lost.

These appalling losses, incurred during that one week of February 1945, were particularly tragic, bearing in mind that the end of the war was in sight. Many of the pilots and aircrews had been flying since 1940 and were looking forward to going home. Some 100 pilots, navigators, radio men and gunners were lost and because of the very low levels at which the operations were carried out, there were few survivors, only a handful turning up as POWs or escapees three months later.

Tailpiece

Cookie is a deep-rooted South African whose father was born in the old Transvaal Republic and his mother in the Cape Colony. He joined the RAF in 1940 and strangely enough his first operational squadron happened to be 14 Squadron in which his uncle had served and lost his life while fighting the Turks in World War I. Cookie was decorated with the DSO, DFC and bar. He lives in New South Wales, Australia.

Outgunned but not Outfought

On 17 February 1941, as a member of 224 Squadron of RAF Coastal Command. I was the captain of Hudson N 7319 when it was attacked by two ME 110s.

We had been sent on 'stand' patrol between Stavanger and Kristiansand which was one of the simultaneous patrols covering the Norwegian coast from Aalesund in the north to Kristiansand in the south-east, designed to acquire information on all shipping particularly iron ore ships moving around the Norwegian coast to the Baltic ports *via* Skagerrak and Kattegat.

Our instructions were to report all shipping and to attack where possible. After leaving Leuchars, our home base, at 1000 hours on the 360-mile crossing, we made landfall about two hours and fifteen minutes later under bright, clear skies.

Turning starboard and commencing the patrol at 4 000 ft, we soon spotted a large ship with several flak ships in attendance. Notes were made for our operational report and a dive bombing attack was launched when four 250 lb bombs were released from 800 ft, all bombs except one straddling the target. The flak was intense during the dive and the climb away to patrol height.

We had just settled back on patrol when I spotted two small dots which could well be enemy aircraft approaching from the direction of Sola aerodrome near Stavanger. The Hudson's defensive armament consisted of two .303 Browning machine-guns fixed in front and two similar guns in a power-operated rear turret, where they enjoyed a wide arc of fire, cutting out when swinging towards the twin rudder. The German pilots knew this and when attacking a Hudson they endeavoured to keep the tailpiece between themselves and the rear turret.

I felt we would be safer near the water to avoid being attacked from below where the Hudson was extremely vulnerable so I opened the throttles wide, locked them there, and with propellers in fully fine pitch, dived for the sea.

After levelling out, I looked around and there were the two ME

Bertie Leach.

110s, one to starboard, the other to port, both as large as life and looking very ominous.

As the one on the left attacked I turned very tightly towards it at the same time lifting the aircraft up a few feet. The sea beneath boiled with shells and bullet strikes, the ME's front armament comprising two 20 mm cannons and six machine-guns!

As we swung towards the enemy aircraft, the pilot made a very tight left-hand turn away, and then the other 110 came in to attack from the starboard quarter, the pilot trying to keep the Hudson's tailplane between his aircraft and the rear turret.

My response was to throw the Hudson into a vertical bank and turn right to get in towards the attack. Again the sea boiled with shells and bullet strikes and the ME broke away to the right. Every nerve was as taut as a harp string as the atmosphere in the aircraft built up to a stifling crescendo. We were on a total high with a feeling that our bodies had reached their maximum pitch of fear, excitement and anticipation.

On the second attack from the right rear ME, an armour-piercing bullet came up through the back of the aircraft and hit my shoulder knocking me against the windscreen. Had I not been leaning over to the left trying to keep an eye on the left-hand ME, the bullet would certainly have gone through my spine.

This recalls a remark made one evening by an officer in the

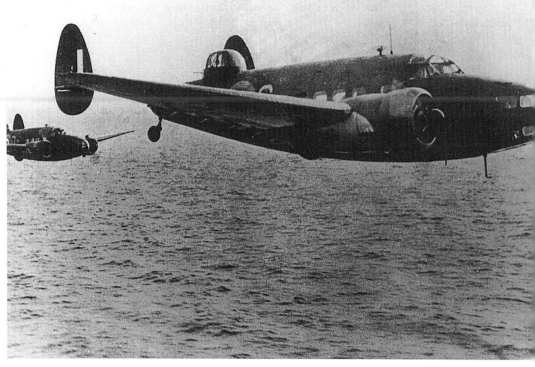

Lockheed Hudsons on patrol.

Leuchars mess. 'Don't worry,' he said, 'If a bullet's got your name on it you've had it.' To which another officer commented: 'That's not what worries me. It's the bullet that has, "To whom it may concern," written on it.'

It is difficult to say how long the action lasted. It seemed like half an hour, but was probably much less. The MEs scored numerous strikes on the Hudson and about two square feet of turret was blown off. The noise of exploding cannon shells inside the aircraft was deafening. I remember looking back into the smoked-filled interior and seeing two homing pigeons which were always carried in case of ditching, crammed together in the bottom of their basket looking really browned off!

After several attacks, my rear gunner Sergeant Eardley, who was miraculously uninjured, set the starboard engine of one of the fighters on fire, the pilot high-tailing it back to Norway. It was just about this time that the other ME must have run out of ammunition, for the pilot decided to have a go at us with a free-firing gun carried in the back of the crew's observatory.

The ME flew very close to port of us and I could see the gunner's face clearly as he fired from close range. It didn't need much manoeuvring to line him up in the front gun sight, and one short burst with the two front Brownings got him in the face, the burst no doubt blowing his head off. It certainly smashed the conservatory and put the gun completely out of action.

All this time the engines had been running flat out and the Hudson must have been clocking 250 mph. As we approached some cloud cover I pulled the aircraft up into a steep climb and at 2 000 ft plus, the comforting folds of cloud enveloped us.

After setting course for home we checked for damage sustained, and miraculously the engines and fuel tanks appeared to be untouched. From the moment I was hit, my right arm was barely usable but at the time this didn't worry me too much. It wasn't painful but I felt as if someone had hit me on the back with the flat side of a spade. On settling down, I probed inside my tunic with my left hand to ascertain the damage and on withdrawing my hand I received a hell of a fright when seeing it covered with blood right up to the wrist. 'Good God!' I thought,'I've been shot!'

Flying Officer Flowers, the second pilot, who was navigating on this trip, was on his first operational sortie. He took over the controls and I went back to where there was space for me to lie down on a canvas stretcher. Sergeant Eardley gave me a shot of morphine from the first aid kit.

We arrived back at Leuchars where snow was banked up high on each side of the runway. Flowers made a belly-landing as the hydraulics had been shot up and the aircraft skidded along the icy runway coming to rest in thick snow. We were all relieved to be back in one piece. I found the bullet which had hit me, stuck in the webbing of my parachute harness!

Tailpiece

Bertie is a South African who joined the RAF before World War II. After a tour of operations with 224 Squadron, he commanded 48 Squadron on his second tour. He was awarded the DFC and was one of the post-war pioneers of South African Airways. He lives in Grahamstown.

Charles Barry

We Owed our Lives to Each Other

Geoff and I were fools, bloody fools that day in January 1945. We had been briefed to photograph factories in Cracow, southern Poland - a piece of cake. Climbing to 28 000 ft from base at San Severo near the spur of Italy, we would skirt the foothills of the Alps, then by-pass Vienna and find Cracow to the left just beyond the Tatry mountains in Silesia. No need to consult maps; we'd flown the route many times before.

But on this day we didn't fly at 28 000 ft. Our Mosquito began pulling vapour trails at 24 000 ft, so rather than try to fly above trail height - supposed to be 2 000 ft thick, but usually considerably more - we opted to fly just below it. No sense in advertising our route to all on the ground, although German radar had no doubt been plotting our aircraft since it crossed the Yugoslavian coast.

The targets in the Cracow area were covered by ten-tenths low cloud, so we decided to divert to alternative targets at Breslau to the northwest. Our track would be across the Blechhamer oil refineries, which we had photographed many times in the past, before and after the Americans had bombed them. There had been flak on those occasions, but never accurate. Our best operating height had been 28 000 ft to 30 000 ft with a cruising speed of 350 mph but today we were down to 22 500 ft because of those contrails, and our airspeed was around 300 mph. That was our big mistake. Why were we such fools? We should have flown around the oilfields.

This was the height at which the American heavies, the Fortresses and Liberators flew and gunners on the ground were homed in on it. At our correct operational altitude, the direction of the flak was usually fairly good; but the shells invariably burst behind us. The Jerries apparently could not calculate our speed. After the war the Germans admitted to having experienced difficulty in plotting Mosquitoes because these aircraft, made mostly of wood, did not reflect radar rays accurately. Even the mass of metal in the engines, in the tail unit and the cladding on the wings, were not enough to give a clear signal.

The first indication of trouble was when flak began bursting near us, at our height and on our course. Some of the black bursts were

Charles Barry.

tinged with reddish-brown which could be marker shells for fighters. Geoff got off his seat adjoining me, turned around and knelt on it placing his head in the top blister, from where he could watch the tail for enemy attacks. This was a vital precaution because photographic reconnaissance (PR) Mosquitoes were unarmed, and early warning was necessary so that the pilot could outrun the enemy.

By now our aircraft was being buffeted about by the flak, and while opening up to full speed, I saw shells bursting in front of us. Suddenly there was a loud crack, followed by a strange roaring, whistling noise. I just had time to look up at the hole that had appeared in the front of the blister before Geoff collapsed to the floor.

I was absolutely horrified. My mouth was dry and I could taste the sulphur of fear as I tried not to panic. Then Geoff turned his head and looked at me as he felt the side of his flying helmet. A piece of shrapnel had ripped it open and shaved off some of his hair - no blood!

His eyes twinkled above the oxygen mask as he switched on his intercom. 'The bastards tried to give me a haircut. Did that shake you?' It did indeed. But his casual quip calmed me and I began laughing with

Ian McIntyre.

relief. Then we were both laughing. The tension had gone and we sorted out our speed and course and carried on towards Breslau.

While approaching the area, and as Geoff prepared to kneel down over the bombsight to guide me on target, I had a feeling we were being followed so turned sharply to port. That was when our luck changed. About 500 ft below and climbing on our track were three long-nosed Focke-Wulf 190 fighters. Had we stayed on that course another half minute we would never have known what blasted us out of the sky.

The turn had put us on a southerly course and I opened up to full bore ('balls against the wall' in the vernacular) as Geoff shouted 'let's get out of here,' putting his head in the blister to watch the tail. 'I have a feeling we are not welcome today.'

We outran those fighters after a 50 mile chase and streaked for home. After landing, a rigger showed me two opposite holes in the fuselage. A piece of shrapnel had passed through, missing the main control wires by no more than an inch!

I mentioned these examples not to emphasize the hazards of operational flying but to underline how much aircrew depended on each

Geoff Jefferys.

other for morale and survival. It was something not always appreciated, especially by pilots. Complete rapport was essential. You worked as a team. Fear was rebuffed by joking.

I was lucky in 60 Squadron SAAF. I had two exceptional navigators, Ian McIntyre on my first tour of operations. Geoff Jefferys on the second. We developed a splendid understanding of each other. Both were unflappable and both had a quick sense of humour, which relieved tension like letting air out of a tyre.

They were different to look at, and in personality, too. Ian was tall, urbane, mild; Geoff short, thickset and aggressive if provoked. Both liked mess parties, but counted their drinks when knowing they would be flying the next day.

Ian was a pupil pilot originally, but was washed out. 'Trouble is, I could fly superbly but I had difficulty in getting down in one piece! So my instructor decided he would save the aircraft and me - in that order - and wouldn't let me go solo,' he would muse.

He could fly well. Often when we were returning to base I would lose height over the Adriatic away from interception and we would swop seats, quite a skilful manoeuvre in a small Mosquito cabin. He would then fly to the spur of Italy and I would take over again.

Both were confident navigators - and we were never lost for words. Ian's popular gambit was to announce casually as he scanned the horizon, 'There's something there on the starboard side. Looks like a Jerry closing fast. I'll tell you when to break.' Then he would pass his hand in front of his eyes and say, 'It's O K. It's a liver spot!'

They were unruffled and precise when calling the run-up on the target. 'Left. Hold it. Flat turn slowly to the right. Hold it. Cameras on. Hold it. Keep running. That's fine. They're a couple of Jerry fighters taking off from the drome but we'll be gone before they reach us.'

One of the positive aspects about photographic reconnaissance is that crews cannot claim to have done the job when they haven't. No room for guesswork or line-shooting. The resulting photographs are checked by skilled interpreters - in our case, RAF WAAF's at MPRW (Mediterranean Photographic Reconnaissance Wing) headquarters and plotted on a large-scale map. If the features aren't covered by the pictures, you missed the target.

Two outstanding jobs by Ian were done in April 1944. The first, on 4 April, was on a recce over a town named Oświęcim in Poland. As we began the run, Ian called over the intercom that one of the long-focus cameras wasn't working. 'We'll make two runs,' he said. 'I'll pick up the target with the starboard camera while flying east and re-cover it on a reciprocal course. And I'll over-run the camera on both.' Which he did at the end of the west run and unknown to us we picked up the infamous death camp of Auschwitz. It was the first picture taken and had important consequences.

Regrettably, post-war it was attributed to the American Air Force and not the SAAF and sometimes still is, although the State archives in Washington have corrected this. I have a copy of the authenticated ops report from the Public Record Office, London, proving we were the crew who took it. The other exceptional job was done just 20 days later over eastern Romania on the Black Sea coast. The Russians were massing to attack on a front known as the Galatz Gap. They had been warned that it was heavily fortified and wanted photographic evidence. It fell to 60 Squadron to get it.

An aircraft was sent on the 1400-mile return journey every day, but the area was consistently covered by low cloud. As an inducement, crews were told that the first to bring back complete coverage would fly a special mission to Russia to deliver the pictures. It was tempting bait; and when Ian and I arrived over the target area on 24 April 1944 in early afternoon, the clouds had miraculously dispersed and the whole twisting Siretul River and its fortifications were clear. We were to be the lucky ones.

Ian was superb. Deliberately and methodically he guided me over the area, aware that a small error at 28 000 ft would be magnified by our long-focus cameras which had a total lateral coverage of three miles, and some of the target would be missed. After about 20 minutes of flying and re-flying over the intricate pattern, Ian, weary from following the target line in his bombsight for so long, switched off the cameras, got back into the navigator's seat and said; 'What do you mix with Russian vodka to make it palatable?'

When plotted, the coverage was a superb example of skilful tracking. He hadn't missed as much as a yard of the fortifications. Wing ops were ecstatic about it; so much so that a senior officer felt it was his duty to fly the pictures to the Russians. So we never found out what made a good mix with vodka!

Almost a year later - on 14 March 1945, according to my logbook - Geoff did an almost identical job on a complex system of German defences near Venice. I recorded in my logbook: 'Geoff pulled off a wizard mapping job here. Definitely one of the best sorties.' The GSO2 of the Military Intelligence Unit (West) agreed. He sent personal congratulations a few days later when the mapping had been plotted.

Both these jobs were team work but the kudos belonged to the navigators. I merely translated what they directed me to do by altering course. Had we been ill-matched we might have squabbled, become ill-tempered; I, because skidding, flat turns are hideously uncomfortable to operate; and Geoff or Ian because, 'why waste time if the bloody pilot won't or can't do as he's told!'

When they were over the bombsight, I kept a lookout for enemy fighters but when they were busy watching our tail from the hatch, I navigated by map-reading. However, we blamed each other if things went wrong. How jumpy you could become 500 or more miles inside

Mosquitoes of 60 Squadron.

Over the Alps at 25 000 feet.

enemy territory, all by ourselves, 30 000 ft up and an engine begins playing up! But it was soon forgotten, and generally ended in a laugh. 'We must not take this war too seriously,' they'd say. Or 'How the hell did you pass Navigation for your wings?' 'Why don't you surprise me by giving me a correct course to fly for a change?'

Ian died in Cape Town some 20 years ago, Geoff in Johannesburg nearly three years ago. Now as I brush up memories of nearly 50 years, I realise what fine comrades and team men they were. We owed our lives to each other.

Tailpiece

Charles Barry flew on two tours of operations with 60 Squadron SAAF in North Africa and Italy. He was well-known for his exploits and expertise as a pilot on photographic reconnaissance work for which he was awarded the DFC and was mentioned in dispatches. Geoff Jefferys was also awarded a DFC. Charles lives in Hurlingham, Sandton.

Small in Stature but a Giant in Character

Pikkie Rautenbach is remembered by his many friends and those who flew with him in World War II and Korea as a man small in stature but a giant in character. He was a magnificent pilot and a fearless leader, and there are some fascinating stories to be told about his exploits during three tours of operations, the first taking place in East Africa and the Western Desert when he flew as an air gunner, the others as a pilot in Burma and Korea.

One morning he was returning from a bombing raid over the Western Desert in a Maryland, when an ME 109 peeled out of the haze bent on shooting his aircraft out of the skies. He manned the top turret gun only to find that the traverse mechanism had jammed leaving him defenceless. He didn't intend to die without a gesture of defiance, so grabbing a fistful of toilet paper packs from a shelf he hurled them out of a window into the slipstream. Unbelievably the enemy pilot winged away without firing a shot, no doubt assuming that the whirlwind of paper represented a secret weapon and he decided to live another day!

After being awarded his wings thanks to assistance from his aircraft's captain, the legendary Bert Rademan, and Field Marshal Smuts, Pikkie was seconded to the RAF serving his second tour of operations fighting the Japs in Burma where his aggressive leadership, uncanny sense of direction and skilful pinpointing of targets predominated.

He crowned this tour of ops with an exploit which appealed to his spirit of adventure. The Japs had surrendered in Rangoon but a few stubborn guards would not release their prisoners from the main jail. Pikkie led a flight of four Thunderbolts to skip-bomb the prison wall and it was the pin point accuracy of his bombs which smashed a hole in the wall through which the prisoners escaped.

After World War II, Pikkie volunteered to fight in Korea with the Cheetah squadron where once more his brilliant leadership, accurate use of weapons and special brand of humour were an inspiration to his squadron.

Pikkie Rautenbach.

The Cheetah's CO, Dick Clifton, regards the diminutive pilot as one of the most memorable flying types he's met during a long service career and pays tribute to his outstanding courage.

'I've witnessed many acts of bravery and flying skill, but there is one episode which remains in my memory so vividly. Pikkie's Mustang was crippled by flak during a strafing attack in a Korean valley and I

A Maryland over the desert.

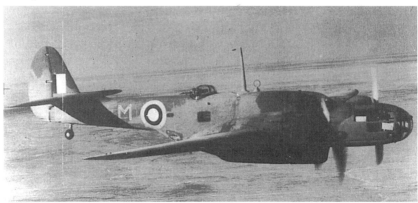

watched him fly his burning aircraft for 30 miles back to friendly lines, determined not to be taken prisoner.

'A less courageous man and less skilful pilot would have climbed his aircraft to a safe height and baled out - but not Pikkie. He flew low, using minimum power to remain airborne. After advising us that he was unplugging his R/T, we saw him crouch with both feet on the seat ready to spring clear. His straps were undone, cockpit canopy jettisoned, and flying with stick alone, he was peering out of the right hand side of the cockpit as flames and smoke obscured forward vision. While passing over the front line he sprang clear, his parachute opened immediately and deposited him safely in friendly territory. At that instant his Mustang struck a hilltop and exploded.

'Two weeks later I was in the Operations Room when Pikkie's flight was briefed to attack an enemy tank and I decided to fly in place of his No 2. While following in the bombing dive I observed his bombs score a bulls-eye converting the tank into a flaming, mangled wreck. Pikkie had got his own back with a vengeance!'

Award of the American DFC.

THE UNITED STATES OF AMERICA

TO ALL WHO SHALL SEE THESE PRESENTS, GREETING:

THIS IS TO CERTIFY THAT
THE PRESIDENT OF THE UNITED STATES OF AMERICA
AUTHORIZED BY ACT OF CONGRESS JULY 2, 1926
HAS AWARDED

THE DISTINGUISHED FLYING CROSS

TO

Captain Johannes G. Rautenbach
South African Air Force

FOR

EXTRAORDINARY ACHIEVEMENT
WHILE PARTICIPATING IN AERIAL FLIGHT

Korean Theater of Operation, 24 February 1952

GIVEN UNDER MY HAND IN THE CITY OF WASHINGTON
THIS   10th   DAY OF   October   1952

Colonel, USAF
Air Adjutant General

SECRETARY OF THE AIR FORCE

Tailpiece

In civil aviation Pikkie was known as a 'South African Flying Legend.' He was an aerobatic champion, an ace crop-spraying pilot and a brilliant innovator. Sadly he met an untimely death in 1976 while flying an aircraft he had designed and built himself. Flying was his life and this was the way he would have chosen to make his bow. He was awarded the DFM during his first tour of operations in East Africa and the Western Desert and an American DFC in Korea.

A Mustang armed with rockets in Korea.

D W 'Pip' Pidsley

The Epic of Rommel's Last Tanker

On the morning of 23 October 1942, there was a keen anticipation in the Western Desert that a mighty clash of arms between the Allied and Axis forces was imminent. The atmosphere was so tense and heavily charged at Lake Mariut, our home base, that I drove into Alexandria about three miles distant to glean some information on the situation.

The normally frequented haunts in the city were deserted and there was no sign of military activity. These ominous observations were given meaning that evening at 2100 hours when the Eighth Army launched a mammoth artillery barrage which lit the horizon with a red glow. The famous battle of El Alamein had commenced.

On 26 October 1942, 15 Squadron awakened to a typically hot cloudless desert morning. The duty crews had been warned the previous evening to expect an operation of some importance and at 1000 hours, the ops buzzer sounded. Six Bisleys were to fly to the RAF base at Gianacles where they would be re-fuelled and the crews briefed.

On arriving at Gianacles we were briefed in a marquee by Group Captain Guy Knocker RAF who outlined the prevailing situation and described the target and the tactics to be employed. He stressed that Rommel was desperately short of fuel for his tanks and mechanised transport and if he didn't receive supplies within two or three days, his chances of halting the advance of the Eighth Army would be severely jeopardised. Consequently, it was clear that the Axis intended to run the gauntlet of the Allied strike forces and sail a vitally important convoy into Tobruk harbour.

The convoy was situated some 20 miles north west of Tobruk and comprised a naval escort of four destroyers, a 5000 ton merchant vessel, a 900 ton freighter and a 3000 ton tanker loaded with petrol which had to be destroyed at all costs. The tanker was the *Prosperina,* known as 'Rommel's last tanker' on which the future course of the desert war would hinge.

The 23 aircraft to take part in the operation consisted of eight torpedo carrying Beauforts, six bomb carrying Bisleys and nine Beaufighters acting as top cover. The gaggle, as this strike force was

Pip Pidsley and his crew (left to right): Monty Yudelman, Pip Pidsley, Taffy Hough.

called, would be led by the Beaufort squadron commander, George Gee. My flight of three Bisleys was to fly on the extreme right and slightly to the rear of the Beauforts with the second flight of Bisleys on the extreme left and the Beaufighters patrolling above. As soon as the convoy was spotted, Wingco Gee would give the signal to attack by firing a double yellow Very light, when the Bisleys would move ahead to engage the convoy and divert attention from the Beauforts and their deadly cargo.

As we emerged from the briefing marquee, all aircrew members were fully aware of the gravity of the situation and understood the reasons for the concern of the Allied High Command, but they did not know that the eyes of the world focused on the mission and many people were anxiously awaiting its outcome. The crews were also in no doubt that an operation of this vital nature would spell death to many of them.

The gaggle took off in perfect conditions from Gianacles at 1230 hours and headed westwards flying in loose formation at about 100 ft above the sea. My flight was reduced to two aircraft when Tubby Bernitz's Bisley failed to take off due to refuelling and starting problems. This left me with Gerald Dustow as my sole wingman. The second Bisley flight was led by Jimmy Lithgow with Sven Leisegang and

Algie Groch as his wingmen. The crew of my own aircraft, apart from myself as pilot, included Monty Yudelman as navigator and Taffy Hough as wireless operator-cum-air gunner.

After approximately two hours and fifteen minutes, while still flying at 100 ft above the sea and about two or three miles from the coast, Tobruk appeared in the distance, but there was no sign of the convoy. Then through the haze, a dozen or more F boats were seen spread out across our track, and instinctively aircraft began to deploy despite the fact that the attack signal had not been given. The F boats gave us a fiery reception.

As Tobruk drew closer, there was still no trace of the convoy and the gaggle edged nearer the harbour to ascertain whether the convoy had perhaps already docked. The enemy defences were on the alert and fired at us with every available gun at their disposal, presenting an awesome sight to our strike crews; but there was no sign of the convoy in the harbour and we pressed on regardless. One of the Beaufighter pilots decided to draw the flak away from the gaggle by flying directly towards Tobruk at about 1 000 ft, a brave act which attained its purpose,

Attacking the tanker 26 October 1942: Pip Pidsley's Bisley is in the foreground; Gerald Dustow's aircraft is at top right, just before plunging into the sea with the starboard engine ablaze. This unique photograph was taken with a small hand camera by the navigator of the Beaufort (following the Bisleys) which launched the torpedo against the *Prosperina*.

but sadly the aircraft was hit by flak, the pilot turning about and flying out to sea, never to be heard of again.

By now the rays of the mid-afternoon sun had lessened the forward visibility, but suddenly the Axis convoy minus the prime target, appeared about ten miles ahead and the signal to attack was given. The moment of truth had arrived. I pulled forward immediately and at the same time spotted the missing tanker with an escorting destroyer. They were further out to sea and about three or four miles astern of the convoy and seeing there was ample space between the tanker and the coast, I decided to attack from the land side towards the open sea so that my approach would be at right angles to the length of the target.

The escorting destroyer assessed my intention initially and sped at full steam towards a position which would force me to pass it within a distance of between 100 and 200 yards. We could see the crew on the destroyer's deck as they fired desperately at us and I remarked to Monty about their apparent panic. He gave me a wry smile as we headed

The hole in the port elevator of Pidsley's aircraft.

towards the shore and then turned to starboard lining up for the attack on the tanker which was now about 500 yards away.

To allow Dusty to keep position on the outside of the turn, I reduced speed slightly but he banked too steeply and to avoid a collision, pulled up over me. This placed him to starboard of me and about ten yards ahead and therefore he was the first to attack.

During our run-in, an intense carpet of incendiary, armour piercing, phosphorous and ball ammunition flak assailed us as we jinked furiously to put the gunners off their aim. A strange calmness prevailed in the cockpit, probably the result of the strict discipline drummed into us during training. While checking vital procedures, I asked Monty whether he'd armed the bombs; a lucky reminder for he'd forgotten and rectified this immediately.

'Drop the bombs when I shout "let go",' I told him and he nodded. We were about 200 yards from the tanker with Dusty slightly ahead to starboard, both flying at deck level. Suddenly the flak switched direction to the vertical, forming a criss-crossed curtain over the ship through which we were obliged to fly. Dusty's bombs fell short but probably caused underwater damage. He pulled up steeply but unfortunately too late and a wingtip struck the top of the front mast, his starboard engine bursting into flames and the Bisley plunging into the sea off the tanker's port bow.

The time had arrived for me to concentrate on the release of my bombs and when about ten or fifteen yards away from the tanker, I yelled 'Let go,' and Monty responded instantly. While pulling up sharply I could see that the distance between the tanker's bridge and its rear mast was smaller than the Bisley's wingspan. I banked steeply to port, passed through the gap and in doing so ripped out the numerous communication wires spanning the masts and bridge.

As we levelled off, Taffy reported that 20 or more enemy fighters were coming in to attack us, so I eased the Bisley down to just above the surface of the sea, in fact so low that its swirling propellors were throwing up a spray off the water. Certainly the enemy aircraft could not get below us and would receive a fierce reception from Taffy and his twin Brownings in the rear turret. Taffy also reported to our delight that three of our bombs had scored direct hits and the tanker's bridge had been blasted into the air leaving a fire raging in the empty space!

We proceeded to the rendezvous which was about 50 miles out to sea and while flying eastwards heading for base, we noticed a Bisley and a Beaufort flying close to one another. Suddenly they collided, flames spurting from their wingtips as they staggered along locked together for about ten seconds before plunging into the sea. There were no survivors and back at Gianacles we learnt it was Sven Leisegang and his crew who had lost their lives.

A 15 Squadron Bristol (Blenheim Mk V) at Lake Mariut, 1942.

At debriefing a comprehensive picture of the strike was obtained as far as the Beauforts and the second flight of Bisleys were concerned.

Ralph Manning, piloting one of the Beauforts, had also spotted the tanker and followed up behind our two Bisleys. Another Beaufort piloted by Norman Hearn-Phillips, known as HP, witnessed the attack on the freighter and then joined Ralph. He had seen Jimmy Lithgow's flight attack the freighter from a very low level. 'They seemed to squat down on the deck to drop their bombs.' The flak was intense and Algie Groch's aircraft was badly shot up, a shell exploding in the nose killing his navigator instantly. As the aircraft pulled up to clear the ship, a wing struck the mast and the Bisley cartwheeled into the sea. Miraculously, Algie and his gunner survived, were picked up by the enemy and became prisoners of war.

The gaggle leader, Wingco Gee, and the remaining Beauforts, then attacked with their torpedoes. The flak remained intense and the rudder of one of the Beauforts was almost shot away, but the pilot survived. Another pilot was not so lucky and immediately after his torpedo had been released, his aircraft flicked over on to its back and crashed into the sea. This time there were no survivors.

While Ralph and HP were preparing to launch their deadly missiles at the prime target, a piece of flak penetrated HP's cockpit severing the Beauforts' electrical circuit and causing the instant release of the torpedo. When Ralph eventually dropped his torpedo, it appeared to run true for an amidships strike, but the tanker's captain was vigilant and turned his vessel towards the Beaufort causing the torpedo to strike his vessel's bow a glancing blow. It then skimmed along the hull towards the stern where a tremendous explosion occurred below the waterline, the tanker becoming temporarily obscured by a column of water and smoke, the latter billowing up into the sky to be seen 60 miles away.

After five hours and thirty minutes in the air, the aircraft which had survived the operation landed back at Gianacles and as the weary airmen staggered on to the tarmac, they received a warm welcome from Air Vice-Marshal Leonard Slater. At Lake Mariut an unforgettable welcome was received from our comrades, an inspiring occasion which caused deep emotions.

Tailpiece

Pip was awarded an immediate DFC for his part in the successful strike. Back in January that year he and Jannie de Wet, another 15 Squadron pilot who lost his life tragically near Kufra Oasis, had mutually agreed

The message to Pip Pidsley from the AOC-in-Chief.

that decorations should be given to the squadron as a whole and not to an individual because success was a team effort.

A few days after the 'strike', Air Marshal Sir Arthur Tedder visited 15 Squadron at Lake Mariut to express his personal congratulations on its achievement. He noticed that Pip wasn't wearing his DFC ribbon and in front of everyone present he chided him with these words. 'If we take the trouble to give you an award, you can take the trouble to wear it!'

Pip was later promoted to the rank of Lieutenant-Colonel and went on to command three other squadrons before the war ended. He lives in Arcadia, Pretoria.

Rod Hojem

Stuka Party

The opportunity to engage in a 'Stuka Party' was the ambition of all Kittyhawk pilots back in those desert days when they were frustrated and angry about being outgunned and outflown by the vastly superior Messerschmitt 109s. The strategy of Stuka dive bombers was to make dawn and dusk raids on our frontline troops, and so, on the morning of 1 November 1942, Squadrons 2, 4 and 5 of SAAF's 7 Wing became airborne just before dawn.

Leading the Wing and 2 Squadron was H E N 'Wildy' Wildsmith who had briefed his pilots the previous evening. I was flying as his wingman on this occasion and we climbed in standard finger formation to 10 000 ft heading towards Gambut. I had a healthy respect for the dreaded 109s and my eyes and neck were doing overtime searching the skies, when I spotted a gaggle of enemy aircraft approaching from the west at about 4 000 ft above us.

'Dogsbody Red 2 to Leader - plus-minus 20 Bandits and Snappers at two o'clock - angels 14 - over.'

A long silence followed and then acknowledgement came crackling back over the R/T.

'Thank you Red 2 - Confirm plus-minus twenty Bandits and Snappers at two o'clock - angels 14 - over and out.'

Wildy never used his call sign but everyone knew his husky voice.

The Stukas, with their ME 109 top cover, were soon recognisable and no doubt one of the German pilots must have shouted '*Achtung* Kittyhawks', for the entire gaggle suddenly turned about and flew back on a reciprocal course. Much to our chagrin and disappointment, Wildy followed suit, at the same time advising us that we must open our Kitty's throttles wide and gain height. A few minutes later, still climbing, we turned around on to our original course and it wasn't long before we understood Wildy's strategy. He had anticipated that the Jerries would try to avoid a confrontation but would return hoping that our aircraft had moved on. Their ruse didn't work and when turning back they were once more confronted by our aircraft but this time their height advantage had been lost. The slaughter commenced.

Rod Hojem.

Acting as top cover, 4 and 5 Squadron kept off the 109s and 15 Stukas rolled over into a steep dive with eleven 2 Squadron Kittyhawks chasing them. Plumes of smoke and dust erupted on the ground from the bombs which the enemy pilots jettisoned on their way down to their customary avenue of escape above the desert scrub. One of the Jerries dropped his bomb as Wildy closed on him blowing a gaping hole in the Kitty's tailplane, but Wildy promptly shot him down.

I closed on a Stuka, fired a short burst and it hit the ground, flipping over on to its back. I then fired at a Stuka standing on its wingtip in a tight turn, but saw my tracers lagging behind it. I consequently found myself, much to my horror, flying in close formation with another Stuka when the grimace on the rear gunner's face was apparent as he

Kittyhawks waiting to scramble.

A downed Stuka

desperately slammed his machine-gun over against the stop. I could imagine him cursing in guttural German as he battled to train his gun on my aircraft!

This burlesque was so intriguing that I overshot the Stuka and was brought back to reality by a stream of tracer from its front guns. A vicious jerk on the stick pulled my Kittyhawk up steeply enabling me to curve back and deliver a two-second full deflection shot. The Stuka dived towards the ground but before I could open fire again, it hit the desert scrub, the right wheel breaking off and bouncing forward in huge leaps and bounds. The pilot flew on for a short distance and then crash-landed, his aircraft churning up a huge cloud of dust. Both he and his rear gunner scrambled out of the cockpit and ran for it as I flew overhead waggling my Kitty's wings in salute, elated but thoughtful about the waste and dire consequences of an unwanted war. I fired at a third Stuka and black smoke began pouring from the fuselage, but I didn't see it crash.

The final 2 Squadron score was eight destroyed and four probables. The 57th Fighter Group USAAF dispatched the three remaining Stukas as they landed back at their base. Lieutenants Angus Allen-White and Dawie Theron of 2 Squadron were shot down during the operation but they both baled out safely. Theron returned with a Nazi flag which hangs today in the SAAF War Museum. Top cover had done well to contain the six ME 109s allowing 2 Squadron to tackle the Stukas unimpeded. What an unforgettable Stuka Party!

Tailpiece

This Stuka party should not be confused with a celebrated 1 Squadron party which took place 3 July 1942. Rod Hojem topped the scoreboard on the November operation by shooting down two confirmed and one probable. He was a brilliant and highly reliable operational pilot who was later appointed as a flight commander in 5 Squadron. His DFC was more than well earned during his operational tour. Rod lives in Durban North.

The opening paragraph of Rod's letter to his father.

No 2 Squadron S.A.A.F
U.D.F. M.E.F.
A.P.O. Durban
Natal

My dear Dad,
We have just come down after the greatest Stuka party of all time. Ten of us bumped into 15 Stukas and half a dozen 109s. We climbed into them and a terrific circus took place.

Arthur Walker

Choppers Were My Choice

'The war is over for you, Whitey - go home.' These words were spat at me by a scruffy Zanla bush fighter as he jabbed an AK 47 in my face just a little too close for comfort. I had climbed out of my Alouette chopper after landing at one of the five assembly points where Mugabe's bush fighters had been ordered to gather at the close of the Rhodesian war.

I remember those months when I flew for 7 Squadron of the Rhodesian Air Force as amongst the most enjoyable in my life. The social life was a warm experience and on flying operations it was a low key war. The enemy death rate was high but our casualties were low in spite of the fact that we were shot at regularly during contact. I ignored the bush fighter's advice and stayed on for a while in the Rhodesian Air Force and when I eventually left, had served under Ian Smith, Bishop Muzorewa and Robert Mugabe.

I had been awarded my wings on Harvards and Impalas in 1977 and when rejoining the SAAF on my return to South Africa in 1980, volunteered for a two-year stint in the operational area. I was soon to discover that chopper operations over Angola provided more than a fair share of the drama and excitement which so many young fellows of my age sought.

On 1 January 1981 I was based permanently at AFB Ondangwa in the operational area in support of 32 Battalion and SAP Koevoet. Alan Elston and I soon achieved great success against Swapo in support of these groups.

From the very beginning there was plenty of action commencing with Operation Zulu when we attacked a Swapo base at Ongiva. In mid-January, six Alouettes flown by Billy Port, Mike McGee, Kevin 'Klip' Reynolds, Willem Ras, Heintz Katzke and myself, were briefed to support an attack on another Swapo base near Zangongo. The range of an Alouette is limited, so mini-bases known as 'HAGs' were set up inside Angola within range of the operational area or the target to be attacked.

In the afternoon of the day before the proposed attack, our six choppers led by Billy Port left for Umbalantu where we were to spend

Arthur Walker.

the night before proceeding to the relevant HAG for the operation in the morning. As we landed, a message was received that we were to fly immediately to the HAG where a patrol had made contact with the enemy near Cuamato and required chopper support.

When flying over the specified area, we spotted an Angolan army base consisting of approximately 120 men. SAM 7s and RPG7s immediately opened up at us with an extremely heavy concentration of fire. The Air Force and Army commanders who had gathered at the HAG to plan the next day's operation, observed our unhealthy situation, for the HAG was only five kilometres away. They concurred that it would be suicidal for us to stay and fight under such perilous conditions and ordered us to withdraw.

While leaving the battle area on his way back to the HAG, 'Klip' Reynold's chopper was hit by 14,5 mm fire. He called up the leader Billy Port: 'Billy, Billy, it's Klip, I've been hit, I've been hit.' Billy's rather matter-of-fact voice and dry humour came back: 'Are you bleeding yet Klip?' The prevailing tension suddenly disappeared as we all hosed ourselves with laughter.

On landing back at the HAG, it was discovered that a supply of 20 mm shells had not yet been delivered for our guns so an urgent message was sent to Ondangwa to oblige without delay. Our choppers were refuelled and while awaiting ammunition, the ground forces decided to attack the Angolan detachment without our support. Before long they called for a casevac (casualty evacuation) which meant that a Puma would be obliged to land close to the target area.

64

By this time darkness was closing in, and since the ammunition had arrived and our guns had been rearmed, Mike McGee and I took off·to locate a suitable spot where a Puma could land. When we reached the target area, the enemy guns began blazing away at us, a frightening sight in the dusk because the fiery trajectory of the tracer was accentuated in the fading light. A Puma would have been shot down immediately in this dangerous climate, so there was only one alternative and that was to put the guns out of action. We were busy swopping fire with the Angolans when my gun ran out of ammunition.

I headed back towards the HAG but hadn't gone far when Mike indicated that he was cornered and in trouble with the enemy guns concentrating their fire on him. I turned about, put all my chopper's lights

Alouette badge.

on, and immediately the gunners switched their entire attention on me leaving Mike to escape from his predicament. I managed to withdraw without being hit too seriously although it is difficult to understand why such heavy gunfire didn't end in the demise of my engineer, Sergeant Danie Brink, and myself.

December 1981 was a memorable month. After Operation 'Protea', our forces had occupied several towns in the area much to the annoyance of the Angolans who had every intention of re-occupying them. There was a HAG at Peu Peu north of Zangongo and one night the rumble of moving vehicles to the north could be clearly heard, making sleep virtually impossible. In the morning it transpired that one of 32 Battalion's patrols had not returned, so Dick Paxton and I took off to try to locate it.

We succeeded on this mission, the patrol leader advising us that the problem had been caused by a faulty radio, and while orbiting and talking to him, we felt bullets hitting our choppers although at first their direction wasn't apparent. We then spotted the convoy of Russian BTR 152 armoured vehicles and personnel carriers, and at least three calibres of guns were firing at us.

A thunderous explosion from 14,5 mm and 12,7 mm bullets seemed to rip my chopper apart and all emergency lights came on, but the engine and vital controls were still operating satisfactorily. I flew away from the contact area towards the Kunene River and luckily the conversation between Dick and myself had been monitored at the HAG when two Pumas flown by Ronnie Johnson and 'Blokkies' du Toit immediately became airborne with troops aboard to assist us.

I landed safely and we both climbed out of the chopper to await the arrival of the Pumas. My pistol was cocked and Danie's rifle was at the ready. Within a few minutes the Pumas appeared· and we fired off some smoke grenades to ensure the pilots would find us. They landed and detailed troops to guard the chopper while arrangements were made to recover it back to SWA. My near disaster had been caused by a bullet passing through the fuel tank and lodging in the gear

An Alouette pilot's eyeview of the southern Angola bush; an unending, featureless terrain sometimes made navigation difficult.

Swapo camp near Cuamato. This camp put up the stiffest anti-aircraft flak of the war until it was eventually overrun by ground forces.

box. I had flown for twelve kilometres without any oil in the latter. Impalas were called in to attack the Angolan convoy with rockets and cannons, but the day was won by Phil Meredith and Dick Paxton in their Alouettes when taking out all 14 BTR 152s and BRDMs.

On 28 December, after an enjoyable Christmas at Ondangwa, we were detailed to drop four 'sticks' of 12 troops to check whether an area north of Evale was free of Swapo terrorists. After dropping the troops, we spotted a small enemy group and immediately attacked it. Suddenly the area became alive with tracer and anti-aircraft fire, and it was obvious that this was an appreciably large contact. We were to discover afterwards that it was an Angolan army group which had moved down the other side of the river intent on re-occupying Ongiva. The group numbered 650 troops with a Russian commander. Our men had their hands full!

Before long they called for a casevac. Serge Bovie and his engineer Dolf van Rensburg uplifted a wounded man but the anti-aircraft fire was intensive; the chopper was hit, crashed into some trees and began burning fiercely. I landed a short distance away and my engineer Sgt Christo Botes and I made our way to it to see if we could help. There was no sign of Serge and Dolf but their casualty had been thrown out and was trapped under the chopper. Botes used an axe to try to cut him free but he was already dead, and since the situation was so dangerous and shrapnel was exploding near us, we decided to withdraw immediately. We were totally outnumbered and would be lucky to escape the situation alive.

Botes ran towards our chopper planning to get the engine started while I returned fire from behind an ant-heap being in no doubt that our chances of survival were slim. What a fool I'd been to volunteer to fly choppers in the operational area. My love for flying and adventure was about to leave me as a corpse in the Angolan bush.

Looking towards Botes I could see him sitting in the pilot's seat and the rotor blades had begun to turn. He gave me the 'thumbs up' and after slithering on my belly towards the chopper, I jumped in and took over the controls. Without fastening the harness or closing the door, I pulled maximum power, bent on getting the hell out of it as quickly as possible.

Keeping low to avoid the enemy fire, I couldn't believe my eyes for in our flight path were Serge and Dolf waving frantically. Still under fire, I landed again, picked them up and hugging the ground, flew the chopper from the jaws of what had appeared to be certain death into a safer climate.

It was a miracle that all of us had remained unscathed for so long under such consistent fire. Apparently the Angolan commander had sent a patrol to check on the burning chopper and Serge and Dolf had taken to their heels chased by the Angolans. I had flown over this patrol and happened to land right behind Serge and Dolf. The relieved expression on their faces when rescued, made it all worthwhile!

Cuamato was one of the towns in southern Angola from where Arthur Walker and his Alouette crew operated. Ground fire from the nearby enemy camps was the most intense of the war.

Tailpiece

Arthur Walker is the only member of the SADF to have been decorated with the Honoris Crux (Gold) and bar. Both awards were made during the operations which have been described in this story. Sgt Christo Botes was awarded the Honoris Crux (Silver) for his part in the rescue of Serge Bovie and Dolf van Rensburg.

Arthur also won the SM for his co-operation with and the development and motivation of the SA Police 'Koevoet' in the SWA operational area. He is the son of the well-known golfer who was English Amateur Golf Champion in 1957 and South African champion in 1959. He is a serving Major with the SAAF and is at present instructing at 87 Heli Flying School, Bloemspruit.

Refuelling position in the Ovambo bush; SAAF engineers worked wonders to create adequate back-up facilities for airborne fighting units in this remote corner of Africa.

Dangerous Moonlight

In modern warfare oil is a necessity. The side that runs short loses. Hitler ensured a foothold in Romania and tried to consolidate his position still further by a thrust to Stalingrad in order to secure his grip on the oilfields around the Caspian Sea. Here he failed, and so Romania remained his major source of oil.

In 1943, the USAAF rehearsed for two weeks in North Africa with full-scale models of cracking and refining plants representing the Romano/Americano oil refineries at Ploesti, north of Bucharest. Eventually a vast low level Liberator attack was launched which turned out to be a disaster and caused only minimal damage. The target was hidden under a smoke screen emanating from smoke pots set off in positions according to the wind direction. Enemy fighters and light flak gunners were very successful and American losses were heavy, not only in the target area but as a result of crews being unable to navigate home once separated from formations.

During 1944, the SAAF and RAF squadrons of 205 Group based at Foggia in Italy, carried out several saturation night raids on Ploesti with considerable losses, yet failed to deal a knock-out blow. Again, smoke was a most effective means of defence as far as the Germans were concerned. The price Hitler placed on oil was obvious for Ploesti enjoyed greater protection than any other target in Europe. Experienced fighter squadrons were based in the area together with radar, searchlights and a large number of heavy and light guns. Another way had to be found to eliminate the oil flow.

Taking advantage of clear full-moon nights, Liberators and Wellingtons of 205 Group turned their attention to mining the River Danube because all oil destined for the Germans' war machine flowed upstream in trains of steel-hulled barges, ten or more being hauled in train by tugs.

The mines used were top secret and were not allowed to be observed even at a distance. They arrived at our squadrons in Royal Navy trucks covered by tarpaulins. Our armourers were ordered to leave the dispersal area while RN armourers loaded the mines into the

A Liberator.

aircrafts' bomb-bays and closed the bomb-doors, not to be opened until over the Danube. Exactly how these mines worked was a tight-lipped secret, and the only crumb of information gleaned, was that they operated magnetically. Their mechanisms were set at random intervals promoting a situation resembling Russian Roulette. It would only be a matter of time before the barges would strike the mines and be blown to pieces. Too bad we would not be around to witness their destruction. This situation was to prove so damaging to the morale of the Hungarian barge crews that they mutinied and were replaced by Germans. Apparently the mines were difficult to detect which was an added hazard for the enemy.

On the afternoon of 30 July 1944, 31 Squadron SAAF was briefed to mine several Danube beds and each crew was instructed to identify their own bed. We were to run in while losing height to precisely 30 ft above the river, adjust speed to 190 miles per hour, drop our mines at three second intervals and then get away as fast as possible. Light flak could be expected from the river banks. After an early meal that evening, we were to be driven to our aircraft which would have been refuelled sufficiently plus 25 per cent for emergencies. As the operation was not a saturation bombing raid, we would fly individually to our specific stretch of river known as 'our bed for the night'! Take off times could therefore be flexible as long as arrival over the bed enjoyed maximum advantage from the light of the full moon. Five minutes were spent rehearsing the details of the drop, the success of which depended on a team effort. When satisfied that the start of our bed had been reached, Happy Holliday would call 'DROP' and the bomb aimer, Laurie Greig, would press his release button and repeat 'DROP'. The second pilot, Bob Hamilton, would then call 'DROP' at three second intervals until all six mines had gone.

Climbing into V Victor through the tail hatch and while heading for our respective positions in the Liberator, we observed the mines which appeared to be overfed and almost touching the sides of the bomb-bay. They were red, cylindrical and much larger than standard bombs of the same weight. Darkness fell as we flew across the Adriatic, and over enemy territory the ground became clearer as the moon's altitude increased. On two occasions we saw an electric flare path switch on and a single light streak along it, no doubt a 'cat's eye' fighter taking off hoping to catch up with us or another of our aircraft.

Happy Holliday asked the beam gunner, Jock van Zyl, to throw out a flare and a few seconds later Leslie Mayes, the tail gunner, called: 'Navigator, I can see the flare and will set my sights on it.' A short pause followed and he continued: 'Quadrant reading ONE-EIGHT-SIX over.' 'Thank you tail gunner from navigator,' and after another pause: 'Skipper, our course correction is FOUR DEGREES TO RIGHT.' Bob Hamilton then chipped in: 'Compass adjusted Skipper.'

Three hours passed before the Danube appeared ahead, and losing height to 1 000 ft we flew upstream to identify our bed, a straight stretch of river with the town of Corabia on its north bank. The moon was now much brighter and ground features were clearly visible. Happy had hardly identified the bed when tracer shells bombarded us from both river banks. According to Jock van Zyl there were two guns on the south bank and twelve on the north bank. As I turned sharply to port, at the same time losing height, the wireless operator, Bunny Austin, advised that he intended to man the right beam gun and when acknowledging his message I reminded him to allow full deflection, quipping that the Jerries don't aim too well when shot at!

In no time we had turned a full circle and were approaching our bed upstream at about 150 ft, still losing height and speed. The radio altimeter had been switched on and set for 30 ft above the water. Its panel was green. We could now clearly see the high cliffs on the north bank as opposed to the much lower ground on the south bank. It wasn't difficult to judge our height by looking along the moonlit banks of the river, but nevertheless, I kept my eye on the radio altimeter panel. It flashed yellow and then red indicating that we were below 30 ft. I eased gently back on the control column and the light turned yellow again. Our speed settled to 190 miles per hour and Bob Hamilton increased power on all engines so that this speed could be maintained. The enemy guns were silent as we approached the bed. 'Ready for dropping,' I called. 'Ready,' replied Happy, Bob and Laurie.

Happy yelled: 'DROP,' repeated immediately by Laurie, and Bob began counting 'TWO THREE DROP' - 'TWO THREE DROP' -'TWO THREE DROP.' Each time Laurie jabbed the release button, a brown light came on for an instant confirming that a mine had been released. As the last mine tumbled, the enemy guns opened up from both banks and immediately our Brownings spat back at the German positions. The smell of cordite inside the aircraft filled the air and lifted our morale considerably. There was a jolt on the control column and V Victor no longer responded to fore and aft control. Fortunately the Lib was well trimmed and as Bob gave the engines full power, I pulled the aircraft out of the river valley by adjusting the tail trimmer - and then turned for home.

The flak had eased and Leslie Mayes had also stopped firing. I had just called for a reduction of power to normal climbing settings when George Peaston in the top turret yelled: 'Skipper, No 2 engine is on fire!' There was a long blue and white flame reaching halfway along the fuse-lage from No 2's exhaust, a frightening sight known as 'torching' which sometimes happens when a turbo-supercharged engine's power is reduced after running on full power for a lengthy period. I put the mix-ture control to auto-lean and the flame vanished.

I couldn't raise the tail gunner on the intercom, but Bunny Austin had just returned to his radio 'office' and assured me that Leslie was OK, but that his intercom wires and gun hydraulics had been shot to pieces. He added that Leslie had switched his guns to manual and had given the Jerry gunners a long parting shot! I called George Peaston in the top turret: 'No communication with tail gunner, so you will have to double for tail and top gunner.' George, a charming and reliable Scot replied: 'That's easy Skipper.'

The danger of the Danube was behind us, but ahead lay the fright-ening problem of how to land V Victor with the elevator cable severed. It was easy enough to fly with manual aileron, rudder and trimmer, but could I land with only the tail trimmer? I had not told my chaps about this hazard for they had enough to cope with and in any case this was my responsibility. After flying for two hours I suddenly remembered that the autopilot had a duplicate set of control cables. I tried the autopilot elevator control and was relieved to find that it worked fore and aft!

By using my feet on the rudder, hands on the aileron and by turn-ing a small disc, I made a reasonable landing and taxied to dispersal.

Next day it was ascertained that not only was the manual elevator cable severed, but the autopilot elevator had almost been shot away. Furthermore, the barrel of Bunny Austin's Browning was smooth as that of a shotgun. He had fired a single burst of 250 rounds at the gun emplacements on the north bank. There is little doubt that this determined action saved us, for the only damage inflicted came from the two guns on the south bank.

Thanks to 205 Group's operations, the flow of oil from Ploesti to Vienna was totally halted. Air Vice-Marshal John Slessor sent Brigadier Jimmy Durrant, the Group's OC, a signal congratulating him on planning and executing the most effective operation in southern Europe. In retrospect, his congratulations were an understatement for, deprived of its major source of oil, the German war machine began to grind to a halt many months earlier than it would otherwise have done and thousands, perhaps millions of lives were saved.

Tailpiece

After the mining of the River Danube operations, Jack and his crew took part in dropping supplies to the Polish Home Army in Warsaw when his aircraft was shot down and three of his crew perished. The story 'Disaster over Warsaw', is told elsewhere in this book.

A Unique Achiever

Jack Parsonson will long be remembered by those of us who served with him in the Desert Air Force for his unflinching bravery, dedication to duty and tenacity in adversity. He is one of the SAAF's unique achievers.

His tour of operations in the Western Desert with 2 Squadron and later as OC 5 Squadron, included a wealth of dramatic adventures. Air battles during this period were an everyday occurrence, the Luftwaffe pilots riding on the crest of a wave with superior aircraft and an abundance of experience. Jack was shot down three times during his tour, returning twice to his squadron to fight again but the third time he wasn't so lucky and spent the rest of the war as a POW.

Amongst his most vivid wartime memories are two operations in which he took part when 47 enemy aircraft were destroyed. On the first occasion, a mixed formation of Junkers 52s and Savoia 72s literally fell out of the sky in flames as 14 were downed.

Three days later, when Jack was leading 7 Wing, there was horrific carnage as 24 huge six-engined ME 323 transport aircraft were destroyed. Jack and his pilots sailed into the hapless enemy aircraft which were undoubtedly carrying a full cargo of fuel. They burst into flames on impact with the water, burning petrol spreading out in all directions giving the impression that the sea was alight. All except one of the ME 323s were destroyed although this was later accounted for by 239 Wing. The total score of 47 aircraft destroyed on both shows included fighters claimed by top cover.

When Jack was shot down the second time, the squadron was attacked by ME 109s and during the ensuing fight, his No 2 spun away in a tight turn leaving him to face four enemy aircraft alone. The odds were too great especially when another four Messerschmitts joined the fray. Jack staved off the inevitable for a while by turning towards his attackers, but eventually they got behind him and he crash-landed, his Kitty riddled with holes and streaming oil and glycol. When he climbed out of the cockpit, the 109s came for him like a swarm of hornets and he dived into a nearby hut which provided protection against these cowardly tactics.

Jack's confidence in his ability to escape captivity a third time, was thwarted by the current between the island on which he had been sheltering and the mainland. He had planned to paddle across the 12 mile stretch of water in his aircraft's dinghy arriving on the mainland in the dark, but due to the fast flowing current he arrived in daylight, was spotted and captured. This was the end of the war for Jack and while in Stalag Luft 3, he heard of his immediate award of the DSO.

He was involved in the 'Great Escape' but while waiting his turn to enter the famous tunnel, the project was discovered by the Germans and he didn't get further than his cell. In so doing he avoided being shot like so many of the other poor escapees.

Jack's qualities as a warrior and achiever are well illustrated by what happened after VE Day. I was told that he was to be repatriated *via* Rome, and I thought what a splendid opportunity to see my friend. General Frank Theron graciously undertook to arrange that he was disembarked in Rome. The Wing's B25 made short work of flying him to Campo Formido in North Italy where 8 Wing was stationed. What a memorable reunion followed! I had visions of a psychologically disturbed person in need of great care and delicate readjustment. Instead Jack by fair means

Jack Parsonson.

Rosy du Toit.

and foul, managed to get a Spitfire to fly. He had a burning objective to get back into flying duty and be considered for further operational duty against the Japanese. His way of achieving readjustment after two years as a POW, was to get involved in the war and make up for lost time.

I recommended him to fill the vacant post of Wing Commander Flying in 8 Wing, to which the AOC, DAF, Air Vice-Marshal 'Pussy' Foster, and SAAF HQ had concurred and he proudly added the extra pip to his crown. He volunteered to fight in the war against Japan but the Atomic Bomb put paid to this intention and he had perforce, to rest on the laurels he had already so gallantly achieved.

A pilot's mess in the desert.

Tailpiece

Rosy became the youngest officer in the SAAF to command a fighter wing on operations. He was decorated with the CBE, DFC and bar, and served with distinction in Abyssinia, North Africa from El Alamein to Tunis, and the Italian campaign. He lives in Durbanville, Cape.

Christmas card from 5 Squadron, 1942 (designed by Padre Basil Barron).

S 'Pi' Pienaar

A Speck in my Rearview Mirror

Archie Lockhart-Ross and I had been briefed for a photographic operation over southern Germany's Black Forest region. Intelligence had called on 60 Squadron SAAF for an emergency flight after underground information had been received disclosing that the Germans were testing a secret weapon in the area.

The date was 15 August 1944 and it was a pleasant afternoon; warm, with a little scattered cloud breaking the starkness of the blue sky. We climbed to 30 000 ft and levelled off, cruising with a speed of 350 mph indicating on the ASI.

I wasn't particularly worried about enemy aircraft, for up to this time no standard German fighter had been able to match a Mosquito's speed, and even if an enemy aircraft took off to intercept, there was ample time to complete the photographic runs before it reached 30 000 ft when we'd be on the way home. Our task was to take photographs and not to seek combat and therefore our Mossies flew unarmed.

While approaching Leipheim airfield, Archie reported an aircraft taking off from an adjacent airstrip. Naturally I kept a watchful eye while he was checking the cameras, types which provided immense detail as long as the pilot flew on an accurate, straight and level course, otherwise the photographs would be blurred.

When glancing in my rearview mirror I observed a small speck on the horizon which a few seconds later had grown into a deadly twin-engined enemy fighter. It was 400 yards behind and about to blast us out of the sky.

I jettisoned the long-range tanks, opened both throttles fully and while turning to starboard, cannon shells severed the port aileron and damaged the port elevator and the main spar. The Mossie flicked over into a flat spiral, totally out of control and when trying to recover, I found that both throttles had jammed in the fully open position and we kept going down.

I pulled back the starboard engine's pitch lever which reduced the revs appreciably, and then the high blowers cut out indicating that since the spiral began, our height had dropped from 30 000 to 19 000 ft. The

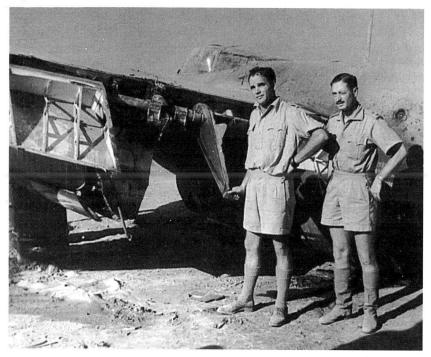

Pi Pienaar (left) and Archie Lockhart-Ross with their damaged Mosquito.

reduction in revs and boost achieved the required result and I was able to recover from the spiral in the normal manner, although obliged to fly with the stick fully over to the right and some right rudder.

As I pondered those dramatic minutes, it was clear that my decision to turn starboard instead of port had been a life-saver because the enemy pilot was taken by surprise. He must have known that under the circumstances, a Mossie pilot would automatically turn to port due to the position of his seat, and if I had adhered to this norm, the full blast of the enemy's cannons would have eliminated us. As it happened, resulting from the damage inflicted, I could only turn to port during the 11 attacks which followed, but I already had the measure of the Jerry who didn't manage to hit the Mossie again.

During the spiral, Archie had been lying in the nose held inert by the 'G' force, and only half-conscious because his oxygen-feed tube had been jerked from its socket. When the Mossie levelled off, he returned to my side, but before there was time to gather our shattered senses, he yelled: 'Look out, here it comes again.'

When the enemy aircraft was approximately 600 yards away, I whipped around to port and was able to turn inside it. If the Mossie had been armed, I could have destroyed my adversary who presented a sitting target while overshooting. We were however, able to identify Germany's latest and fastest twin-engined jet fighter, the ME 262, which was still on the secret list.

It occurred to me that perhaps the Mosquitoes which had gone missing over recent months, had been the 262's guinea-pig victims and we had been earmarked as the next. Undoubtedly the pilot intended to play a cat and mouse game with us knowing that we were unarmed and he could practise his skills from all angles. However, he was to learn that the 262's phenomenal speed was the main cause of his failure for he could not turn sharply enough when making an astern, quarter or beam attack, and on each occasion I was able to turn inside him. During three head-on attacks, he didn't seem to have a clue for his aircraft's tracer streaked harmlessly over us.

Archie was a star turn throughout those dramatic attacks for he warned me every time the 262 was approaching and was approximately 1 000 yards away. This enabled me to turn timeously to allow for the jet's exceptional closing speed. During each attack, appreciable height was lost but at the same time we were edging closer to Switzerland.

When the 262 came in for the tenth attack, our height had been reduced to 9 000 ft and I thought that it was only a matter of time before superiority conquered, so I said to Archie: 'If we are going to die, let's take this blighter with us,' and yanking the Mossie around, I headed straight at the 262 - but its pilot had a different idea and hopped over us. Our position was somewhere near Lake Constance when the 262 made its twelfth and last attack; another fruitless head-on attempt after which it broke away and disappeared, probably short of petrol.

The engines were still running at full boost and most of the instruments were jammed when Archie gave me a course to steer for home. We had been flying in and out of cloud, but over Schwaz the Mossie plunged into uniform cloud which, excepting one break, remained solid as we flew across the Alps with a clearance of only 500 ft. When Archie estimated our position was over the plains of northern Italy, I let down through the cloud and couldn't believe my eyes when seeing Udine airfield immediately beneath. It was a German base crawling with fighters and very heavily defended - always well avoided by Allied airmen unless briefed to attack it.

'Hold tight,' I yelled to Archie as I pushed the stick forward and we skimmed along one of the runways on the deck. The Mossie's screaming engines must have put the fear of hell into the soldiers who scrambled and dived in all directions, but before they could man their guns, we were heading for the safety of the Adriatic and our base at San Severo. Archie spotted four aircraft high above us and I froze on the controls, but they turned out to be Spitfires!

As San Severo appeared ahead, I tested for stall and found it to be well above normal. Apart from this, the Mossie's hydraulic controls had been shot away, so the landing gear was not operating, and there was no throttle control. I made a wide low circuit of the dirt runway, warning Archie to free the top hatch and let it go at the moment of impact with the runway.

A 60 Squadron Mosquito.

The approach was made at 200 mph and when over some trees on the airstrip's boundary, I cut the switches on both engines, the speed falling off as I steered the Mossie towards the runway. There was a jarring thump as the belly hit the ground throwing up a huge cloud of dust while slithering to a halt. When I looked for Archie, he had already evacuated the Mossie and was standing alongside shouting: 'Get out man, get out!'

Tailpiece

Pi and Archie were able to supply 'Intelligence' with the first detailed information on the ME 262. They were both awarded immediate DFCs, but before toasting this occasion with their squadron mates, they celebrated their safe return and the fact that they would be sleeping in their own beds that night!

Pi was to become the most renowned captain in South African Airways logging up 18 648 flying hours and introducing SAA and the South African public to the jet age. In 1975 he climbed to the top of the ladder to become SAA's Chief Executive. He lives on his small farm on the banks of the Vaal River near Parys in the Orange Free State.

Acknowledgement

The story of Pi Pienaar's encounter with the ME 262 appeared in Carel Birkby's *Dancing the Skies*.

Karen Birkby has kindly authorised the use of a number of extracts from her late husband's book.

An ME 262, the speck in Pi Pienaar's rearview mirror.

Captains Victorious

Many of South Africa's World War II friends have forgotten the SAAF's valiant efforts in those faraway days, but my memory will never fade. I am one of several Australians who had the honour of serving with 24 Squadron, SAAF. The pilots, aircrew and ground staff were an outstanding bunch of fellows for whom I will always hold a healthy respect and affection.

I served with some of the squadron's distinguished commanding officers, flight commanders and aircrew, far too many to mention by name and therefore I will deal mainly with the captains of the crews with whom I flew most of my operations.

I must stress from the start that there was no glamour attached to any individual in a bomber crew. Success was entirely due to a group effort. My role in the team was navigator/bomb aimer.

I flew on several raids with Jack Mossop who was also the CO at the time. He was a Permanent Force officer like many of the early 24 Squadron COs, a skilled, methodical pilot, always keen to fly and lead by example.

No doubt the most unforgettable operation I took part in with Jack, was on 21 March 1942. An urgent convoy was to be pushed through to Malta and it was hoped that the Desert Air Force would be able to neutralise as many enemy landing grounds as possible. No 24 Squadron's target was Barce airfield in Cyrenaica and nine Boston aircrews were briefed to attack the airfield in three waves of three aircraft at half-hour intervals, the intention being to disrupt long range bomber activity.

As it happened, the first wave of Bostons led by Jack with myself as navigator/bomb aimer, were the only aircraft to reach the target. The others turned back because of weather conditions which made flying and navigation extremely difficult. An escort was not provided as the distance to be flown by the Bostons was considered to be too far for the fighters. To baffle the German radar, an initial course was flown out to sea and around the Cyrenaica-hump but unfortunately cloud and

B A 'Aussie' Coleborne, RAAF in 1941, just after joining
24 Squadron SAAF.

unstable air forced Jack to skip around the sky while endeavouring to avoid some towering cumulus clouds, making it very difficult for me to navigate accurately and ascertain our precise position.

Luck was on my side for as our Boston crossed the coast I recognised a prominent landmark. A quick change of course brought us to the target. The bombing run was made at 7 000 ft, all bombs falling across the corner of the airfield where several aircraft were parked. As planned, we then dived to approximately 100 ft above the ground reaching a speed of approximately 300 mph.

It was a lovely spring morning as the three Bostons were cruising along smoothly just above the ground, their crews elated by the successful operation and thinking about breakfast they would shortly enjoy, when suddenly the top gunner's voice broke the silence: 'Fighters astern.' There was a pause and he added: 'It's O K, they are ours - I think!' A couple of rude words followed and then our two Brownings began to chatter along with those of the Bostons on either side of us.

Jack opened the throttles fully and the Bostons battled along eastwards out-gunned by at least three ME 109s. Although the chase didn't last longer than a few minutes, our own aircraft and one of the other two in our lot were hit in vital areas. Amongst the three crews, one member was killed and several wounded including Jack and our gunners. Both damaged aircraft were obliged to belly-land in isolated territory when I was lucky to escape with burns while helping to rescue the wounded from our burning Boston - but that's another story.

In June 1942, having recovered from the Barce drama, I returned to 24 Squadron where Bert Rademan, the popular charismatic CO, introduced me to my next captain, 'Squiffy' Smith, and his crew. My sojourn with this crew was to be one of the happiest and most fulfilling of my operational career. It covered the period known as the Gazala Gallop when our forces had been out-thought and outmanoeuvred by General Rommel and were on the retreat. The task of the Desert Air Force was to hammer the Afrika Korps unmercifully as it chased our forces eastwards. Then came the tough days in July when Rommel threw his armoured formations against the El Alamein line where the Allied armies eventually turned defeat into victory.

I flew 39 raids with 'Squiffy' and his crew in just 42 days and when asked to forsake this crew and navigate for flight commander Dirk Nel, I was naturally saddened. 'Squiffy' was a wonderful character with a hearty spontaneous laugh, a practical joker with an amusing repertoire of sleight-of-hand tricks.

Perhaps one of my most treasured memories of 24 Squadron was its high morale. The aircrews and ground staff worked exceptionally

Bostons and bombs at an advanced landing ground, 1942.

hard. Dirk Nel was an unflappable character and during the time we flew together I only saw him lose his cool twice and, to some extent, this was my fault. When he flew a course, the compass needle never seemed to move from the lubber line. At first I used to give the compass bowl a tap to see if the needle was stuck. The pointers on the ASI and altimeter dials also stayed on their pre-arranged figures. Dirk was a fine leader, keen to fly on as many operations as possible and play his part in helping to bring the war to a quick and successful conclusion. He was a true Afrikaner with a keen interest in the soil.

We were a happy crew and flew on some extremely successful raids together, but once again my service with a first class crew was terminated when Dirk breezed up to me one morning in his usual jocular manner: 'Congratulations Aussie, we are sorry to see you go, but Bert Rademan has been put off ops and Blackie Blackwell of 12 Squadron is taking over as CO. He wants you as his senior navigator/bomb aimer.' Blackie turned out to be a magnificent CO. It wasn't easy for him to step into the shoes of a colossus such as Bert Rademan, but like Bert, he was a true leader and before long had won the total respect and affection of the squadron and where he went, every crew member in the squadron followed unquestionably.

I flew on 24 raids with Blackie and became closer to him than any other pilot with whom I operated. He never adopted a 'know-all' attitude and was always willing to listen to everyone's point of view. He understood the part played by crew members and he was a leader who

Retreating Axis forces hammered.

took the brunt of all vital decisions. He often remarked that it didn't matter how good or daring a bomber pilot, he was quite useless unless the entire team was up to scratch.

A memorable op which Blackie led, shows that he was not afraid of making immediate, vital decisions. The Battle of El Alamein commenced on 23 October 1942 and the following day the squadron was briefed to soften up the German positions where our forces were planning to break through. Generally the desert skies were cloudless, but on this occasion there was a uniform layer of cloud situated slap over the target area. Under normal circumstances a bombing run would be made at 9-10 000 ft and if cloud obscured the target, bombs would be dropped through the cloud on ETA. However, with the close proximity of our own troops, visual bombing of the target was essential.

It was not the kind of day for dealing out death and destruction. The squadron took off in glorious weather. The battleground could be seen from a long distance away, the gun flashes accentuated by the uniform layer of white cloud covering the area.

There were two choices; either to abort or to fly under the cloud. If the former decision was taken we'd let down the army which was relying on our help to defeat the Afrika Korps. On the other hand if our aircraft attacked under the cloud, they would be sitting ducks for enemy flak, inviting heavy casualties.

There was no hesitation when Blackie made his decision and even before he spoke over the R/T, I knew what he was going to say; 'Aussie

German fighters scramble to intercept.

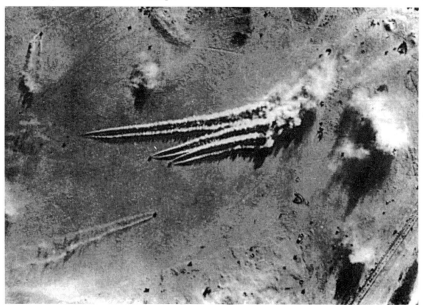

Crews board transport to be taken to their aircraft (just visible on the horizon) for an operational sortie.

- we'll have to go underneath the cloud. What do you estimate the base to be - 6 000 ft?' 'I hope it's not less,' I replied. 'Can you get everything reorganised in time?' he asked. 'I'll have to,' I said, but I can tell you that I wasn't too confident about succeeding.

It must be borne in mind that a navigator/bomb aimer pre-planned his bomb aiming strategy from an agreed height and when a drastic change was made with limited notice, it wasn't easy to adjust and still obtain accuracy. An asset as far as I was concerned during these torrid moments, was that I was so busy estimating the height of the cloud base and fiddling with my bomb-aiming sight, that there

A Boston prangs on returning from operations.

89

wasn't time to think about the sport which the German ack-ack gunners would enjoy as our aircraft trundled across the target area scarcely a mile above them, outlined conveniently against a brilliant white background of cloud.

Blackie throttled back and our Bostons lost height as we ran in towards the target. The cloud base turned out to be a little under 6 000 ft and I'm pleased to say that the squadron's bombs fell within the target area, a fact later confirmed by the army. The ensuing flak hammered the Bostons and the toll was heavy, but it could have been much worse. Two observers were killed, two crew members wounded and one aircraft belly-landed on returning to base.

After victory at the Battle of El Alamein I will never forget the punishment meted out to Rommel's forces as they retreated in full flight. The squadron formed up in vics line astern and bombed enemy transport which was boxed up nose to tail on the main coastal road where there was total confusion.

Today I look back and remember with pride, all those who like me were part of that squadron for a part of its long and successful operational record in the 1939-45 War.

Tailpiece

Blackie Blackwell paid the following tribute a week before his death. 'I guarantee that worldwide one couldn't find Aussie's equal as an observer. He was calm, collected and infallible. When his aircraft was shot down after the Barce airfield raid, he walked for more than 24 hours wearing out the soles of his shoes and eventually finding help. His control of bombing, his navigation and general behaviour under stress, were admirable. He was awarded the MBE and DFC and should have received the DSO.'

Jack Mossop asked whether his tribute could also be included in the tailpiece so here it is: 'I owe my life to Aussie's courage, fortitude and extraordinary navigational ability. While pulling the wounded gunners out of the blazing Boston, his face and hands were severely burnt and in spite of this and the fact that his maps and navigational equipment had been destroyed in the aircraft, he walked back to our lines through trackless desert and was able to provide DAF HQ with such an accurate pinpoint of our aircraft's position that we were located and rescued.' Aussie lives in New South Wales, Australia.

Dick Clifton

Mustang / MiG Mêlée

In mid-winter 1951-52, with the ground fighting in Korea stabilised roughly along the 39th Parallel, the primary task of the United Nations Air Forces became the interdiction of the enemy's main supply route. Attacks on this route by Mustangs of the USAF 19th Fighter-Bomber Wing to which 2 Squadron SAAF was attached, were carried out by small formations which dive-bombed the railway line and then attacked pre-briefed secondary targets such as storage areas, with rockets and guns.

Early in February, when the weather was still so cold that the Cheetahs were obliged to keep their beer in the fridge to prevent it from freezing, the theme was varied for a brief period by the skip-bombing of railway tunnels. A tunnel was approached 'on the deck' along the railway line, and a couple of 500-pounders were dropped just short of the entrance by each aircraft before it zoomed up abruptly to avoid the surrounding high ground.

In theory, if the aim was accurate, the bombs which were fused to explode 15 seconds after impact, would bounce on frozen ground, disappear into the tunnel, emerge at the other end and explode in the open. If falling short of the entrance, they could explode dangerously close to the following aircraft. Consequently, no one was sorry when this crazy experiment was dropped.

In any event, Fifth Air Force HQ decided at this time that the flak was becoming too concentrated south of the Ch'ongch'on River and switched fighter-bomber operations further north towards the Manchurian border. Here initially, there was less flak, but the target area was within easy reach of the Chinese MiG 15s operating from Antung air base across the Yalu River. The politicians had decided that to extend the war into Manchuria might escalate the conflict too dangerously, so Antung remained an official MiG sanctuary. I emphasise 'official' because I have seen gun-camera films of MiG kills by USAF F86 Sabres which showed the enemy aircraft with their wheels and flaps extended, suggesting that they were shot down in the Antung circuit.

Dick Clifton is decorated in Korea.

The new plan of attack, known as 'Operation Saturate', involved using large formations of fighter bombers to attack short sections of railway line causing maximum destruction and swamping the enemy's ability to repair railcuts overnight and move supplies before the fighter-bombers returned at dawn next day. This meant operating at Wing strength, so 2 Squadron SAAF and the 12th, 39th and 67th USAAF Squadrons each mustered as many Mustangs as possible in multiples of four, the basic section formation.

Flying 36 aircraft off a narrow PSP (Pierced Steel Planking) airstrip in the shortest possible time was chaotic until 'Monty' Montgomery, the Cheetah's immensely popular Squadron Operations Officer solved the problem by marshalling our aircraft like the starter on a racetrack. Monty, an ex-35 Squadron Sunderland flying boat pilot, had nearly completed a tour of operations on Mustangs, when he was grounded because of acute sinusitis, so he was a natural to take over from 'AQ' de Wet who had ruptured himself lifting an oil drum for the Ops Room heating stove. What a character Monty was! His standard opening when answering the phone was: 'Hello you big *poep.*' This often had to be corrected hurriedly to: 'Oh! Good morning sir.'

To execute Monty's idea, squadrons taxied out in a pre-briefed order, sections of four taking the runway together nose to tail, relying entirely on his marshalling signals, as forward vision was limited both by the Mustang's long nose and the clouds of fine slush raised by the slipstream of the preceding aircraft. Our exuberant Ops Officer stood off to one side of the airstrip armed with a large red flag. When raised and held steady, it signalled 'Stop'; waved round and round above his head meant 'Open the throttle against the brakes'; and lowered briskly to point down the runway, indicated 'Let go the brakes and roll'. Pilots didn't see much of the aircraft ahead of them until their own aircraft's tail came up, but having flown Mustangs himself, Monty could be relied on to judge a safe gap. This unusual procedure continued until all aircraft were airborne at close but safe intervals.

The Wing formed up, each section in close finger formation while circling the base. The leader then gave the order: 'Battle formation go,' and set course for the target. It was indeed a tremendous thrill to lead such an armada; to observe each squadron and section take up their battle stations, knowing that every man depended on you to lead him unerringly to the target and bring him safely home.

Cloud cover en route to the target, some 200 miles distant, was a leader's greatest problem because map reading and dead reckoning were his only means of navigation. Known heavy anti-aircraft gun concentrations were avoided if possible by slight detours and if gun flashes on the ground or black puffs of exploding shells were spotted, it was advisable to lead the entire formation into a 'corkscrew', constantly changing altitude and direction.

Instead of navigating directly to the target, some suitable, easily recognisable, feature was chosen as the 'IP' (Initial Point) to head for. Up to the IP, our battle formation left no blind spots where enemy fighters could surprise us, but here, turning towards the target in a stream, we were more vulnerable to attack until re-formed in battle formation after bombing. Initially 'Operation Saturate' was a 'piece of cake'. Targets were almost flak-free and a top cover of F86 Sabres patrolling at height in the target area, kept the MiGs out of our hair. Soon, however, the enemy tumbled to the change in tactics and moved flak to the new target area, so it became the practice to send one squadron in ahead of the main formation to suppress the flak.

I have in my scrap book a signal from Colonel Toby Moll, the SAAF's Senior Air Liaison Officer with the USAF Far East Air Force HQ in Tokyo, which was prompted by one such mission. It begins: '25 Mar for Clifton from Moll. Congratulations on aggressive display against MiGs. This is further evidence that 2 Sqn is upholding fine fighting tradition of SAAF.'

On 20 March 1952 I had led eight SAAF Mustangs on a flak suppression mission in support of the rest of the Wing which followed at a short interval to attack the railway line between Sinuiju and Sinanju. On the way to the target one of the second section's aircraft developed a rough engine, so I sent the pilot back to base under escort, for we were already deep in enemy territory. The remaining two pilots, Vin Kuhn and Hans Enslin closed up with my section.

I had been unable to contact the promised Sabre top cover and from the IP to the railway line we saw no other aircraft friend or foe. Heavy flak opened up, the flashes pinpointing the target, so we wasted no time attacking. As I pulled out of my bombing dive in a climbing turn to observe results, the sky suddenly seemed full of MiGs, no doubt attracted by the black puffs of bursting shells which had greeted us before the attack. Dave Taylor, my number 4, was hit while pulling out of his dive and there was momentary chaos while I urged the 'Cheetahs' to re-form battle formation.

Joe Joubert, Mac McLaughlin and Hans Enslin slid into finger formation as I circled to allow them to catch up. Vin Kuhn with two MiGs after him, managed to fight his way into the protection of a cloud bank. I positioned behind and above Taylor's Mustang which was losing height while heading south, streaming smoke and glycol. He did not answer when I called him repeatedly and was obviously in serious trouble.

Then the MiGs attacked in real earnest. A pair came in extremely fast from nine o'clock high on a quarter attack which I parried in the conventional way by turning our formation towards them. They were

A Cheetah Squadron Spitfire

flying too fast to get in behind us and were forced to break upwards. We turned back to cover Taylor, but before I could locate him, the MiGs came in again from three o'clock high and the same manoeuvre had to be repeated.

As we straightened out I was watching these two when Joubert's sharp eyes spotted another MiG sneaking up behind and below me. 'MiG six o'clock below shooting at your leader,' he reported and as we broke to port, the enemy overshot relatively slowly with air brakes extended, turning to the left in a shallow climb. Like one man we turned sharply towards the MiG, Hans being in the most advantageous position to bring his guns to bear. 'Keep shooting, you're hitting him!' I shouted as I saw a white blur on the MiG's port wing root where 50 calibre explosive incendiaries were hitting home. There was a puff of black smoke, probably from the after-burner as the MiG dived away at high speed followed by the remaining enemy aircraft, no doubt disconcerted by the discovery that Mustangs could hit back.

We were then able to turn our attention to locating Dave's aircraft but he had vanished. We flew back and forth in the area where he was last seen, searching in vain. Other aircraft operating in the vicinity had been ordered to join in the search when I reported to our control centre, but they too found no trace. This was not really surprising considering the weather and the mountainous and heavily wooded terrain. It seemed certain that Dave had gone down. He was posted 'Missing believed killed in action'. His death, like that of the other 33 SAAF pilots who were killed in Korea, was a sad blow to the squadron. Second-Lieutenant Taylor, like all others who flew with me on that mission, was a young Citizen Force volunteer. He had recently joined the squadron and although relatively inexperienced, it was simply bad luck that he was the one to be hit. With their superior performance, the enemy jets should have done much more damage. If it hadn't been for brilliant formation flying by those who stuck with me and some clever manoeuvring by Kuhn on his own, they could have got us all.

My No 3 (deputy leader on the mission) Joe Joubert certainly saved my life by spotting the MiG sneaking up on me. The 30 mm shells must surely have hit me seconds later if Joe hadn't warned me in time, for I was an easy target flying straight and level. Joe, who later became Second-in-Command of the squadron, was doing his second tour in Korea, having flown 100 sorties on his first tour. His love of flying led him to follow a career with South African Airways when he left the SAAF shortly after the Korean war.

The others on that mission also happened to be rather special people. Vin Kuhn was promoted soon afterwards straight from Second-Lieutenant to acting Captain to lead 'Dog' Flight which he did with distinction. This was a very popular choice which gave a boost to the

Squadron's morale. 'Happy' Mac McLaughlin, who rose to high rank in the Royal Rhodesian Air Force, was a born leader right from the start. Sadly, Hans Enslin died in an accident shortly after the Korean War. I remember so well how thrilled he was to have hit the MiG and how excited he became when we all watched his gun-camera film clearly showing his hits. What a pity he couldn't claim more than a 'Damaged' but we had lost sight of the MiG still apparently under control.

There was a great party that night to celebrate our successful mêlée with the MiGs and to pay homage to Dave Taylor in the traditional SAAF manner. Everybody made a fuss of Hans and I recall vividly a picture of him grinning from ear to ear each time his health was toasted.

Peter Bagshawe has asked me what my feelings were during the mêlée. Being an ex-fighter pilot himself, I suspect that he knows only too well, but wants me to spell it out. In the Western Desert in 1942 where I flew Kitty 1s in that same 2 Squadron SAAF, I had been shot down and wounded by the 20 mm shells of a Messerschmitt 109. Ten years later in Korea, I had no illusions about the hazards of air combat with superior fighters. There is no point in pretending that I wasn't frightened. I was well aware of what a 30 mm shell was capable of. Fortunately, however, when the adrenalin is pumping fast and the furious activity of air combat blots out normal emotions, there isn't really time to be frightened for more than a few seconds at a time.

Another strange phenomenon is that there is always a comforting illusion of safety when airborne inside a fighter aircraft's cockpit - the reason, no doubt, why pilots are reluctant to bale out when their aircraft are crippled. The worst fear stems from anxious anticipation of the unknown. Once airborne on a mission, this anxiety evaporates and is replaced by a feeling of exhilaration. It takes something quite traumatic to dispel this grand feeling of invincibility. The encounter with MiGs was certainly traumatic, so, let's face it - I was terrified, but weren't we all!

Tailpiece

When Dick was shot down during the Desert War, he was lucky to escape with his life. Seriously wounded he baled out, landed in the sea near El Alamein and was rescued by an Australian soldier just as he was about to pass out from exhaustion and loss of blood. He commanded the Cheetah Squadron during the Korean War at the time it was awarded the United States Presidential Distinguished Unit Citation. He was a career officer in the SAAF acting in 1974 as a Major-General and has retired at Knysna, Cape Province.

Graham Lock

Death in the Desert

While compiling 15 Squadron's history, I unearthed the following unhappy saga from the SADF archives in Pretoria. The editor's tailpiece includes some interesting comments by the CO of the squadron at the time, Lieut-Col John Borckenhagen.

On 20 April 1942, a detachment of three 15 Squadron Blenheims based at Amariya in the Western Desert, was sent to Kufra Oasis, 550 miles south of Gazala. The oasis was a likely base for possible enemy land action against Egypt, and 203 Group at Khartoum considered cannon-firing Blenheims suited to attack any ground force which might attempt to seize the oasis. The attachment was led by Major J L V de Wet with Second-Lieutenants L T H Wessels and J H Pienaar as his wing-men.

The nearest supply base was at Wadi Halfa, 650 miles from Kufra, so Major de Wet was advised, according to the record, not to fly on more than one sortie per day. On 3 May, satisfied that compasses had been swung at Amariya, he briefed his pilots for a practice flight of 281 miles. The next morning the Blenheims duly took off with four day's rations and water aboard. De Wet refused a weather balloon test for wind strength and shortly after the aircraft had departed, the forecast proved to be incorrect, stronger winds blowing with 65 degrees of difference.

One of the aircraft established radio communication with the ground station but the other two, crewed by poorly-trained operators, failed to make contact. The ground post at Rebiana, only 83 miles away, had been warned to expect the Blenheims and to hold fire, but they did not appear. The post at Bzema, 51 miles further on, saw nothing of them though visibility was good.

The three Blenheims had become hopelessly lost and a request to the direction finding station for a course back to Kufra proved to be fatal. Major de Wet's radio operator stopped transmitting before an accurate bearing could be obtained and only a snap bearing was received. The aircraft radio operator recorded the figures 3, 0 and 5 so Major de Wet altered course to 305 degrees which he flew for an unrecorded period and then turned about on to a reciprocal course. At about 0900 hours, an engine on one of the aircraft started cutting so the Major ordered all three aircraft to make a forced landing.

Pilots and navigators then endeavoured to determine their position, but found no flight details had been recorded in their navigation logs. De Wet took off on a course between east and south but returned after failing to find Kufra.

That afternoon, Wessels flew on a course of 220 degrees also returning after flying only 26 miles. It was ascertained later that if he had continued for 82 miles on that course, he would have found Kufra.

Using fuel from the disabled aircraft, a third flight was made by De Wet on a course of 223 degrees when the R/T operator managed to transmit calls on the direction finder frequency. The Blenheim returned once more without any joy. No orders had been given to conserve water and the stranded crews used most of it to keep cool.

Kufra Oasis.

Furthermore, no attempt was made to display air recognition strips, or to burn petrol to guide searchers.

At Kufra the Cypher Officer sent off a signal to 203 Group HQ and the DF stations at Heliopolis and Mersa Matruh asking for information. The Sudanese Defence Force signalled that its post at Taizerbo had heard aircraft faintly to the west and had sent out patrols to Rebiana, Bzema and LG 7. Shortly after 1300 hours, Kufra asked for a search aircraft and 203 Group agreed to send a Blenheim from Khartoum the next morning and to brief a Bombay at Wadi Halfa.

That morning Major de Wet had the remaining petrol drained into one of the Blenheims and when Pienaar did not return from a flight, it was assumed that he had found Kufra and had informed the authorities of the situation. In actuality Pienaar's aircraft had made a forced land-

The desert between Wadi Halfa and Kufra Oasis.

ing. Meanwhile the signal to call the Bombay at Wadi Halfa only arrived in the early hours of 5 May when repeated phone calls to the officers' mess were not answered. Eventually someone was raised, but it was too late. The Bombay had already left for Khartoum. Over and above this, the Blenheim, which had flown to Wadi Halfa with instructions for the Bombay crew, went unserviceable.

During the night De Wet's men fired Very lights and bursts of machine-gun bullets from gun turrets and in the morning the last of the water was issued - one bottle per man. Tormented by thirst, they drank the oil from the sardine tins and the syrup from canned fruit - but they could not eat.

Middle East HQ, RAF, ordered three Bombays from 216 Squadron, Khanka, to proceed to Kufra. From Khartoum, 203 Group sent a senior officer to meet the aircraft at Wadi Halfa and organise a search. Fate foiled every move. The officer's aircraft made a forced landing on the way and he completed the journey by goods train. He arrived too late to meet the Bombays, two of which had already left for Kufra, while the third had returned with engine trouble.

Meanwhile a signal from one of the Blenheims had been roughly fixed on 4 May and again the operator had stopped transmitting before an accurate fix could be attained. A patrol was sent out by land to a point 60 - 70 miles from Kufra. A Sudanese unit and nine members of the 15 Squadron detachment went along leaving early on 5 May. Visibility was six miles in the morning increasing later from 12 to 18 miles. During the afternoon the patrol picked up a strong signal and decided the Blenheims must be close, but night fell without sighting them.

Major de Wet's men were in grim shape. A sandstorm blew up and they sprayed fire extinguisher fluid on to their bodies to allay the unbearable heat. The intense cold gave some relief but their flesh burst out in blisters which developed into sores. Gentian Violet from the medical box provided little relief; morphia afforded more. Then the men turned to alcohol in the instruments, breaking open and drinking the compass and bombsight fluid. 'It's stimulating,' De Wet recorded in his diary. He wrote: 'The boys are going mad and want to shoot each other - very weak myself. Will I be able to stop them, and from shooting me - please give us strength.'

The sandstorm raged on. The search Bombays could not take off from Wadi Halfa until 1100 hours and when approaching Kufra found visibility down to 50 yards at 3 000 ft. They flew past Kufra, blind, turned about and made a forced landing 40 miles short of the oasis where they were stranded. They were unable to acquire a direction from Kufra for the crews had not been supplied with the call sign of the newly-established station. Meanwhile the ground party struggled across the desert but having got to within five miles of the position given by the fix, could get no further. The broken nature of the ground made air co-operation essential. At Kufra the visibility had fallen to a couple of hundred yards.

A Bombay transport aircraft.

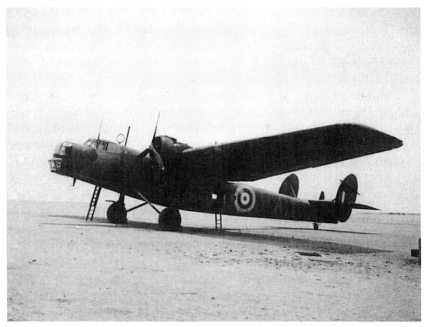

Next morning, 7 May, no search aircraft had reached Kufra and the garrison commander sent out a second patrol in a sandstorm; in fact the first patrol had been halted by the visibility which was down to a hundred yards. The stranded Bombays could not take off all day and when they were eventually able to get off the ground, it was decided that there was not enough fuel for a search and they returned to Wadi Halfa remaining there for an entire day.

Major de Wet's diary records: 'We expect to be all gone today. Death will be welcome - we went through hell.' His last lucid thoughts were recorded in a weak hand. 'We can last if help arrives soon - they know where we are but do not seem to do much about it. Bit of a poor show isn't it? But we will try to stick it out to the very .... It is the fifth day, second without water and fifth in a temperature of well over 100, but Thy will be done, O Lord. *Ons kan niks doen behalwe lê en wag. Miskien kan ons nog weg uit die hel op aarde. Hou duiwels [duime?] vas hoor.*'

Wellingtons ordered from 162 Squadron at Bilbeis were delayed for two days by engine trouble. Then the first aircraft could not find Kufra because the pilot had been given an incorrect call sign for the Kufra direction finding station.

After a five-and-a-half hour search on 9 May, Squadron Leader D G Warren found the Blenheim flown by Second Lieutenant Pienaar. The crew were dead in the shade of the wing, the aircraft's tanks empty, its engine over-boosted (a clear sign of panic) and every evidence of a fearful struggle to live. Death by thirst, a doctor maintained, had occurred the previous day. There was no navigator's log on board but only a map and sketch. When Squadron Leader Warren attempted to reconstruct the Blenheim's course from these, he discovered the navigator's bearings had been calculated on the mis-identification of a hill feature. On 11 May, while other aircraft searched in vain, Warren returned to the Blenheim and set course for the features he considered to be represented on the map. Only 24 miles away he saw the two Blenheims pushed nose to nose in the shade of a hill, and extremely difficult to pick up. No ground strip had been put out but a parachute had been draped on a nearby feature. He saw a figure struggling to spread out a ground strip. This was Air Mechanic N Juul, the sole survivor. Three revolvers were found, all the ammunition expended. One of them was in Major de Wet's hand.

A Court of Enquiry blamed lack of experience by pilots and observers in desert flying; failure of observers to keep accurate logs; and the inability of wireless operators to carry out their duties in the air. Unserviceable aircraft, poor signals organisation and bad direction-finding procedures on the ground had hampered the search. Death had occurred early because of the crew's ignorance of survival techniques.

Tailpiece

I asked John Borckenhagen who was OC 15 Squadron at the time of the Kufra disaster, to comment on the findings of the Court of Enquiry. Here is what he had to say:

'Over the past 47 years, neither the official account in the Pretoria archives nor the articles appearing in the press and magazines, have told the entire truth about this horrifying episode and how it could have been avoided.

'Strangely enough, I wasn't summoned to attend the Court of Enquiry, at which no one mentioned the all-important fact that during this period, the direction finder at Kufra was not fully operational, and at-times was not operating at all! It is my belief that this is why the Blenheims were not homed to Kufra.

'Apart from this, the tragedy would not have happened if Major de Wet had obeyed my order at Amariya. All levels from HQ Middle East downwards knew that the Kufra MF/DF station was unserviceable and this is why I personally briefed De Wet not to fly any long range patrols until the direction finder was serviceable.

'I must mention, that as soon as I was informed about the missing aircraft, I flew to Wadi Halfa with the intention of refuelling before proceeding to Kufra, but the *khamsin* was blowing strongly and visibility was poor. Under these circumstances, it would have been suicidal to have attempted the flight without the assistance of the direction finder.

'After waiting three days for the weather to improve, I made the journey in a Sudan Defence Force truck, arriving at Kufra on 8 May after a sleepless, 40 hour nightmare journey. The poor fellows were buried next to their aircraft where I read a simple burial service.'

Graham Lock is a serving Major and pilot with 15 Squadron SAAF based in Durban. He flew on operations in the Border War.

Accent on Take-Off

It was a cold day in Italy and one needed to be wrapped up warmly when flying in an open cockpit. The 7 Wing Spitfire IX pilots favoured flying with open hoods while taking part in dive-bombing and strafing operations. The reason for this unusual but practical procedure was to facilitate a pilot's exit from the cockpit should he be obliged to bale out or crash land after his aircraft had been fatally hit by flak.

A Wingco Flying, who spoke English but with a pronounced Afrikaans accent, the long nose of a Spitfire IX and a bulky Irvine jacket are the features in this story.

I was the leader of twelve Topper (2 Squadron) aircraft briefed for a dive-bombing mission and it happened to be the Wingco Flying, Colonel A C 'Bossie' Bosman's turn to act as Airstrip Controller and to oversee our take-off from Trigno on the Adriatic coast.

The engineers who had built the strip, had bulldozed flat a narrow length of beach. Layers of hessian, coir matting and chicken wire formed a foundation on which lengths of PSP (pierced steel planking) were laid to form the landing surface. The planks were perforated to allow rain and, on one memorable occasion, the sea, to drain away.

The strip was too narrow for a formation take-off so aircraft became airborne one after the other at safe intervals. A Spitfire IX pilot had to be careful not to raise his aircraft's tail too high when taking off otherwise its long airscrew blades could hit the ground causing extensive damage. This fact and the length of the Spitfire's nose, completely blocked the pilot's forward view of the airstrip during take-off forcing him to keep straight by glancing down left and right towards the sides of the airstrip.

We carried two bombs, one under each wing. Immediately before a pilot bombed a target, he turned on two switches situated near the instrument panel to energise the bomb release mechanism. When in the dive and ready to release the bombs, he pressed a countersunk button on the throttle lever. On this occasion my No 4, Puck Healey, was unaware when climbing into his Spitfire, that the sleeve of his bulky Irvine jacket had knocked down one of the switches which readied the bomb release on the starboard wing.

'Bomb' Finney, (left), with his flight commanders
Klippie Stone and Bushy Moon.

As we taxied out along the dispersal track, Colonel Bossie who
was one of the SAAF's greatest fighter pilots, took up his position as
controller, halfway along and just off the airstrip. He stood in the control pit surrounded by a low wall of sandbags, a microphone in his hand
and on my request authorised the squadron to take off. I rolled forward,
turned down the runway and opened the throttle. After my Spit had
run about 100 yards, my No 2 turned down the runway, paused a few
seconds and then roared after me. Soon it was Puck's turn and when
his aircraft was just short of the control pit, the drama began.

Part way down the runway, Puck decided to open the throttle
wider to increase speed. As he did so his thumb squeezed the bomb
release button which for an unknown reason had not been countersunk
in the throttle lever. Consequently one bomb was released but didn't
explode when first hitting the PSP. All this happened as Puck's Spitfire
was nearing the control pit. When Colonel Bossie saw the bomb bouncing along behind the aircraft, he hastily ducked behind the sandbags
and started burrowing through to Australia! A few seconds later the
bomb exploded and fortunately Puck was situated a short distance
ahead of it. He didn't hear the explosion which was deafened by the
noise of the aircraft's engine, but he couldn't understand why the Spit
had lifted into the air so quickly and abruptly!

The right side of the airstrip was a mangled mass of steel plating and after a while Colonel Bossie tentatively stuck his eyes above the sandbags and to his horror saw Barrie Haynes had commenced his take-off run. He had already turned up the airstrip, his Spitfire's nose blocking his view of the events taking place ahead of him.

Colonel Bossie grabbed the mike and yelled: 'That aircraft yus taking off, throttle back,' an order with which Barrie complied, but Puck who had just become airborne and was over the swamp at the end of the airstrip, thought the order was addressed to him and that Colonel Bossie had said, 'That aircraft yus TAKEN off, throttle back!' Puck obeyed the order and throttled back. Bossie heard his engine crackling and backfiring as the Spit wallowed over the swamp and he shouted: 'That aircraft yus taken off, open up, open up,' which Puck did. Barrie, still on the airstrip, heard the order as, 'That aircraft yus taking off, open up, open up,' so he continued his take-off.

Believe it or not there was still time for Bossie to give one more order and he yelled: 'That aircraft on the runway, keep lef, man, keep lef!' As Barrie swept past the control pit he kept left, his starboard wingtip just missing the twisted PSP - and then he throttled back and braked, for there was not enough runway left for a take-off.

Unaware of the events which had taken place during Puck's take-off, the four of us who were already airborne, including Puck, made a wide circuit of the airstrip waiting for the rest of the squadron to join up, but Colonel Bossie gave instructions that we were to proceed to the target and after the operation, not to land back at Trigno. 'Commander',

Bomb's Caterpillar Club membership card.

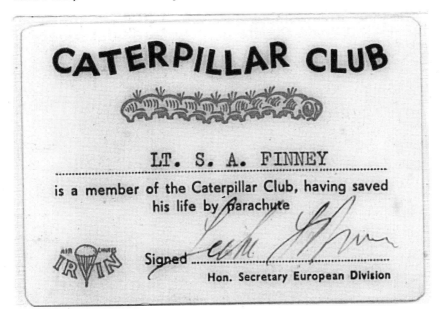

CATERPILLAR CLUB

LT. S. A. FINNEY

is a member of the Caterpillar Club, having saved his life by parachute

Signed ....

Hon. Secretary European Division

IRVIN

the area controller, would re-route us to another airstrip. On the way to the target I noticed that Puck's aircraft carried only one bomb instead of two, a fact which puzzled me, but this was soon forgotten in the heat of the attack. 'Commander' instructed us to land at Biferno which we duly did and returned to Trigno by road, keen to hear what had transpired during our take-off.

While all this drama was taking place centre stage, another situation had arisen which could have ended tragically. Bob Kershaw of 7 Squadron was happily walking along the taxi track which was about 50 yards from the airstrip, when he saw the bomb fall off Puck's Spit. The seriousness of the situation didn't register at first but just before the bomb exploded he threw himself flat on the track. A piece of shrapnel cut him across the forehead just above one eye, but apart from this he only suffered bruises.

Years later Puck, then an engineer with the Natal Roads Department, was chatting to another engineer in Eshowe, Zululand. On discovering that they had both served in Italy during the war, the Eshowe man remarked, 'On one occasion my unit was sent to repair an airstrip on a beach where some pea-brained pilot had dropped a bomb on take-off.' His surprise when Puck silently pointed at himself, can best be left to the imagination!

Tailpiece

'Bomb' was a popular personality who served in the Western Desert, Sicily and Italy. He was fortunate to escape with his life, once when shot down and wounded and on another occasion when colliding in mid-air and having to bale out. He flew three tours of operations, was an OC of 2 Squadron and was awarded the DFC and bar. He lives in Westdene, Johannesburg.

Split Seconds Between
Life and Death

'Two ME 109s dived out of the clouds, engines screaming, black crosses plainly visible, their machine-guns firing in short staccato bursts. Our aircraft hadn't a hope under the circumstances and both were hit almost immediately. One of them plummeted to earth, a blazing torch; the other was also on fire and so low down that I could see every detail. As the pilot baled out, it seemed impossible that he could survive, for his aircraft was not more than a couple of hundred feet above the ground with what appeared to be insufficient time for a parachute to open.

'After leaping into space he tumbled over and over and suddenly, during the split seconds between life and death, his parachute billowed open, his feet struck the ground almost simultaneously and he rolled away from the heat of the burning aircraft which had plunged into the ground just before him.'

These lines were written in a letter to my uncle by Lieutenant G W R Butcher, an intelligence officer with the Natal Mounted Rifles who happened to be on the spot and had witnessed the drama. I was the lucky man to escape death on that morning of 6 September 1942 and sadly it was my good friend Terry Whelehan who lost his life - as brave a man as I will ever meet.

Towards the end of 1942, 7 Squadron SAAF had been re-equipped with Hurricanes. Shortly afterwards, the CO, Doug Loftus, left to assume command of 7 Wing and Terry replaced him. Another good friend, John Wells, was promoted flight commander at the same time as me. Throughout August heavy equipment had been rolling forward towards the El Alamein line and a decisive battle was imminent.

On 5 September, John Wells was appointed CO of 274 Squadron RAF and the next day 7 Squadron was briefed to provide medium cover on his first operation as leader of his new command when attacking enemy transport straddling the main road in front of the First South African Division on the El Alamein line. Top cover was to be provided

Walter Stanford.

by 127 Squadron RAF while 7 Squadron's contribution was a flight of six Hurricanes led by Terry, with Lieutenant Ray Burl as his No 2, myself as No 3, Lieutenant A G Turner as my No 2, Lieutenant J S Botha as No 5 and Lieutenant J H Haire as his No 2.

We flew westwards to the bomb line and before long could see the famous white road running south from El Alamein. John Wells spotted his target and, at the same time, 'Commander' called up, warning that 20 plus bandits were in the area. As John peeled over into his bombing dive, I saw the ME 109s diving down from behind and above 127 Squadron. Obviously they had not been seen and my warning was too late, for the tail-end Hurricane was sent spinning down on fire, another following a few seconds later. The squadron turned about and this was the last we saw of our top cover.

The 109s then dived in our direction and Terry led us between them and 274 Squadron which had almost completed its attack on the enemy transport. With hearts pounding we awaited the onslaught, and down came those 109s at a speed which left us with no alternative but to form a defensive circle. Alas - this did not save Lt Haire who was the first to be shot down. I managed to fire a good deflection shot at the enemy aircraft which got him, but I was far too busy to observe the result.

Calmly, Terry Whelehan warned that 109s were behind us and we turned desperately, opening all taps, but the speed required to defend ourselves adequately could not be attained. The 109s kept diving on us, pulling up to 600 or 800 ft above for another attack until all three of our No 2s had been shot down. Botha had got separated and was nowhere to be seen.

And so Terry and I were left on our own to face an impossible situation. Another attack came from the starboard side and Terry, realising that we two friends were facing the odds together, spoke in his usual quiet controlled voice: 'Wal, is that you? Let's give them socks.' I felt good alongside such a brave man. These were the last words my friend uttered, for as we turned, a 109 got him. Out of the corner of my eye, I saw the burst of cannon shells hit his Hurricane, flames engulfing it entirely. I was stunned as I realised that my best friend was burning to death and I was helpless to do anything about it.

Within seconds, another ME 109 came for me. I was in a 90 degree steep turn and saw the wicked blue-white streak from its nose, and like a good shot at golf, I knew the pilot's deflection was right. 'Whoosh!' My Hurricane's gravity tank containing 30 gallons of 100 octane petrol situated just behind the dashboard, ignited and I was enveloped in flames. What an unbelievable situation had arisen! Like Terry, I was being incinerated in the cockpit. No thoughts of past life crossed my mind at this stage, although I would willingly have dived my Hurricane into the ground to avoid further agony.

Luckily my instincts took over and I rolled the aircraft out of the tight turn, unlocked the Sutton safety harness and jumped outwards with a huge heave of my legs. By this time the height above the ground could only have been a few hundred feet which didn't leave much time for my parachute to open. I pulled the ripcord and as the 'chute opened I was suspended immediately above the blazing remnants of the Hurricane which had already dived into the ground. Suddenly a gentle wind from the sea produced a slight drift and I landed about ten yards from the burning wreck.

It was a painful struggle to free myself from the 'chute because my hands were skinless and bleeding. I had landed right in front of our infantry which, as already mentioned, turned out to be the Natal Mounted Rifles. Some of their men ran towards me gesticulating and indicating that I must not move. It was then that I noticed little mounds of earth which were covering the mines between which my chute had been dragging me!

I eventually extricated myself from the harness and lay waiting for help. Fortunately, one of the first to arrive was the NMR's Medical Officer, Captain Harry Curwen. I had known Dr Curwen in East Griqualand and at the University of Cape Town where he was the two-mile champion. 'Hallo Harry, do you remember me?' I said weakly.

'Yes, old boy,' he replied, although not having a clue who I was, with the skin burnt off my face! He gave me a shot of morphine in both shoulders bringing blessed relief.

I was taken by field ambulance to Burg El Arab and then to Alexandria and Palestine. Hospitals followed in Haifa, Nazareth and Jerusalem, then Cairo, and finally back to South Africa and some plastic surgery at the famous Brenthurst Clinic in Johannesburg.

After the losses on this operation and those suffered during the Battle of Alam Halfa in early September, 7 Squadron was pulled off operations to lick its wounds, re-equip and replace its depleted complement of pilots.

Tailpiece

Along with Doug Loftus, Terry Whelehan and John Wells, Walter was a foundation member of 2 Squadron SAAF in East Africa. They were all lucky to survive a tour of operations in 1941 in the Western Desert when 26 out of 32 pilots were lost, mostly against the Luftwaffe's Marseille Wing.

The occasion should also be recorded when Walter's alertness probably saved the lives of Field Marshal Smuts, Generals van Ryneveld, Venter and Theron who were visiting front line Forces on the Italian front during June 1944. They were flying in a Ventura which was escorted by six Spitfires of 7 Squadron led by Walter. Their destination was Orvieto, 7 Wing's new airfield near Lake Bolsano, not far from the bomb line at that time. The weather was poor and the Ventura's crew could not locate the airfield in the murk. There was no radio contact for this had been discontinued during the move forward from the old airstrip and had not yet been re-installed. Walter realised that within a matter of minutes the VIP aircraft would trundle over the bomb line and could well be shot down by enemy flak with incalculable results for South Africa. There was no radio intercommunication with the Ventura so Walter flew up alongside it indicating to the pilot that he should turn about and follow him. After some anxious minutes, Orvieto airfield was located and the Smuts VIP party, unaware of their narrow escape from disaster, landed safely.

Walter left the SAAF with the rank of Lieutenant-Colonel. He was decorated with the DFC and after the war received the CBE for his services to Basutoland, (now Lesotho). He lives in Somerset West.

Tony Harris

A New Ball Game

On 20 February 1945, when based at Forli in Italy with No 4 Squadron SAAF, I was flying as wingman to the CO, Major Hilton-Barber, on a reconnaissance mission over north-east Yugoslavia, when we spotted a train with smoke curling from its funnel. Our Spitfire IXs peeled over to the attack amidst an accurate curtain of flak from guns mounted on a platform in the rear truck.

We made 11 strafing attacks on that train which included the flak truck, leaving the engine billowing steam from its punctured boiler and several of its trucks burning, but unfortunately my Spitfire's coolant tank was holed and it soon became apparent that the chance of making it back to base was a doubtful possibility. I decided it would be sensible to bale out over the adjacent mountains which were known to be Partisan territory.

I called my leader over the R/T and told him of my decision, but he disagreed. 'The leak is small and you should be able to fly back to Forli,' he said. 'Carry on and I'll join you after a quick recce of shipping in Trieste harbour.' That was the last I saw of him. Heading back towards Italy with smoke pouring from my aircraft, the engine cut three miles from the Italian coast. I was flying approximately 1 000 ft above the sea and after transmitting a 'mayday' call, I prepared to bale out.

I didn't set the tail-trim sufficiently nose-heavy before turning the Spit over on to its back and became jammed under the windshield. Luckily I managed to kick the stick forward which pushed the nose up and I was catapulted into space. After the parachute had opened, the aircraft put up a peculiar performance turning through 180 degrees, missing me by approximately 50 ft before plunging into the sea.

On the way down I heard a strange hissing noise sounding like the wind passing through the parachute shroud lines, but was in fact the wind escaping from my 'Mae West' through the valve which I'd forgotten to tighten during the bale out preparation. When surfacing, I loosened the parachute harness and disentangled myself, but without a buoyant 'Mae West' to keep me afloat and with my hands frozen and useless from the intensity of the cold water, I couldn't open

Tony Harris.

up the dinghy pack and jettisoned it. The shore was only 800 yards away and while struggling desperately to reach it, I became totally exhausted, passed out and literally 'drowned'.

I regained consciousness some two hours later in an Italian house with a German officer, Lieutenant Brunzel, and an Italian man working on me. I must have spewed up half the Adriatic before coming around! My helpers had seen me bale out and had rowed out in a boat to rescue me. Lieutenant Brunzel very kindly gave me an Italian overcoat which not only provided warmth, but also covered my uniform. This was to save my life on more than one occasion during the days ahead when after bombing and strafing attacks by Allied aircraft, an enraged population could have lynched me.

The Fascist interrogator at Mestre, where I was taken, shouted: 'How many people did you kill this morning?' and spat in my face. When he had finished with me, I was tossed into a cell. The temperature was subzero, my clothes and boots were still soaking wet and with shock setting in, I began to shake and tremble uncontrollably. During the night three Italians, one woman and two men, were dumped in the cell and they huddled around me for the rest of the night, the warmth from their bodies and their humanity no doubt saving me from freezing to death. All three of them were shot at dawn outside the cell's door. I was so horrified and sickened by this dastardly act that when the guard brought me eggs and bacon for breakfast, I couldn't eat a morsel despite the fact that I'd received no nourishment for two days.

I was transferred to Verona jail and on the first night Allied aircraft bombed the marshalling yards on the outskirts of the city. All prisoners were moved to an air raid shelter and before entering I was able to obtain a superb view of the fireworks caused by the raid. 'What a wonderful sight' I said aloud and the jail's OC who was standing nearby, heard my remark and scolded me outside the shelter while the shrapnel was falling around us!

From Verona I was moved to Padua for another interrogation and when this was completed, two German officers, a captain and a lieutenant, both over two metres tall and who were travelling to the 'fatherland' on leave, were instructed to escort me to a POW camp. We set off on foot initially until the two Jerries laid claim to an Italian Fiat. By nightfall I'd mended ten punctures and the patching material ran out, so the Fiat was abandoned and we foot-slogged it once more. At nightfall the two officers commandeered an Italian house smashing some of the furniture for firewood and lighting a fire in the lounge. For the first time since baling out five days previously, I was able to dry my clothes.

The next night was spent in the Lake Como area where there was a German barracks which my two guards visited in search of food. Walking behind them down a long dark corridor, I decided to escape and dived into a recess in the wall flattening myself against it. The Jerries soon noticed my absence and walked back along the corridor passing the recess without seeing me, but by this time I'd realised it wasn't an opportune time to make a getaway, so followed up behind them, stuck a thumb into the nearest officer's back and said 'boo'. They were not amused and reminded me that if I tried to escape again they would not hesitate to shoot me.

In the morning we boarded a troop train which was bombarded during the night, the troops showing a furious, aggressive attitude towards the attacking aircraft. I was thankful that the overcoat hid my uniform otherwise they would undoubtedly have turned on me. My guards answered any questions about my identity by disclosing that I was an Italian deserter. Eventually *via* Innsbruck and Munich, the train arrived at Hulle, 15 miles south of Berlin where it stopped, for the capital city and its suburbs were experiencing heavy air raids. As we hurried to the air raid shelters, hysterical hate was once more displayed by the German troops and the overcoat may have once more saved my life.

On the way from Hulle to Frankfurt, I visited the toilet. There was

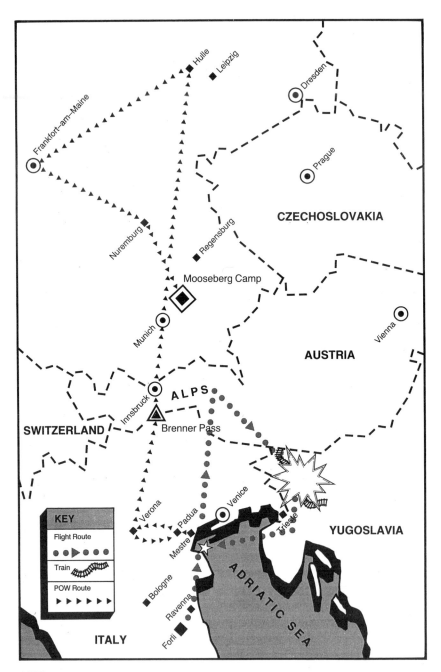

POW route

no lock on the door and suddenly a German officer walked in, closed the door and offered me his pistol - butt first, saying in good English: 'To aid your escape.' 'Thank you very much,' I replied, ' but the war is almost over and I do not intend to escape.' After a brief conversation he scribbled his name and address on a piece of paper and asked me to deliver it to an address in London's Fleet Street.

The prisoners in the camp at Frankfurt were mainly Americans and after being deloused, I was issued with an American uniform and boots. Soon, General Patton's advancing army threatened to over-run the camp, so all POWs were crammed into cattle trucks and moved to Nuremberg where Bob Kershaw was a fellow prisoner.

Incidentally, there were 62 of us in our truck! Food was very short and a horse would be driven into the compound daily and shot. Several hours later we would queue up for a bowl of watery soup and ersatz bread, our food ration for the day. The insects in the soup were an added delicacy!

We didn't remain for long at Nuremberg and all 28 000 POWs, including Bob and I, were force-marched to Mooseberg. Along the route the lengthy, winding column was strafed by American Thunderbolts with ghastly results. I had spotted the aircraft circling and warned the guards that an attack was imminent, but my warning was ignored. As the Thunderbolts moved into echelon formation and the leader winged over to the attack, I grabbed the nearest guard and we rolled down the embankment into a shallow ditch. Another guard who got the message, left it too late and as he followed us, a shell decapitated him.

At Mooseberg camp we were greeted by hundreds of red-tabbed soldiers who had been captured three years previously at Tobruk. I enjoyed telling my American friends that these South Africans had been in the bag before Roosevelt had declared war. Most Americans knew nothing about South Africa.

Shortly after arrival, an ME 262 pilot showed off his aerobatic skill and the performance of his jet. A pride-flushed officer later sauntered up to Bob Kershaw and asked him what he thought of the performance. 'Rather ordinary' replied Bob, 'but if you had performed at 150 instead of 1 500 ft, it would have been a great display. The proud German officer climbed back into his aircraft determined to prove his expertise but exceeded our expectations by hitting a concrete pillar during a shoot up and writing himself off in a ball of flame and red hot-metal.

Suddenly the war ended and I was flown to England. It was only then that my wife Betty and the family heard that I was still alive and well.

Tailpiece

It will be gathered from this tale, that Tony had a strong constitution and no wonder, for he is the celebrated double Springbok who along with Danie Craven, comprised the legendary half-back combination in Philip Nel's rugby Springboks which won the test series against the mighty All Blacks in 1937. He also played cricket for South Africa and toured Britain in 1947 with Alan Melville's team. The war was a new ball game to Tony and he was fortunate to win and survive. He has retired in Plettenberg Bay.

A Fighter Pilot's Odyssey

So many memories involving high drama and wonderful comradeship have faded over the years, but some, both trivial and dramatic, are clearly recollected including my first operational flight with 1 Squadron. They began with a covering patrol over Winston Churchill's aircraft when taking off on a return flight from the Western Desert to the United Kingdom. My first baptism of enemy fire was experienced a few days later.

The squadron was escorting a tactical reconnaissance Hurricane flying at only 4 000 ft behind the El Alamein Line, when the unfamiliar black, oily puffs of 88 mm flak intermingled with red and yellow medium flak, burst around our aircraft forming what appeared to be a formidable, impregnable barrier. Suddenly a voice shouted over the R/T : 'Donald Duck'- a code word which was new to me, but on seeing one of our aircraft diving out of control with black smoke pouring out behind, I realised that the unfamiliar 'code' was a warning for me to 'duck' because an enemy aircraft was on my tail! After throwing my Spitfire into a tight turn to the left, an ME 109 with a yellow spinner flashed by on the right leaving me unscathed.

The 109s kept attacking as the squadron turned back over the bomb line, and at debriefing, a reaction set in from that initial frightening experience. 'I'm going home,' I told the CO, Peter Metelerkamp. His reply was psychologically brilliant. 'So am I and I'm coming with you!' Peter was a brave, competent CO and would have enjoyed a great future if a freak shot from a JU 88's rear gunner hadn't cut short his illustrious career.

One of the pilots who joined 1 Squadron with me was Ralph Chaplin who was nicknamed 'Cheese'. He was a unique personality, at times scathingly cynical, but always deeply religious and possessing a whimsical, dry sense of humour which he used at all times, particularly when the odds were against him.

This trait was well illustrated by the hectic dogfight which ensued as 20 ME 109s and Macchi 202s attacked our Spitfires over Gabes. Five enemy aircraft were accounted for by the Spits. The mêlée included

Don Brebner and his canine crew.

head-on attacks and near collisions. In fact one Spitfire was rammed by a Macchi and both aircraft were destroyed. During the fight, Cheese chased every enemy aircraft in sight and expended all his ammunition without witnessing a single strike. He didn't make any claims but remarked at debriefing that all the Macchis he'd fired at had obviously been built with self-sealing fuselages!

The factors which influenced the course of Cheese's life were the facial scars and deformities resulting from a crash during his training. Aircraft recognition was not one of his strong points as an op near Cape Bon attested. While escorting Kittyhawks, the squadron was jumped by a large number of ME 109s and a hectic dogfight ensued. No casualties resulted but on returning to base, Cheese was indignant about the audacity of those 'bloody Ities' for their head-on attacks on his aircraft. Large sections of his fuselage and port wing had been shot away and on further interrogation it was realised that the culprit was an FW 190 and not a Fiat G5 as identified by Cheese. Only the FW 190s heavy cannon could have been responsible for such damage!

Apart from one short leave back home, after which Cheese joined 4 Squadron, he refused any other break from operations until the end came in May 1944, when his aircraft burst into flames while dive-bombing over Ancona. He will always be remembered and respected by those of us in the SAAF who knew him; a little fellow with a stout heart and a very lovable nature, his droll sense of humour endearing him to all.

Over the many months and years of 1 Squadron's history, fighter operations were its forte during the numerous successes earned in Abyssinia, North Africa, Malta, Sicily and Italy.

One of the last sweeps in Italy was a typical Lieut-Col Bosman 'hush hush' affair. Colonel Bossie as he was known, was the 7 Wing sweep leader, an extremely clued-up fighter pilot with incredible eyesight and a proud record in the Desert War. He approached me, almost clandestinely, to select four pilots including myself to join him on an

Cheese Chaplin.

unusual but exciting operation. He'd flown solo on many occasions, not only to test the latest modifications which had been fitted to his aircraft, but at the same time to reconnoitre the Foligno area where he had discovered that enemy aircraft were active just before dusk.

We set course for Foligno at 1900 hrs heading north into the darkening evening. I led the top cover comprising four aircraft, with

Bossie Bosman (left), with his air mechanic.

Spitfires over Italy's snow-capped mountains.

Colonel Bossie and his No 2, Trevor Wallace, below, and sure enough on approaching Foligno, eight ME 109s and FW 190s could be seen flying around the main and satellite airfields with four more circling above. The game was on and we went in for the kill with a vengeance. During the mêlée Colonel Bossie destroyed 2 ME 109s and along with Trevor Wallace flamed another on the ground. Douglas Judd and I each claimed a long-nosed FW 190 fitted with a Daimler Benz engine from which both pilots baled out, and Bill Kayser claimed a 109 damaged. It was a highly successful operation and full marks to Colonel Bosman!

I was a great admirer of Colonel Bossie. He was always on the go, eager to try anything, but at the same time he was very excitable and when in this state of mind, was difficult to understand. In July 1944, six of us were chosen to escort King George VI on his Italian tour. The King's UK Beaufighter escort advised us not to fly too close to the Avro York or we could be placed under close arrest for dangerous flying. As a result, we flew so far away from it that an interception couldn't fail! However, the King was happy with our performance and sent congratulatory messages every evening.

On the occasion when the King visited our base at Foiano, the York landed and taxied to a spot which happened to be next to a typical

120

desert 'loo' surrounded by a low sack cloth where Col. Bossie was sitting enjoying his morning constitutional!

Over a couple of drinks that evening Colonel Bossie told me what happened. 'Well, Don, old *boer*, what could I do? My pants were around my ankles and if I stood up it would be rude, but to sit in the presence of the King of England would be even more disrespectful, so I just *sommer* bobbed up and down! To crown everything the King bent forward and shook my hand!'

Colonel Bossie would have made a first class ambassador for South Africa had he lived, for he loved royalty in any form. Another amusing incident was when he and I drove up to Kandy from Colombo in Ceylon for an interview with Lord Louis Mountbatten in an attempt to persuade him to arrange a ship back to South Africa, for the Wing had been refused permission by the SA Government to act as an occupation force in Japan.

Lord Louis was in short sleeves when we visited him, for the heat and humidity were almost unbearable. He was charmingly co-operative in solving our problem and after thanking him profusely for his help and understanding, we returned to Colombo. On the journey back in the Jeep over a long, winding road, Colonel Bossie remarked: 'Don, did you look at Lord Louis's arms closely ? If you did, you would have seen the blue blood coursing through his veins!'

I was Colonel Bossie's best man at his wedding in Pretoria, and happily a son was to be born who could carry on the family name, for his father was tragically killed in an aircraft accident near Khartoum along with some of the cream of the SAAF who had recently celebrated victory.

Nose-mounted cannon in ME 109F.

In August 1944, 7 Wing was converted to dive-bombing and in the course of time became particularly accurate at destroying bridges, buildings, transport and trains, the latter being extremely satisfying because of the pyrotechnic effects. Every leader had his own private 'hunting ground' and mine was in the San Marino area which always abounded with Mercedes Benz staff cars and despatch riders, both fair game in my opinion!

Tailpiece

Don shot down four enemy aircraft during World War II. He was appointed OC of 7 Squadron in Italy and was awarded the DFC. Just before the war ended, his operational enthusiasm encouraged him to return to a target which had already been attacked, and he paid the penalty for this unwise decision. He flew his crippled Spitfire back 80 miles before the engine caught fire, forcing him to bale out. Unfortunately he pulled the ripcord too late and the parachute opened seconds before his body hit the ground with a resounding thump. The result was a fractured spine which, in spite of surgery, still gives problems. He remains ambulatory, is physically independent and manages to run a private practice. He lives in Parktown North, Johannesburg.

A Buccaneer to the Rescue

The armourer Flight-Sergeant didn't like it one bit. 'Captain, our orders were to load your aircraft with 72 standard HE rockets. I cannot change that on your request!'

He was quite correct of course. The type of weapon used in an air attack is determined after careful target analysis, and we were going to give close air support to our armoured fighting teams mopping up the Swapo camp at Chetequera. It had been decided by Strike Command that 68 mm high explosive rockets were the ideal medicine. As it was, we had recently returned from a similar sortie over Cassinga, after helping the Parabats with some heavy machine-gun positions which had been troubling them following their silken let-down into that little town which had suffered a surprise attack at sunrise by some Canberras with anti-personnel bombs, and seven Buccaneers, each off-loading eight thousand-pounders.

I could not explain the reason for this highly irregular request, but repeated it nevertheless: 'I want every third rocket to have an armour-piercing head, and that is final! And please hurry up; we must be airborne in fifteen minutes.'

Navigator Ernie Harvey looked even more perplexed when we ascended the ladder and lowered ourselves into the Buc's large but cluttered cockpit. He was, however, soon too busy setting up the Nav. Computer to say anything. Those moments prior to start-up for a strike mission are very tense, very personal, and can only be appreciated by one who has lived them. More so for the Navigator/Weapons System Operator who has no control over the aircraft in any way, and is completely at the mercy of his pilot.

After the engines have been started, nerves loosen up, as the task at hand requires the crew's total attention, and soon we were crossing the border into Angola at something under the speed of sound, on track and on time for Chetequera.

Ernie was just about to check in with Tactical Headquarters at Ondangwa when things started going mad on the Ops frequency. Dick Warncke, having relieved us at close air support, reported an armoured

Dries Marais

convoy consisting of tanks and BTR 152 personnel carriers was approaching Cassinga from the south. This spelt DRAMA, as about 20 Puma and Frelon helicopters were on their way to Cassinga to uplift the paratroops, who apparently had been involved in one hell of a fight and were virtually out of ammunition. It seemed that the helicopters and the armoured column were going to arrive at the same time. We heard two Mirages being scrambled, and the flight leader reporting that they had no rockets, only 30 mm cannon, but with no armour-piercing rounds to stop the tanks. I again made a decision against all planning, and understandably drew some comment from my navigator who had the very difficult task of keeping us on track to our planned target over the featureless Southern Angola countryside.

'Do you still have the Cassinga maps with you?' I enquired. Ernie said 'No', but, bless him, he had not cleared the target co-ordinates from the navigation computer which, incidentally, was the only one installed in our squadron at that time. The next moment I had track and distance (and time to go) on my Horizontal Situation Indicator, and not being able to get a word in on the, by now, completely cluttered frequency, I took up the indicated heading and felt the thrust of power from the two Rolls Royce Speys as I opened the throttles.

We were ten minutes from Cassinga when I was for the first time able to break in over the radio chatter and ask permission to terminate our flight to Chetequera and attack the tanks, mentioning that we were carrying armour-piercing rockets. Major Gert Havenga, who manned the Ops frequency at Tactical HQ, also a Buccaneer pilot and never afraid of assuming responsibility, did not hesitate: 'You are cleared, and I will back you up.' What a man!

Surprise and *Concentration of Force* are key principles of any assault action, and by the grace of God we again achieved them that

124

Sabbath of 4 May 1976. As I rolled into my dive attack on the tanks which had by now reached the outskirts of Cassinga, in front of me, just settling into their attack, were the two Mirages. The 30 mm HE rounds of the first one exploded ineffectively on the lead tank and I called out to the second aircraft to leave the tanks alone and go for the personnel carriers. The pilot confirmed my request and the next moment I was overjoyed with pride as I witnessed my closest friend, Major Johan Radloff, whose voice I had immediately recognised, take out three BTRs with a single burst from his twin cannon. Ernie gave me a selection of 12 rockets which also flew true, and then we had to break off violently to avoid flying through the debris from the exploding tank.

Turning round for another pass, we could see the first tank burning like a furnace, and on this run, the lead Mirage pilot destroyed no fewer than five BTR's with a long burst, running his shells in movie-like fashion through them. *'Dis hoe die boere skiet, julle ... sems!'* were my thoughts, and then our second salvo of 12 rockets, every third one with an armour piercing head, also struck home.

In a matter of seconds, two tanks and about 16 armoured personnel carriers had been completely destroyed, and then the Mirages were down to their minimum combat fuel and they had to retire leaving us to deal with the rest. We decided to concentrate on the tanks, and then things started happening. Most of the BTRs were trailing twin-barrelled 14,5 mm anti-aircraft guns, and some of them were now deployed and shooting at us. Even one of the tanks was firing with its main weapon and I remember being amused at the gunner's optimism at hitting a manoeuvring target travelling at 600 knots.

Ernie, on the other hand, was far from amused as he was not, like me, in a state of aggression and experiencing tunnel vision. Keeping a good look out all around, he was actually aware of several AA positions firing at us. He was even less impressed at my dismissal of the problem, but my whole system was now charged to take out the remaining tanks.

As we turned in again, these two tanks left the road and disappeared into the bush. We destroyed another BTR, but decided to save our ammunition for the tanks. Flying around trying to locate them, I became annoyed with one AA site which kept up a steady stream of tracer in our direction and decided to take it out. It was, in fact, the gun which had been towed by the BTR we had just destroyed, and to this day I can only have respect for the discipline and courage of the gun crew and some troops who kept up their firing - even with their small arms - until my rockets exploded amongst them, killing the lot and destroying the gun.

As I broke off from this attack, the huge gaggle of helicopters

A Buccaneer of the SAAF

passed underneath us and landed in the pre-planned area to pick up the troops. By this time I had learned that the Chief of the Army, Lieut-General Viljoen, was on the ground with them, and that there was grave concern for his safety. Then, as the helicopters were landing, the remaining two tanks reappeared on the road and started shelling the landing area which was in a shallow depression. Because of this, and the inability of that particular type of tank's inability to lower its gun far enough, they were fortunately overshooting by some 300 yards.

We were in a perfect position for an attack from the rear on the front tank, and calculating that we had 12 rockets left, I asked Ernie to give me only six, leaving another salvo for the other tank. Timing was critical as the tanks were beginning to find their range. I realised that they HAD to be stopped. It was a textbook, low angle attack, and the 'Buc' was as steady as a rock in the dive. It was like lining up on a trophy kudu bull after a perfect stalk, but when I pulled the trigger, nothing happened - no rockets, not even one. I jerked the aircraft around, almost in agony, cursing Ernie for having selected the wrong switches. He was quite adamant that he had selected the switches correctly, and then we went in for another attack, but with the same heart-stopping result. Without really thinking it out, I opened the throttles wide and kept the aircraft in the dive, levelling off at the last moment, and flying over the tank very low and doing nearly Mach One.

Turning, we went in again from the front, this time doing the same

126

thing with the tank once more shooting at us. I assumed that the crew would have no idea that we were out of ammunition, and hoping to intimidate them, we continued to make fast, head-on low level mock attacks. The Buccaneer from close up is an intimidating aircraft. Flying low, it makes a terrific amount of noise compressed into a single instant as a shock wave, and if this had an amplified resonance inside the tank, the crew would have to be well-trained to stay with it, were my thoughts!

Again I can only praise God, for I remember distinctly having felt during those minutes which followed, being an instrument in His hands; myself a perfect part of the aircraft, and He the Pilot. As it was, the tank crews were eventually sufficiently intimidated to once again seek cover in the heavy bush, enabling the helicopters to load their precious cargo and get away safely.

Tailpiece

After returning to base at Grootfontein, 17 hits were counted on the Buccaneer including a 37 mm AA hit through the left flap as well as several hits through the engines, although not one was fatal. Dries was awarded the Honoris Crux (Silver) for an action of bravery while his life was in danger. Navigator Ernie Harvey received the Chief of the Defence Force's Commendation medal for his truly commendable actions. Dries Marais works as an aeronautical consultant specialising in accident investigation.

Peter Bagshawe

Kittyhawks at War

A naval commander of some repute once wrote: 'There are no great men in this world but only challenges which ordinary men are obliged by circumstances to accept.'

Kittyhawk pilots of the Desert Air Force accepted the challenge, but it was sad that they could not have shared their leader's medals, having all faced the same odds with the same courage and dedication.

Many young men paid the full penalty for helping eliminate Nazi tyranny. Many left home as beardless boys who scarcely needed to shave, yet on joining their squadrons, they grew up in a matter of a week or a month as a result of facing the strain of frequent operations against the enemy and the knowledge that death was their constant companion.

The six Kittyhawk squadrons which comprised 239 Wing were from South Africa, Australia and Britain, the pilots of the RAF squadrons hailing from several countries, South Africa predominating.

Kittyhawks in echelon.

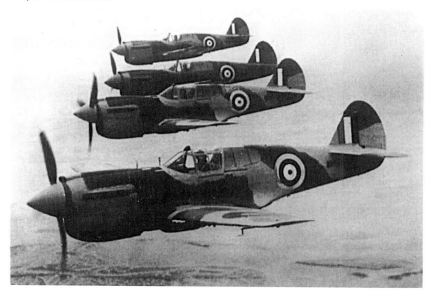

South African pilots on a battle-ready Kittyhawk.

An unusual aspect of these squadrons was their pilots' messes in which rank was of no consequence, the exception being the squadron commander who was respected as head of the family.

This situation, along with the diverse assortment of nationalities, produced the type of camaraderie which made a mockery of the cynics who claim that mixed nationalities breed disharmony and discontent. It certainly did not impair the discipline and efficiency of these squadrons in battle as their operational record proves. The pilots often sang each other's national ditties with great gusto, 'Sarie Marais' being one of their favourites.

Kittyhawk pilots were the toast of the Desert Air Force resulting from their victories against the German and Italian air forces as well as from their prolific support to the Eighth Army in the desert and to the Allied armies during the Italian campaign.

It can be said without fear of contradiction that Desert Air Force Army co-operation and close support operations produced a new dimension of efficiency and an expertise which had not been experienced in warfare up to this time, Kittyhawks making a tremendous contribution towards this success.

By the time British and American forces had joined hands in Tunisia the bulk of the enemy air forces had been either swept from the skies or destroyed on the ground, the way being paved for even more effective support to the Allied armies in their struggle against fanatical Nazi opposition in Italy. Kittyhawks made a formidable name for themselves as fighter aircraft in the Far East and the Western Desert in spite of the superior quality of enemy aircraft. As a result of their magnificent performance in support of the army, they found their true place in the combat spectrum as ground attack and dive-bombing aircraft. Sturdy in structure, providing ideal weapon platforms, they could absorb heavy punishment from flak. Their ground attack operations not only involved close support to the army, but also hitting the enemy and their lines of communication wherever they could be found. While an important battle was in progress, the squadrons flew up to three and occasionally four operations a day.

An excerpt from a Desert Air Force operation's report indicates that during one particular month in Italy, 239 Wing flew 900 000 miles which equals a trip to the moon and back and sixteen times around the equator. Over 2 000 tons of bombs were dropped and 700 000 rounds of ammunition expended, an impressive total for single-engine aircraft carrying only a moderate bomb load.

Armed reconnaissance was a regular operation entailing an area search for targets of opportunity. Other missions included the disruption of enemy lines of communication by bombing roads, railway lines and canals. The bombing and strafing of all types of rolling stock, airfields, factories, shipping, supply depots, fuel and ammunition dumps,

A Kitty flipped over on returning from an operation.

occupied buildings and bridges, were just a few of the vast variety of operations entered in a pilot's log book.

Bridges were one of the most frightening targets which Kittyhawk pilots were briefed to attack. They were certainly the most costly as far as casualties were concerned. The description which follows of a squadron attack on a bridge, paints a lucid picture of the hazards involved.

Italy's geographical structure, excluding its northern plain, consists of rugged mountain ranges overlooking valleys ringed with a network of rivers. The successful defence of bridges was therefore an essential prerogative to both the German and Allied armies allowing them to move their troops and supplies across the rivers during offensive and withdrawal operations.

No wonder the Italian campaign was often called the 'Battle of the Bridges' and not surprising that the Germans, who did not enjoy control of the Italian skies, used every type of flak at their disposal to defend the bridges.

There was no chance for a squadron to achieve surprise when attacking a bridge since the enemy was always alert and waiting. If the target was to be destroyed, there were no short cuts, and the rules for acquiring success had to be adhered to by each pilot. Firstly, an accurate 60 degree angle of dive was required, and secondly, a well-controlled dive had to be executed ensuring skid and slip-free accuracy as the bombs were released.

A Kittyhawk being serviced at the dispersal area.

All that remained of Monte Cassino.

The attack was initiated from 6 000 ft with aircraft stepped back in loosely spaced-out echelon formation which enabled pilots to make individual attacks. The pilot's nerves were as taut as violin strings as they braced themselves for the moment when the flak would shatter the existing tranquility. The enemy gunners usually held their fire until the wing over into the dive in spite of the fact that the approach to the bridge had already broadcast the squadron's intention to attack.

The leader felt like a shepherd leading his sheep to the slaughter during the run-up to the target which had to be made in straight and level flight until it was directly under one of the wings of his aircraft's landing lights, this being the best way of acquiring an accurate 60 degree angle of dive.

He closed the throttle, pulled the nose up and winged over into the dive pointing the Kitty's spinner at the nearest end of the bridge. At the same time, an intense carpet of flak arose with enemy guns firing from both sides of the river; ominous, sooty black bursts of 88 mm shells surrounding the aircraft.

The airspeed increased at a mind-boggling rate and the altimeter unwound crazily as the Kittyhawk plunged through an ever-thickening barrage of flak. It didn't seem possible that a pilot could fly through such an intense screen of red-hot lead and live to tell the tale.

The ASI indicated 450 mph and the altimeter 1 500 ft above the ground when the moment of truth arrived for the leader. If a direct hit was to be scored on the bridge, precision accuracy was essential.

He positioned the spinner over the centre of the bridge, corrected the skid and slip recorded on the instrument panel, held the controls steady and released the bombs. Seconds later he yanked back on the stick and as the aircraft levelled out, he applied full throttle to add impetus to the zoom which would carry him out of the jaws of death, God willing!

As the Kitty pulled out of the dive, not only was the full expanse of its belly exposed to the enemy, but at the same time the 'G' force phenomenon took over - the abrupt change of direction at speed draining the blood from the leader's vital nerve centres, leaving him totally blind for a few seconds, which seemed like minutes as he was carried up and away from the target.

He felt like a ping-pong ball bouncing on top of a water spout. He could hear the roar of the guns and the shells exploding around his aircraft and he wondered how much longer his luck would hold out.

When his vision returned he started some drastic evasive action in a desperate effort to mislead the aim of his tormentors, and then, as suddenly as the flak had begun during the initial dive, it ended, and calm skies prevailed.

The enemy gunners had abandoned the chase as far as he was concerned and were concentrating their full fury on his fellow pilots. At 6 000 ft he circled the agreed upon rendezvous and observed the pilots diving down through that lethal corridor of flak and he understood why a pilot was occasionally branded for lack of moral fibre. Mr Luck was his co-pilot on bridge-busting operations.

The close support operations on which Kittyhawks made their name were called 'Cab Rank', the brainwave of a celebrated South

A bridge across the River Po destroyed by dive-bombing.

African, Wing Commander David Haysom DSO, DFC. During an important battle, a flight of six aircraft would patrol the rank flying up and down between two landmarks behind the bomb-line. The controller, who was usually a tour-expired squadron commander, would be situated on a hill or a high building overlooking the battle front from where he kept in touch with the army and flight commanders by radio.

When the Army Commander required air support, he called up the controller and described the target to be attacked providing two references on a gridded topocadastral map with which both the controller and flight commander had also been issued. The first reference confirmed the general target area with an alphabetically marked square which in turn, was divided into numbered squares from which the area immediately surrounding the target, could be pinpointed. A flight leader seldom experienced difficulty in identifying the target while patrolling the rank, but if in doubt, he usually 'spotted' it while diving down to the attack, his bombs acting as markers for the rest of the flight. Cab Rank proved to be a reliable and effective method of close support to the army whether the target was a tank, an enemy HQ, a troop concentration or just a lone, troublesome gun.

The victory fly-past of the battle scarred squadrons of the Desert Air Force was a nostalgic episode for everyone concerned since it meant the ringing down of the curtain on the last page of the last chapter comprising the outstanding record of a legendary force.

Tailpiece

At the end of the war, I was OC 250 (Sudan) Squadron RAF and a citizen of the United Kingdom. When all South Africans and Australians had returned home, I was detailed to form one squadron from the remaining three RAF squadrons, to dispose of 250's Kittyhawks and re-equip with Mustangs. It was a sad moment for me one morning when witnessing the last of DAF and 250's Kittys fly south towards the scrapyard. I saluted their glorious deeds during four years of constant operations against the enemy and still remember them with respect and affection.

Walking Home

Many pilots had to walk home. I tried it myself a few times, but found this particular hike possibly the most interesting.

My first operational sortie in a Spitfire lasted two hours, but it took me two days to get back to the squadron. This was the commencement of my second tour in January 1943. For familiarisation with this dainty bird of prey, I was positioned to fly No 2 to the Commanding Officer, Major 'Snowy' Moodie. The mission, considered a relatively easy exercise, was to escort a specially equipped Wellington bomber detonating magnetic mines in Tripoli harbour on the day the city was evacuated by the Axis forces. All went according to plan. There was no enemy interference from air or ground and the 'Wedding-ring Wimpy' enjoyed a successful hour with its escorting Spitfires. We left the area and set course for home.

Seventy miles south-east of the city, the terrain below appeared very different from the usual sand and flat expanse. Undulating wadis and broken outcrops of rock stretched away to the horizon in a monotonous grey brown of Libyan waste. I was thinking how unfriendly it all looked, and how unsuitable it would be for a forced landing, when white puffs of glycol vapour spewed from the starboard exhaust. My thoughts had become a reality!

The engine roughened up quickly and the oil and water temperatures rose dangerously, so I cut the ignition switches and selected a suitable landing area. This wasn't easy, but it was to be my lucky day and after gliding down in eerie silence between two low hills of rock, I slithered AX-C to a wheels-up belly-landing over a sea of stones and small boulders. It was an undignified tail-up finale and approximately a 100 yards ahead was a sheer drop!

I climbed out of the cockpit and waved to the two Spits circling above checking my situation. On their departure I felt I was the loneliest person on the African continent. The time was nearly midday and I decided to adopt the law of the western desert and stay with my aircraft. Unscrewing the armourplating behind the cockpit and extracting a water-bottle, a small tin of emergency rations and a first-aid kit, I waited instructions.

'Bushy' Langerman (left) with his CO 'Snowy' Moodie.

After about an hour, a strange sensation told me that I was not alone. Standing up from my reclining position on the shady side of the fuselage, I saw a group of approximately 20 Bedouins dressed in the familiar dirty-white 'night shirts', had surrounded me. Not one word was uttered as an old man walked towards me holding a little boy's hand. He stopped and pointed to the lad whose head was covered in festering sores and I got the message. Allah had sent me from the skies to do something about it.

My first-aid box revealed, amongst other oddments, water purifying tablets, disinfectant and a roll of sticking-plaster. I solemnly applied some powder and then covered the wounds with the sticking-plaster. For the first time the old man said something, calling out loudly, whereupon the entire circle dropped down on their knees and prayed in the familiar Mohammedan way. They disappeared as mysteriously as they had arrived.

About 1730 hours, Major Moodie and Doug Rogan flew over my aircraft dropping instructions, a revolver in its holster and a screwdriver in case I hadn't been able to remove the armourplating and recover rations. I still have the sheet of message pad instructing me to leave the aircraft and walk south-west and that within approximately nine miles I would meet an army truck used by the advancing 7th Armoured Division. I set off about 1800 hours when the sun was sinking low, but a full moon was taking its place. I donned my flying helmet not only for warmth but in case it was required the following day, and I slipped the screwdriver into the side of my flying boot.

After about five hours of climbing up and down rocky hills in the

The note dropped by Snowy Moodie after Bushy's forced-landing.

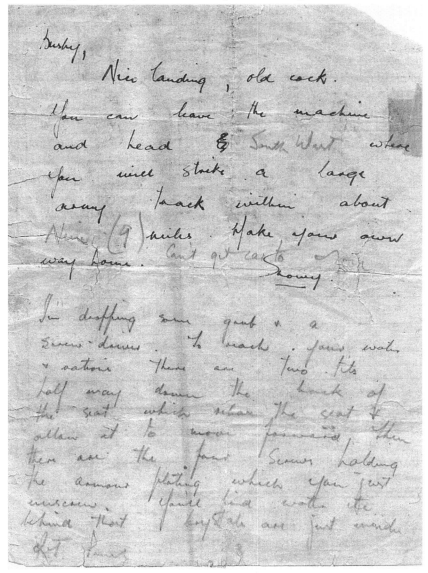

bright moonlight, I realised that something had gone wrong. There was no track, no transport and all the time I appeared to be moving further and further away from civilisation, so I decided to turn about and head for the coast road about 30 miles to the north.

At three o'clock in the morning, from the top of the wadi, the moonlight revealed what appeared to be dispersed tanks about a mile away. The 'tanks' turned out to be large dead, almost petrified, thorn bushes in a sandy river bed. Next to one bush was the plastered dome of an old well, about ten feet in diameter, its lid secured with a dead tree trunk. By this time my water-bottle was running low and anticipating a long hike in front of me, I prayed that the well would not be as dry as its surroundings.

Water was there, sweet and cool, but in order to reach it I had to unravel the R/T leads from my helmet, and these together with the webbing, allowed sufficient length for bailing with the holster weighted down with a few rounds of ammunition. I drank my fill, replenished the bottle and continued walking north.

At sunrise next morning a dog barked. Civilisation turned out to be a cluster of small, low, dark-brown tents in the middle of nowhere. A few small areas of tilled earth, about a quarter of an acre in extent, and a number of goats and fowls completed the camp site. From the first tent, a man appeared and beckoned me in. The interior was only about four feet high and I crouched low on entering, squatting next to him in the one of the two sections. The other was sealed off with a curtain of goat skin. My host produced an egg which he had cooked on the embers of a small twig fire in the middle of the 'room'. A goat was then fetched and pushed through the curtain behind which I heard it being milked - obviously by his wife whom, no doubt, I was not allowed to see. The small calabash of warm goat's milk was like the nectar of the gods and this generous hospitality was reciprocated with the presentation of the screwdriver. In this nomadic existence, my gift was received with warm and genuine gratitude.

After seven hours of walking and a few hours of sleep, I arrived at a small village made up of square white buildings straddling the main road. The first building turned out to be a small store. The owner stood behind a rough counter and there were about five other occupants seated on the ground in front of it. My entrance obviously caused a stir, a few members of the party standing and some whispering, indicating a general uneasiness. The owner kindled a small fire in the middle of the floor and a clay container of coffee was heated. It was thick, full of grounds and very sweet. While sipping the brew, there was a general flurry from an adjoining room and two Senussi NCOs in immaculate uniforms appeared. I grabbed my revolver, but with solemn dignity they stopped in front of me and in a gesture of surrender, each

Bushy with Doug Rogan.

presented me with their daggers which I stuck in my revolver webbing and went on drinking my coffee.

Sign language and drawings on the sand floor revealed that I was only five miles from the small town of Marconi. Marching my two prisoners about 30 yards in front of me, I arrived in Marconi about two hours later where I commissioned the local mayor and his doctor to drive me to the nearest British troops. The night was spent with the 1st Tank Transport Company before I returned to the squadron.

So ended my first Spitfire operation but fortunately 250 more sorties lay ahead.

Tailpiece

'Bushy' was involved in many precarious adventures during his three tours of operations. On one occasion he and six other 4 Squadron pilots were outnumbered in a scrap with more than 24 enemy aircraft and only two of the seven returned safely to base. The other five, including Bushy, were shot down; three were killed but he survived. Shortly after crash-landing and jumping out of his burning aircraft, it exploded.

'The walking home' saga was 'old hat' to Bushy. He later commanded 2 Squadron and was awarded the DFC. He lives in Parktown North, Johannesburg.

Jack van Eyssen

Disaster over Warsaw

Before recounting the story of Liberator KG 939-A's ill-fated operation over Warsaw on 14 August 1944 while dropping supplies to the *Armia Kragowa*, (home army), an account of why and how the airlift took place is necessary.

During the deliberations at Versailles after World War I, the only truly astute delegate, General Jan Smuts, warned that the imposition of the 'Polish Corridor' would not necessarily be the reason, but could certainly be the excuse for hostile action against Poland in the future. His warning became a reality in 1939 when history repeated itself. Nazi Germany and the Soviet Union, having signed a pact, attacked Poland simultaneously from both east and west and after fierce fighting, the country was subdued and partitioned according to the wishes of Hitler and Stalin.

Immediately after this humiliation, the AK movement provided a priceless intelligence service to the UK and USA and in 1944 it was granted full combat status by a joint decision of Britain and America. The AK harassed the Germans wherever they could and inside Warsaw during 1944, plans were laid for a concerted effort to prove to their enemies, to themselves and to the free world that Poland's spirit had not been crushed. Warsaw was the headquarters and nerve centre of the AK, and the organisation was urged to rise in revolt by the Russians who were now on the Allied side and had promised immediate assistance. On 1 August 1944, the die was cast and the AK rose against its oppressors. After fierce fighting in most parts of the city, the valiant Polish freedom fighters captured 70 per cent of Warsaw but there was no sign of the promised Russian intervention. With food and ammunition running low, superiority was slowly whittled away by German reinforcements.

Winston Churchill decided that arms and provisions should be flown to the beleaguered Polish garrison from Italy, a return flight of almost 2 000 miles. The distance from UK was too far and Stalin flatly refused permission for Allied aircraft to refuel on Russian soil. South African Brigadier J T Durrant, who commanded 205 Group RAF of

Jack van Eyssen and two of his crew (left to right) 2 Lt R G Hamilton, Capt J L van Eyssen, Lt R F Holliday.

which 2 Wing SAAF was a part, was not happy about this decision. He visited Air Vice-Marshal John Slessor to tell him so and was surprised when admitted into the presence of Churchill in an adjoining office. Durrant pointed out to the British Prime Minister that an airlift would not help to promote a military success and the loss of aircrew and aircraft would be unrealistic. While Churchill agreed with him, he nevertheless insisted that the operation should take place, if only for reasons of propaganda and morale.

No 2 Wing's 31 and 32 Squadrons and 148 and 178 Squadrons of the RAF, all attached to 205 group, were detailed for the Airlift because their Liberators possessed the range and the load capacity. A new look had to be taken at the payload versus the fuel load. On conventional bombing raids, sufficient petrol was uplifted for the distance plus 25 per cent reserve for emergencies. On the flight to Warsaw, the maximum fuel load the tanks could hold was 2 300 gallons and the percentage reserve was only ten per cent. Twelve canisters were carried on the bomb racks, each crammed with light machine-guns, ammunition, hand grenades, radio equipment, food and medical supplies. In addition the canisters were fitted with small parachutes to break their fall and prevent their contents being damaged.

When planning the operation, two chilling prospects arose. Firstly, due to the long days in the northern hemisphere at that time, the enemy coast would have to be crossed in sunlight both on the outward and return flights, providing an easy target for enemy fighters; and secondly, a small complement of aircraft could not saturate the enemy defences which included searchlights, flak and fighters. A zig-zag course was therefore essential to miss the main interception areas.

Our Liberator, K6 939-A, became airborne from Foggia at 1700 hours taking the full length of the runway before rising sturdily into the air and setting course across the Adriatic. The sun was still shining as

142

the enemy coast was reached but darkness soon enveloped us and the Danube appeared below on ETA. To the north lay the Carpathians and bad weather. The Lib was tossed about in angry clouds and was lit up frequently by lightning, the propeller discs at times creating blue circles and blue flames which trailed from the wing tips and other projections. This was known as St Elmo's Fire - frightening but harmless.

North of the mountains, the weather cleared and another alteration of course bypassed the dreaded Cracow which was a Luftwaffe night-fighter training centre. After a final course alteration, music from Radio Warsaw could be heard and then a glow on the horizon was apparent. After losing height towards the city's outskirts we were shocked to see row upon row of buildings burning, sending a pall of smoke thousands of feet into the air illuminated by the light of the raging fires. Obviously a life or death struggle was taking place in that unhappy capital city.

We flew north along the Vistula reducing height to 200 ft before turning around a cathedral in the north of the city and then heading south keeping the river on our left. At this stage bomb doors were opened, and letting down to 150 ft using optimum flap, I kept the Liberator under control while flying at only 130 mph. A greater speed could have snapped the shroud lines of the canister's parachutes.

On observing a green letter 'K' flashing on the ground, we dropped our canisters on it from roof-top height and I opened all throttles bent on a quick getaway. At the same time the Liberator was heavily engaged by 35 mm anti-aircraft guns and both engines on the right wing were set alight. I turned east towards the Russian lines and told Bob Hamilton to stop the burning engines and to try to douse the flames, but the fire extinguishers were useless and were of no effect. It was difficult to hold course, for the two live engines on the left wing tended to turn the aircraft to the right.

Seventy feet above the ground was too low for a parachute jump and the engines were burning too fiercely to risk a belly-landing. George Peaston dramatised the situation further when reporting that one of the two good engines on the left wing had also caught fire, so without hesitating I told Bob to re-start the two burning engines on the right wing. He turned on the fuel and switches and held down the feathering buttons. The inner engine took full power but the other did not even turn over.

With three engines on full power I climbed the Lib to 1 000 ft. Pieces of red hot metal were falling from the wings and an explosion seemed imminent when I gave the order to abandon aircraft, held the alarm bell down for about half a minute and then made my way to the catwalk where Bob Hamilton was waiting to see me out. I ordered him to jump and as he did so I followed immediately behind, pulling my ripcord at the same instant. Within seconds of my 'chute opening I hit

The shrine, built by Kowalski, on the precise spot where van Eyssen's Liberator crashed.

the ground, but Bob's 'chute didn't open and he was killed instantly. He'd probably counted up to three before pulling the ripcord not realising that the Lib had rapidly spiralled earthwards after my departure from the cockpit. I feel certain that Sergeants Mayes and Hudson were both killed by flak for their bodies were still inside the aircraft which crashed close to where I had landed, generating an enormous fire.

The four other survivors left the aircraft immediately after I'd given the order to abandon ship. George Peaston landed on the roof of a Polish professor's house; 'Happy' Holliday took refuge under a bed in

144

another friendly Pole's cottage, while Bunny Austin, who had always been a man for the girls, had a welcome stroke of luck for he landed inside a girls' convent and took refuge in bed with a girl called Ursula! Years later he returned to Poland, met up with Ursula, helped her to escape from Warsaw to Paris and then wrote a book about her. We five survivors ended up at a Russian Divisional Headquarters where, after interrogation, we were driven east for about 70 miles to a village where 16 days internment followed before we were flown to Moscow and eventually back home.

Many South Africans perished during the 'Warsaw Airlift' and some were lucky to survive. Bob Burgess who, as second pilot, flew his crippled Liberator eastwards and landed on Russian territory after his captain had become disenamoured with the flak and baled out without a word of warning. Bob was awarded an immediate DSO and at 20 years of age he was the youngest ever recipient of this prestigious award. Another lucky pilot was Nick Groenewald who found himself falling through the dark after his Lib was blown to pieces over Warsaw. His parachute pack was in his hand like a briefcase and he managed to clip it on to his harness, landing safely but with facial burns.

During the worst nights of the airlift, between 4 August and early September 1944, 194 sorties were flown to Warsaw of which 85 aircraft reached the target area and 39 were lost. The task was too great to save the gallant Polish army which was destroyed while the Russians sat idly by, barely 20 miles away.

Liberators dropping provisions over Warsaw.

Tailpiece

The airlift may have failed, but it served to cement a bond of friendship between Poles and South Africans based on mutual respect and a sincere friendship. A patriotic, public spirited Pole, Bornislaw Kowalski, erected a shrine in the woods near the village of Michalin which marks the exact spot where Jack's Liberator crashed in flames at midnight on 14-15 August 1944. In his garden, Bornislaw built another shrine in which a light burns day and night in memory of the three airmen who died that night. Their remains rest in Cracow Cemetery with the other South African, RAF and Polish Air Force casualties who lost their lives in the 'Warsaw Airlift'.

Jack also took part in bombing the Ploesti oilfields and when these attacks failed to achieve the required results, he became involved in the alternative of dropping mines in the River Danube, a story which features earlier in this book. For his heroic contribution to the success of many operations and his stoic courage over Warsaw, he was awarded the immediate DFC. He lives in Waverley, Johannesburg.

I Flew with Pat Pattle

Unfortunately the suitcase containing all my memorabilia about World War II between 1940 and 1944, excepting my logbook, was stolen from my tent at Suez while I was awaiting embarkation back to South Africa. Sadly the logbook didn't reflect details of any value about Pat Pattle other than recording that on one occasion while I was flying as his No 2, we shared the destruction of a Cant 100T.

I joined 80 Squadron RAF in May 1940. One flight operated between Sidi Barrani and Mersa Matruh landing grounds and the other was based at Alexandria, responsible for the defence of the harbour. For the next six months 112 (Shark), 32 and 80 Squadrons were virtually the sole aerial defence of Egypt.

In November the Squadron moved to Eleusis near Athens and then to Larissa in central Greece which became our main base. I was detailed to proceed to Trikala on the Albanian border to establish an advanced landing ground, and it was from here that Pat gained many of his victories.

Our CO, Squadron Leader Bill Hickey, was shot down shortly after our arrival in Greece and his replacement was 'Tap' Jones, with Pat as his senior flight commander. At this time, as far as I can remember, Pat's score was 26 confirmed victories and by the time I was shot down, his score had increased to 35. He flew on virtually every patrol 80 Squadron put up and on his return, the usual greeting from his ground crew was: 'How many this time, sir?'

I remember he used to stay on the airfield if he'd been shot up, to make sure that his erks patched up the holes so that the aircraft would be serviceable for the next sortie. He was entirely without fear. On one occasion I was duty pilot on the airfield when it was strafed by 12 ME 109s. No funk hole for Pat who ran out on the tarmac waving his hands above his head and screaming abuse at the Jerries until they had disappeared. I will never understand how he survived the torrent of shells which rained down on every portion of the airfield.

I came out of hospital, rejoined the squadron at Eleusis airfield and shortly after, on 12 March 1941, Pat was posted as CO to 33 Squadron

Bunny Hosken.

RAF. I never saw him again and we were all distraught on hearing of his death on 20 April 1941. Those of us who knew him well, thought he was indestructible.

He was shot down while going to the assistance of one of his pilots, an Irishman Timber Woods, who was outnumbered by several enemy aircraft. Pat wasn't well at the time and shouldn't have been in the air. He swept into the fray, pulled up behind the Irishman's adversary who was flying an ME 110, and set it alight. Perhaps, if Pat had been his usual fit and alert self, he would have faced the odds as he had done on so many other occasions, and won; but the superior numbers got him in the end and another Hurricane pilot saw him slumped forward against the dashboard of his burning aircraft as it dived vertically towards Eleusis Bay.

During the months I operated with Pat, I found him to be a kind, friendly person with a fine sense of humour and a tolerant, humble nature; a true South African gentleman. Undoubtedly he was a brilliant, dedicated pilot and in my opinion, if he had flown in the western European theatre of operations as opposed to the desert and Greece using tired Gladiators and Hurricanes, he could have held an all-time world record for the number of enemy aircraft destroyed by an individual pilot. As it happened he was the top scoring British and South African ace with 41 confirmed victories and it has been maintained that his final score was 47 which could not be confirmed because all records were lost during the evacuation from Greece.

Pat's success as a fighter pilot stemmed from the effortless way in

148

Pat Pattle

which he flew at all times. He was a born fighter pilot and knew precisely how to get the better of his enemy, and then with his excellent sense of timing and brilliant marksmanship, he seldom missed destroying his adversary. We were all very sore that he was not given more recognition. His decorations only included the DFC and bar and he was mentioned in dispatches, although if he had survived, his outstanding courage would undoubtedly have been justly rewarded.

Tailpiece

Bunny joined the RAF in Nairobi during 1940 where he held a civilian pilot's licence with an Auxiliary Air Unit. When Greece was overrun by the Germans, he was evacuated in a Sunderland flying boat. He lives in Sandhurst, Johannesburg.

Willem van den Bos

The Loss of a Champion Athlete

On Tuesday 14 August 1951, Second-Lieutenant Christiaan Lodewyk de Jongh of the South African Air Force was reported missing in action on a raid against the North Korean capital city of Pyongyang. At the time of his disappearance, Ian de Jongh was the holder of the South African high jump record and was one of the country's most promising athletes. I had come to know him when he was a cadet before joining 2 Squadron in Korea. My friend Derek Doveton was courting his sister Helene, better known as 'Tutu' de Jongh. Their marriage (I was best man at the wedding) proved to be shortlived as Derek was killed in action in Korea on 15 February 1951. Given that background, I had a special interest in Ian's progress.

To appreciate the grim irony of Ian's loss, it is necessary to go back to Monday 30 July of that year. Rumours had been circulating for some time in the 18th Fighter-Bomber Wing (No's 12, 39 and 67 USAF squadrons and No 2 SAAF Squadron) that a 'big show' was in the offing. Briefing that morning confirmed the accuracy of these rumours. There was to be a mass raid on Pyongyang. Sixty F-80 Shooting Stars were to go in first with proximity-fused bombs and rockets for 'flakbusting', followed by 64 F-51 Mustangs of the 18th F/B Wing with napalm tanks, (a petrol-naphtha jelly which burns fiercely and sticks like glue while it burns), to attack selected targets in the city. Finally, 60 F-84 Thunderjets, 60 F4U Corsairs, and 40 B-29 Superfortresses were to complete the raid.

Weather on the way to Pyongyang was poor and at the starting point for our run in we were advised that only a few of the flakbusters had managed to find their targets. However, our Wing leader decided to attack and we streaked in at rooftop height. The enemy had been alerted by the attempted flakbusting; 20 mm and 40 mm flak providing a hot reception although our height was so low that most of it went over our heads. Hugging the ground along a valley I saw two flak gunners on either side shooting at one another in a frantic effort to get us.

We dropped our napalm tanks on target, starting some impressive fires, and while still on the deck, followed the planned exit route down

150

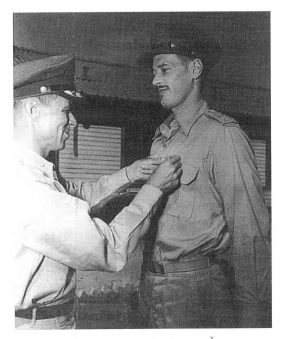

Willem van den Bos decorated in Korea.

the Taedong River. Not one of our 64 aircraft was hit, which proved the value of surprise. Most of the Thunderjets behind us found their targets but the Corsairs enjoyed little success and the Superfortresses none at all. Deteriorating weather and intensifying flak took their toll. JOC (the Joint Operations Centre from which all land and air operations were directed) ordered a repeat operation in the afternoon but the weather had closed in to such an extent that the attack was abandoned. A comment in my diary for that day reads: 'A good thing too. I don't like this practice of repeating a show twice in one day with everything the same down to the last detail.'

On the morning of 14 August we were briefed for a similar operation. On this occasion I was to fly as reserve accompanying the formation as far as the bomb-line in case a pilot was forced to drop out. As it happened nobody turned back so I deposited my napalm tanks on a lone stationary vehicle just north of the bomb-line and returned to base. The raid proved to be only moderately successful, poor weather having once more hampered attacks. JOC insisted on a repeat operation in the afternoon and our Wing was briefed to attack locomotive repair shops and turntables in the Pyongyang railway marshalling yards. To my mind the effectiveness of napalm against such targets was minimal, but who was I to argue with the 'top brass' at JOC?

This time I was part of the show and in the same flight as Ian de Jongh. Weather over the target was again poor, the flakbusting was not effective and the gunners were more than ready for us putting up an almost impenetrable curtain of flak. The napalm tank under my port wing hung up and no amount of juggling with switches and jettison

Ian de Jongh.

levers could dislodge it. With close on half a ton of napalm tank under one wing, the Mustang is not the most manoeuvrable aircraft tending to crab through the sky dropping the loaded wing sharply at every opportunity and responding very sluggishly in a turn away from the loaded wing. With every aircraft at full power on the exit run, I soon fell behind the rest of the flight, still trying to shake off the stubborn tank. It was at this stage that I heard Ian on the R/T: 'I've been hit!'

Looking ahead I could see the tell-tale plume of white glycol vapour streaming from his Mustang's radiator. He banked sharply to starboard heading west towards the coast where rescue launches were waiting offshore to pick up downed pilots; and coaxing my handicapped aircraft into a turn to starboard I tried to follow. Suddenly the napalm tank fell away, which almost caused a spiral dive to starboard. After recovering from this unexpected manoeuvre I caught sight of a Mustang ahead streaming glycol, but it turned out to be a 39 Squadron aircraft. As I drew closer it dived into a paddyfield bursting into flames on impact with no hope for the pilot. Reports indicated that Ian had been seen heading west and had disappeared into scattered low cloud. To this day his fate remains shrouded in mystery.

That afternoon raid turned out to be a traumatic experience for the 18th Fighter Bomber Wing. The 39th lost its Commanding Officer and two other pilots; the 67th lost a pilot and we lost Ian, while more than half the aircraft that returned to base were damaged by flak. In retrospect, I think my erratic flight path in trying to shake off the napalm tank may have helped me to come through that raid unscathed. The results? Five pilots lost and very little damage done to the targets. A comment in my diary for that day reads: 'I have come to the conclusion that the planning staff at JOC has no idea of weapon effect and is using these raids purely as a political lever at the cease-fire talks which are currently in progress at Panmunjom. Altogether a bloody stupid raid.'

The South African Amateur Athletics Union subsequently honoured Ian's memory by instituting the Ian de Jongh Athletics Meeting, held annually at the Pilditch Stadium in Pretoria.

Willem van den Bos in his Spitfire at Potchefstroom Air Force Station, preparing for a weapons display.

Tailpiece

Willem was shot down in both World War II and the Korean War. The first occasion was over Yugoslavia in March 1945 when flying on an armed reconnaissance with an RAF Spitfire squadron. His flight attacked a train with smoke curling from the engine's funnel, but it was a well-planned German trap and Willem's Spitfire was crippled by an intense flak barrage forcing him to crash-land in a forest. The aircraft's wings were torn off, the safety harness snapped and he was catapulted forward, his face smashing into the gunsight. With a severely damaged hip, a bloody, lacerated face and a mouthful of loose teeth, Willem scrambled out of the smoking cockpit and crawled to a safe distance from the wreck before losing consciousness. He woke up in Zagreb Hospital where some friendly Partisans had taken him and he spent the rest of the war as a POW.

On 5 September 1951, as a member of 2 Squadron in Korea, his Mustang was hit by snipers while flying at low level searching for a downed American pilot. He crash-landed once more but this time he was unhurt and was rescued 40 minutes later by a helicopter. He returned to the squadron and completed his tour of operations on 21 October 1951.

Willem has enjoyed a distinguished career in the SAAF over the post-war years and although he took an early retirement to become a senior lecturer at Cape Town University, he is still involved in the aviation world as chairman of the Cape Town branch of the SAAF Association. He lives in Constantia, Cape.

Rows of napalm bombs ready for loading.

Danie Laubscher

Light Aircraft 'Nail-Biters'

Back in the 1970s when South Africa was assisting the FNLA and the Unita forces in Angola against the MPLA, before the Cubans intervened, I was operating a Cessna 185 aircraft on call for a number of possible requirements including communications, reconnaissance, casualty evacuation and control of artillery and mortar barrages. During this period I recall three typical missions which caused me some concern to say the least.

A Packet of Lexingtons

I was stationed at Unita's Luso HQ in Eastern Angola and one morning I was detailed to fly two black colonels, one from the FNLA and the other from Unita, to a small village called Cago Coutinho which was controlled by Unita, but the airfield was the responsibility of the FNLA.

I was to discover that total disunity and mistrust existed between the two groups. After 90 minutes flying, the airfield appeared ahead, individual mushrooms of dust swirling above it, an unusual phenomenon. I don't believe in heroics unless imperative and decided to circle at 1 000 metres to await developments. The FNLA colonel indicated that I should land, but the Unita colonel wasn't happy about the situation and I was inclined to agree with his sentiments.

After circling for a short while, the dust settled and I landed. While taxiing, a group of black soldiers suddenly appeared out of the surrounding bush waving AK 47s and signalling me to stop. One doesn't argue with AK 47s so I obeyed, and the Unita colonel climbed out of the aircraft and disappeared into the bush with the soldiers.

I was reluctant to taxi to the parking area and indicated to the FNLA colonel that he should disembark and go his own way. He refused and I had no option but to taxi to the parking area where another group of unfriendly soldiers was brandishing AK 47s from all directions.

The colonel waved vigorously at the soldiers and I noticed he was sweating profusely with fear - but suddenly there were flashes of white ivories and the apprehensions of both parties melted as the soldiers

Danie Laubscher.

recognised their superior officer and concluded that the Cessna was on their side.

Not wanting to offend anyone, I shook hands with all the soldiers who must have numbered about 100 and I doled out Lexington cigarettes which were carried in the aircraft in case of such an emergency. The good deed had almost been completed when a couple of mortar shells landed too close for comfort. I wasted no time and dived into an adjoining slit trench, a prompt although foolhardy decision because the 100-plus soldiers then landed on top of me, still clutching their lethal weapons!

Five minutes later all was quiet, and we climbed out of the trench. My priority was to get the hell out of it soonest, but the colonel would not hear of this. He intended to hold a meeting with his men and then he wanted me to fly him to see his General at Huambo. The more I argued with him the more he ignored me.

Naturally I was unable to advise him that the SADF was pulling out of Angola in the morning and I certainly did not intend to be around when these people learned of this plan, so I advised the colonel that the aircraft needed a service and if this was not carried out, the engine might cut dead while I was flying him to Huambo. I would return and fetch him in the morning.

We were still arguing about my proposal when the mortar shells began falling again and at the same time an FNLA soldier reported that a group of Swapo troops had joined Unita. Desperately, I looked around to see whether there was a chance of making a quick getaway in my Cessna and noticed an FNLA soldier who was having his wounds treated. 'I'll fly him to hospital,' I shouted in an accommodating voice and without waiting for a reply, I manhandled the soldier towards the Cessna and bundled him inside. The engine burst into life immediately and there was no time for any safety checks. I opened the throttle fully and took off on the taxi track!

When airborne there was a frightening knocking against the side of the aircraft and I was convinced that bullets were striking the fuselage. I dived the aircraft until its wheels were just above the bush but the noise persisted. The FNLA soldier was so petrified that his eyes were rolling around like marbles!

The noise was coming from one area and I suddenly realised that in my haste to take off, the co-pilot's safety harness and buckle had been left dangling outside the aircraft and it was the slipstream which was blowing the buckle against the door and causing the racket!

I climbed to a safe height, opened the door and pulled in the harness. We smoked a packet of Lexington on the way home to soothe our shattered nerves!

A New Meaning To Life

During Operation Savannah, January 1976, I found myself and my Cessna at Silva Porto, the Unita HQ approximately 550 miles north of Rundu. In addition to my aircraft, the SAAF detachment consisted of one Puma, two Alouette helicopters and a Dakota. Every second week the Dak carried supplies to Lobito Bay and returned with a supply of soles and shrimps. While this bounty lasted, festive moments were enjoyed by everyone.

One Sunday morning after one of these fiestas, I had been encouraged by the prevailing adverse weather conditions to burrow into the bedclothes for a real 'sleep-in,' but my slumber was rudely disturbed by the Ops clerk. 'Your presence is urgently required at Operations Control.'

I dragged on my flying clothes, opened a tin of viennas and swallowed a few. At the airfield, a mug of coffee was scrounged from a Unita soldier and I reported to Major Coetzee at Ops Control.

'One of the helicopters has been shot down and there is one survivor at the wreck who needs immediate medical attention. There is no airfield near the scene and so a Dak cannot be used. The distance is beyond the range of a helicopter and therefore a Cessna 185 is the only alternative. A safe landing can be made on a tar road near the site of the crash.'

The passenger seat was removed from my aircraft and replaced by a foam mattress. A radio message from the crash area indicated that a steady rain with a ceiling of 300 metres was prevailing. My map showed that there was high ground on the direct route, but if a north-westerly course were followed across lower-lying ground, a tarred road would be picked up which would lead past the wrecked helicopter.

I took off accompanied by a doctor and followed a north-westerly course, soon striking the adverse weather. I lowered one notch of flap and the Cessna crawled under the low cloud. While turning back from time to time and probing forward again in search of alternative routes, I was well aware that our lives were in jeopardy, but the life of a comrade was at stake. Should all fail, an escape route was available by spiralling up through the cloud and returning to Silva Porto.

Patience prevailed, the tarred road appeared beneath and I followed it to the right under a cloud base which had lifted to 200 metres. Soon the remains of the helicopter loomed up ahead and I was advised by radio that a specific section of the road had been cordoned off for a landing. When circling I could see that the trees were too close to

Danie's Cessna C185 on an airstrip near Silva Porto.

the road on the allotted stretch so I chose another section of road on which I put the Cessna down safely.

An ambulance appeared and I recognised Commandant Verster in spite of his badly burnt face. I removed the right rear door of the aircraft and he was laid down gently on the mattress, the excruciating pain he was suffering being reflected in his eyes. The doctor climbed into the aircraft and wriggled into a comfortable position next to his patient, at the same time attaching a drip to the starboard sunshield.

As I replaced the door, the Commandant lifted his hand slowly and with tears in his eyes he thanked me for helping him. Those few seconds brought a new meaning to life and I promised to fly him back to base in the shortest possible time.

I climbed my little Cessna into the clouds, tuned the radio frequency to Silva Porto and following a self-designed let down procedure, landed on the airfield where an ambulance was waiting. The Commandant was whisked away for an emergency operation and that night he was flown to No 1 Military Hospital. Today he has retired and owns a little farm near Montagu.

A Bottle Of Cabernet

Early one Monday morning, I was jerked out of bed and summoned to the Ops room. My briefing was to aid a Combat Group which had made contact with the enemy near Cauindo. Mike James, our operations officer, accompanied me and after one hour's flight I spoke to the team's leader over the radio. He asked me to search for a 'Buffel' armoured car which was missing. I picked up Cauindo and identified a SAM 7 missile through my binoculars, self-preservation compelling me to give it a wide berth while searching for the 'Buffel'. There were plenty of tracks but no sign of the lost vehicle and while returning to base, instructions were received to land and re-fuel at Ionde. As it happened, no fuel was available there and a quick calculation disclosed that sufficient petrol was in the Cessna's tanks for 50 minutes flying. Ongiva was precisely 40 minutes away.

I took off and using minimum power, followed the road to Ongiva. With one tank empty and the gauge on the other showing red, a safe landing was made. There was ample fuel available on the airfield but the pump was unserviceable and a replacement was not due until later in the day, so Mike and I did the sensible thing and caught up on some sleep.

When the pump arrived, the Cessna's tanks were filled to capacity, for instructions had been received to return to Cauindo. Becoming airborne again at 1800 hours, we reached Cauindo at dusk, when the Combat Group requested a fix of its position, a request which was com-

Patrolling the Angola/Namibia border.

plied with after some flares had been set off in the bush. After relaying some messages to the Combat Group's HQ, I set course for base in total darkness.

At this time of year electrical storms are a feature of the weather pattern and the Cessna's radio compass picked up one storm centre after another which I was able to skirt around, and deciding that thunderstorms in the southern hemisphere move in a north-easterly direction, I estimated a course for base accordingly.

After about 45 minutes, the fuel indicator warned that one tank was empty so the second tank was selected. At that stage no immediate problem existed thanks to a 30 minute reserve tank, but my sub-conscious mind was aware of the fact that the course for base was only an estimate and could be incorrect. After flying for just over one hour, the rain was pelting down and there was no sight of the ground beneath let alone the lights of Rundu.

Then, after I had been flying for about 90 minutes, the moon suddenly appeared and at the same moment the Okavango river was observed beneath. The sighs of relief were shattered by the realisation that we were to starboard of course and at least 30 minutes from Rundu with precisely 30 minutes of fuel left in the tanks.

I broke the news to Mike who reacted like a good intelligence officer and suggested that the situation may not be as chronic as it appeared. I contacted Rundu on the radio and informed the operator of our position. Mike and I discussed our course of action should the worst happen. I was wearing a parachute but he was without one, so obviously I couldn't bale out and leave him to his fate. The only alternative was to force-land on the edge of the Okavango swamp and take a chance with the crocodiles!

With about 45 kilometres to go and with the fuel indicator needle well in the red, I spotted Rundu's lights in the distance. The last 15 minutes seemed like an eternity and the lights didn't appear to get any closer. The fuel needle was at the end of its traverse and Mike and I had run out of conversation. However, the engine refused to quit.

Control advised that I was clear to land straight ahead on 080 degrees. The airfield was seven kilometres away and our height was 700 metres, when the engine coughed, the fuel gauge needle matching the fluctuations of my heart. In desperation I flicked the fuel pump switch to on and off; there was a momentary pick up and then the engine died. I quickly completed emergency drills and with the prop in coarse pitch for maximum glide, I informed Control of our position. The altimeter read 600 metres and I estimated the distance to the runway was three to four kilometres.

The Cessna crossed the perimeter at 100 metres above the tarmac and was chased by the fire tender and ambulance, its red lights flashing - and then at long last the Cessna's wheels squeaked on the runway and I said a silent prayer of thanks. At dispersal I struggled out of the cockpit and while standing on the tarmac, my legs were trembling and my flying suit was damp with sweat. The officer who greeted us suggested that de-briefing could be left until the morning, and in any case Mike had a more sensible idea. 'Come Danie' he murmured, 'Let's off to the mess and open a bottle of Cabernet!'

Tailpiece

Danie is a serving Major in the SAAF based at Potchefstroom. In 1981 he was awarded the Honoris Crux (Silver) for his courage when marking a target holding up the advance of SADF forces. While under enemy fire he attacked a Swapo gun emplacement at low level with smoke rockets, putting it out of action.

Bob Klette

Death was not our Destiny

By 0900 hours on Sunday 13 August 1944 it was clear that 31 Squadron would not be required to fly that night and our thoughts turned to the cool, crystal clear waters of the Adriatic at Manfredonia Bay not far from our base camp at Celone in Italy.

My crew and I were stepping out to join the exodus of would-be swimmers from camp when our attention was caught by a cloud of dust preceded by a jeep approaching us in haste from the direction of the Ops tent. It was the CO's navigator, Lofty Thorogood, with the terse instructions, 'No one to leave camp - briefing at 1100 hours.' This didn't satisfy our curiosity, for crews were only told that they were to fly to Brindisi after an early lunch for further briefing.

At Brindisi, we parked our Liberator G for George and ambled over towards the 148 Squadron 'Ops room' where many other crews, both RAF and SAAF were assembled.

Inside was a huge wall map of Europe and a route from Brindisi to Warsaw was marked with tape. We were totally ignorant of what was happening in that war zone and wondered what was in store for us.

The mission was to drop supplies to the beleaguered Polish patriots in Warsaw and the background was rather sketchy. The briefing detailed the route, the position of the dropping areas in Warsaw and the height and speed of approach (500 ft and 140 mph). The Met officer forecast cloud with tops at 16 000 ft; handy for ducking into if night fighters showed up. A Polish pilot assured us that the trip there and back was 'a piece of cake'. He did it every week and advised that the high buildings to the south of the city should be avoided.

With canisters full of guns and ammunition packed in her bomb-bays, G for George crossed the Adriatic in fading light, Brian Jones our navigator called for a northerly course, and the long flight across the Carpathians commenced. As night fell, all eyes were on the lookout for tell-tale glows in the sky which would indicate night fighters. Not much chatter from the crew - consisting, apart from Brian, of second pilot Alf Faul, mid-upper gunner Herbert Brown, wireless operator Eric Winchester, waist gunner 'Smiler' Davis and tail gunner Henry Upton.

Bob Klette

All too soon the promised cloud loomed up ominously and although our height was above the forecasted ceiling of 16 000 ft, we plunged into the murk which turned out to be the brute of a cumulonimbus, vicious turbulence rocking, swinging and bumping the Liberator. It was like riding in a rodeo, the compasses spinning in all directions from north to south and east to west. Losing height didn't help; gaining height brought rapid icing on the leading edges of the wings as well as sluggish flying; so back to 20 000 ft. Eventually we were through the worst and Brian's calm voice came over the R/T suggesting that the mountains had been cleared, and the descent could commence; but I flew on for nearly half an hour before complying with his proposal. It was one hour fifty-five minutes after entering the cloud that we emerged with the altimeter reading exactly 1 000 ft, and below, stretching into the distance, was Poland.

Brian pinpointed Cracow and we turned eastwards to observe the Vistula River as a clear landmark beneath. While following the river northwards, a pin-point of light grew rapidly into the shape of a city in flames. This was Warsaw - an unforgettable sight. The river divided the main city to the west from its satellite Praga to the east, and bridges linked the two clearly demarcated cities, flames illuminating the buildings and streets of Warsaw.

We could visualise our heroic Polish allies waiting patiently for the supplies to be dropped while another mental picture was of trigger-happy ack-ack gunners preparing to welcome us.

While nearing the first bridge I reduced height rapidly and as the bridge disappeared beneath, half-a-dozen searchlights beamed on the Lib and the heavens opened up with streaks of tracer and balls of flaming onions following from the east bank. Instinctively I pushed the stick forward and pulled it back again, roller coasting along through the muck.

The noise was deafening as the flak thumped against the aircraft and our own guns fired flat out. There was little hope of accurate shooting by our chaps due to the rocking of the aircraft although there was an excited shout from Herbert Brown who was overjoyed when eliminating a searchlight. Smiler Davis and Henry Upton were wounded during this battle but fortunately not too seriously.

Number 2 engine spluttered to a stop and the aircraft slewed to starboard. Keeping straight was not easy and while Alf was feathering the engine and Brian was guiding me over the dropping zone, number 3 engine also petered out. The problem now, with only the two outer engines functioning, was to maintain height, but I managed to stay at 500 ft while Brian talked me into position and after our load had been dropped he yelled. 'Canisters away, let's get the hell out of here,' and he gave me a course to steer for home.

We turned southwards away from the flames of Warsaw, the inky blackness ahead showing no sign of a horizon and inside the aircraft, the artificial horizon along with other gyro instruments, had gone for a total loop. A second or two later there was a severe jarring and scraping under the Lib's belly and then silence. The tall buildings to the south which the Polish pilot had warned us about, was my immediate conclusion as I tensed myself for inevitable death - but nothing happened. Various thoughts went through my mind: Had we crashed? Was I dead and in heaven? Then I stole a quick glance below to the left and couldn't believe my eyes. The Lib had made a perfect belly-landing on a grass surface. 'My God, we're on Mother Earth,' I yelled, but the intercom was dead and only Alf heard me.

We jumped out and ran to the aircraft's nose where Brian had been trapped and was hacking his way clear with an axe carried in that section of the Lib. After freeing himself he joined us and we turned about intending to discover how the rest of the crew had fared, but while running around the port wing with its two engines spewing petrol on to the ground, the beam of a searchlight suddenly settled on us and at the same time a machine-gun opened fire. Throwing ourselves flat on the ground we crawled along towards the wing tip but my progress was suddenly halted by something which caught in my equipment. I gave a tug and with a SHhhh...... my Mae West began to inflate! Had the situation not been so traumatic, the scene could have been like something from a comic opera. I saw my shadow lengthening and felt my chest rising from the ground! Feeling a bit too vulnerable, I shed the Mae West and, still hugging the ground, scuttled along to catch up with Brian and Alf. The searchlight went out and the machine-gun stopped firing. 'Stay down,' I yelled, sensing a trap. I doubt whether anyone heard the warning, but sure enough the searchlight came on again along with the repetitive bursts of machine-gun fire. (We were to learn later that the spirited young Brown had made a dash for it, possibly at this moment, and was hit in the back of his thigh.)

A moment or two later, Very lights hovered over the Liberator. There were voices in the dark and a gun seemed to be firing at the aircraft where, as far as I knew, our wounded gunners were trapped, so Brian, Alf and I stood up and surrendered. Three Luftwaffe types, one a corporal, walked up. '*Ah, Jannie Smuts se boys*' said the corporal eyeing our red tabs! A conversation proceeded in a mixture of German, Afrikaans and English when it was ascertained that we had landed on Warsaw Airport, unbelievably flying straight into the hornets nest! I didn't mention that G for George had landed herself with practically no help from me!

Tailpiece

Bob and five of his crew were escorted to a room in the airport building where a Luftwaffe officer volunteered to arrange for Bob to visit Herbert Brown who had been taken to hospital. This visit did not materialise and Herbert wasn't seen again although the International Red Cross confirmed that he had been hospitalised in Warsaw. He was reported missing after the Russian advance but was not traced. Bob and the rest of his crew became POWs and fortunately the war only lasted another 10 months when they returned home. Bob lives in Somerset West.

Peter Atkins

A Tribute to Bert Rademan

It is not easy to pay an adequate tribute to a man of the calibre of the late Bert Rademan. He was a magnificent pilot, almost without peer as a squadron-leader in World War II and, above all, a great but modest gentleman.

A brief summary of his flying career would not be out of place. He joined the South African Air Force in the 1930s but, having won his wings, left the Air Force for South African Airways. At the outbreak of the war he was recalled to the Air Force and experienced his first taste of operations in East Africa where his expertise and courage while leading a squadron resulted in the award of the DFC. But it was in the Western Desert where his outstanding talents were to be exposed.

He took over 24 Squadron in less than auspicious circumstances. The Bostons had been plagued with teething troubles and when these had been solved they were sent out on two unescorted raids in which two out of three and four out of six planes were lost. In the second of these raids, Lt-Col Jack Mossop was seriously injured and command of the squadron was temporarily in the hands of a Permanent Force officer. Squadron morale was at a low ebb but it did not take long for Bert to change that!

He had taken over a short while before the furious Gazala battles were to be fought and proceeded to lead the squadron through its greatest triumphs. During the battles and the long retreat to El Alamein, 24 Squadron flew 1 000 sorties in less than seven weeks and with 12 Squadron did much to hinder Rommel's advance. So much so in fact, that Air Vice-Marshal Dawson stated: 'But for the Bostons, the Eighth Army would have been fighting in Palestine.' Bert became tour-expired just before the final battle of El Alamein and subsequently commanded 22 Squadron both in South Africa and Gibraltar.

No one who served in 24 Squadron in its halcyon days is ever likely to forget Bert Rademan. He was our ideal of what an operational commanding officer should be. He was an inspired leader who led every tough raid. How he did this without offending his flight commanders was a masterpiece of discretion. Of course he knew the targets before the rest of us. If he was due to lead and the target was a relatively easy

Bert Rademan

one - there were no easy ones - he would wander into the Ops tent and declare he did not feel like flying and substitute his name at the top of the standby list in favour of one of the other leaders. If the raid looked like being really tough and he was not due to lead, he would have a look at the standby list and mutter something about the others 'hogging the raids' and replace the name of the leader with his own. It did not take we humble followers long to learn that if the CO was leading we could expect a sticky do.

The tremendous efforts of the Bostons would never have been possible but for the magnificent coverage by the fighter squadrons - largely our own. Naturally it was essential that the Bostons flew in the tightest possible formations in order to ease, as far as possible, the problem of the fighters. Bert's way of ensuring this was to have two of the finest of formation pilots, Dirky Nel and Andy Jordan, flying on him. This resulted in every other pilot competing furiously in the hope that one day they, too, would have the privilege of flying on the CO.

Bert was imbued with great charisma and inspired intense loyalty. While grousing and bitching was very much part of our lives, there was never a single word of criticism of the CO. He was a gregarious man and when he wasn't flying, was either out on the landing ground chatting happily to the hard-working ground crews or sitting in his favourite canvas chair in the Ops tent holding court. It was not unusual for the flying types to become involved in heated arguments. Bert would listen with an amused grin and then take the steam out of the argument with a mischievious comment. Not so long before his death we were talking about the Desert days when Bert remarked that he'd lost two stone in weight in the desert. I suggested that due to the intense heat, lousy food, no booze and little enough water, we all lost weight. With his usual grin Bert replied, 'I was shit scared all the time. That was a big weight loser!' What a man!

After the war he returned to South African Airways as a senior commander. When the first of the Boeing 707s was ordered, Bert and Pi Pienaar were the first South Africans to fly them, and Boeing officials rated them both as superior to the pilots of all the other airlines converting to the 707s.

After he retired it was tragic that his courage was again to be tested to the full in a losing battle against cancer.

All in all, they just don't come bigger and better than Bert Rademan and his death was a tremendous loss to all of us who knew him. His decorations included the DSO and DFC.

K B McDonald

War over Burma

Wartime Burma. In most minds these two words conjure up a vision of jungles, monsoons, bitter bloody fighting and a bridge over a river called the Kwai.

It was all of that and more. From the Air Force's point of view, there was no Battle of Britain-type air-to-air combat when one was continually subjected to vicious man on man dogfights. There were air-to-air encounters between Hurricanes and Japanese Oscars and Zekes during the early stages of the war - and later on Thunderbolts and Spitfires diced with Jacks, but kills were not a daily occurrence.

Our task was mainly interdiction, army close support, armed reconnaissance and, when Thunderbolts arrived on the scene, long-range high altitude escort mainly to American Superfortresses.

Not many SAAF pilots were involved during the retreat from Singapore to the Indian border. The only two who come to mind are Percy Bodley, who was eventually on Mountbatten's staff as an air transport advisor, and John Viney who was flying Blenheims at the time. It was only late in 1943 when the SAAF called for volunteers for secondment to the RAF, that they began appearing in any numbers in the South East Asia Command (SEAC).

During winter, flying conditions were ideal with ceiling and visibility unlimited (CAVU), but during the monsoon period they were unbelievably poor and treacherous. Flying school had indicated that clouds would not be found above 30 000 ft but on one occasion while returning from an escort mission to Rangoon, we were flying at 30 000 ft above a gaggle of Superforts, when a line squall was encountered with tops about 15 000 ft above us which forced us to make a detour of around 200 miles. Thank heavens for the Thunderbolt's range and the Superfort's leading navigator!

Due to the continuous call for close support, the squadrons in Burma soon became experts in this type of operation and it is no line to say that targets were frequently bombed when only 30 yards from our own troops, a remarkable performance which the SAAF emulated in Korea a few years later.

K B McDonald.

Our Hurricanes were grand old faithfuls but we weren't sorry to bid them farewell. The Thunderbolts were a great improvement - six-and-a-half tons unloaded, eight x .5 Brownings; a bomb load of 3 000 lbs or a mix of napalm and long-range tanks, an endurance with over-load tanks of eight-and-a-half hours, a ceiling of 40 000 ft, and an incredible radius of turn at altitude. I watched Neil Cameron, the CO of 258 Squadron, pull inside a Jack over Bangkok at 25 000 ft and lit-erally saw it in half with his eight x .5s.

The MG fire power came in useful on another occasion after the fall of Mandalay when the Japs were retreating south over a road/rail bridge which was heavily defended by all sorts and calibres of ack-ack guns which had accounted for numerous Liberators and B25s. As expected we were briefed to attack this target and fortunately Intelligence had a good idea of where the gun emplacements were sit-uated.

In collaboration with 258 Squadron, 24 aircraft were laid on. Both squadrons were to fly in two parallel lines in a wide line astern. No 79 Squadron's OC Gatty May's aircraft, was to be loaded with three x 1 000 lb bombs with 11-second fuses and he would fly as No 6 in the right-hand gaggle. We planned to approach on a southerly course, some distance from the target, endeavouring to look as though the bridge was the last thing we were interested in.

The raid took place in the late afternoon so that the beady-eyed little yellow men would be looking into the sun. One word from Neil and we all made a 90 degree diving turn towards the target area. Well out of range, I would say about 1 000 yards, all pilots except Gatty, who concentrated on his bombing, opened fire covering a wide area surrounding the bridge. The effect of 184 x .5s on the Jap ack-ack crews must have been formidable for not one puff of flak was seen and Gatty laid his eggs neatly under the centre pylon as we streaked away on the deck. The bridge was destroyed and not one aircraft was touched.

A SAAF pilot who should be mentioned in this story although he was not engaged in flying operations, is Lt Cecil (Buck) Rogers, a brother of General Bob. Buck volunteered to serve as a Liaison Officer with General Orde Wingate's second long range penetration operation. The idea was for a large military force to be dropped behind the Jap lines to disrupt their lines of communication. They would be sustained from the air and would on occasions be supported by air attack against their opposing forces. Eventually after the completion of the operation which would coincide with the onset of the monsoon, they would be expected to work their own way back to friendly territory.

This task sounds simple. In any theatre of war it was a hazardous undertaking, but under the conditions in Burma it was sheer bloody hell. Buck eventually came out, was posted to Ceylon to recover from four months of 'Hades' and to marry Helen, a WREN he'd met on the ship when sailing from Suez to Bombay. Buck flaked out at the wedding reception and spent the next four months recovering from blackwater fever, malaria, dengue fever and a host of other maladies for which Burma was infamous. His delightful sense of humour must have suffered a severe strain after this unfortunate situation had caught up with him on his wedding day!

Talking of humour, not long after Ginger Lacey, ace Battle of Britain pilot, took over 71 Squadron, a young Australian sergeant pilot ferried Ginger's Spit to an RSU at Imphal for a major service. Painted on the side of the aircraft were 27 swastikas and one Rising Sun representing Ginger's 28 victories. The Yank who marshalled the Spit into the maintenance area stood mouth agape when the sergeant pilot climbed out of the aircraft. 'Say guy, is this your ship?' he drawled. Quick as a flash the Aussie replied: 'That's —— all, you should see my CO's aircraft!'

In the early part of 1944 the 14th Army was experiencing a rough time on the Arakan front which except for the coastal belt was dense jungle and mountains. Casualty evacuation was very difficult as airstrips could not be built for Dakotas, there being no flat ground of sufficient length. A few short strips were hacked out of the jungle to take L 5s, and Tiger Moths were modified to carry one stretcher in the space behind the rear cockpit. Only the most serious cases were evacuated in this way. The others were brought out by roads which were little more than tracks!

I don't know who suffered most, the patient or the pilot. Trying to make the flight to the nearest Dak strip as smooth as possible, was a terrible strain especially over the mountains. How we never lost any aircraft will always remain a mystery. Perhaps the Japs were unable to assess the amount of deflection to allow, but in any event no aircraft were hit and many badly wounded 'Pommies' owed their lives to the dear old Tiger.

Before one of these flights I was taken by the Medical Officer to meet the casualty before flying him out. He was a private in the Queen's Own Scottish Borderers and had been caught in a mortar blast which had removed most of the flesh covering his stomach. The Doc decided to change his dressings before we left. The patient was heavily dosed with pain killers but was lucid and cheerful, and when hearing my Scots name he said: 'Aye lad, that's a good name ye've got.' When the dressings were removed I heaved and almost fainted at the sight of his wound which was teeming with maggots. The M O explained that they were controlling the gangrene and must remain in the wound until hospital treatment was received.

K B leaves Japan for Korea in his Mustang.

We took off at 1130 hours which was the worst time of the day to fly, for the thermals over the mountains were extremely rough and when we landed at Ramu one hour and 20 minutes later, I expected to find a corpse in the back. Much to my relief, a brave 'Jock' grinned weakly and said; 'Y'see laddie, I told Y' we'd be alright.'

This episode had a sequel some three or four months later when I was in Calcutta on a spot of leave. While walking down the main thoroughfare, a jaunty little Scot grabbed me by the arm: 'Sir, ye dinna remember me?' I had to admit that I didn't and he continued: 'The fellow with nae stomach that ye flew out of the Arakan.' Needless to say we proceeded to the Grand Hotel and knocked back a few ales in celebration. I hadn't expected him to recover.

During April 1944, while visiting a friend at Chittagong, I was privileged to listen to an extremely dramatic display of cool-headedness by a Beaufighter navigator. My friend was doing a stint in the flying control tower at Chittagong so I'd decided to keep him company during a period which was expected to be an uneventful night shift.

Around 2230 hours we heard a faint transmission of what was obviously a conversation between two aircrew members who had their radio toggle on transmit instead of intercom. The signal grew louder as the aircraft flew nearer to Chittagong and it became clear that the pilot had been wounded and the navigator was talking him home.

The pilot's voice was slurred and vague while the navigator's was calm and collected and sometimes even jocular. He could well have been a flying instructor from the way he corrected the pilot's errors with statements like: 'Watch it skipper, we're losing height, ease back on the stick slightly,' or 'Skip, we're turning port, take her right a bit, OK that's fine.' This went on for about an hour and then he said: 'Skip, I think we had better land at Chittagong as it's still the hell of a long way to Cal [Calcutta].'

This remark pushed the controller into action. The flare path was already on but he also organised the chance lights, alerted the fire tender and ambulance and advised the base CO and the hospital. Shortly after, the navigator realised the radio was on transmit instead of intercom and advised the pilot to rectify the error. Our contact with them was lost for a short while but then the navigator called up informing us of their predicament and his intention to talk the pilot down to a 'wheels up' landing.

By the time he had reported that they were 20 miles away, the CO and the Medical Officer were in the tower and the latter suggested that the pilot should be told to select maximum oxygen which could clear his brain a little. This advice was taken and the navigator reported that it appeared to have helped. Suddenly, out of the darkness and into the glare of the floodlight runway came the Beau on a perfectly normal approach. It touched down on its belly halfway along the runway and slithered to an abrupt halt.

The pilot reported later that he couldn't remember the landing but only the navigator's constant chatter. When one considers that the navigator in a Beaufighter was positioned amidships with no physical contact between himself and the pilot, and he was not able to operate any of the controls, the feat accomplished that night was all the more remarkable.

The war in Burma became known as the 'forgotten war' for it received only a fraction of the publicity accorded to the other war-theatres. One of the main reasons for this was poor communication due to the totally undeveloped areas which prevented access by war correspondents. However, there is little doubt that the fighting men consisting of British, Indians and various Commonwealth troops, could justify their claim to be the greatest fighting men in the world. It was indeed a privilege for us to do what we could to support men such as these.

One of the most unpleasant tasks we were called upon to undertake on operations was the disruption of work on the Burma/Siam railway line which was maintained by Allied POWs at a death rate of one man per sleeper laid. It was on this line that the celebrated bridge over the River Kwai was situated. Pilots often reported seeing POWs waving and obviously urging them on, even though aware that for every sleeper re-laid, one of their number would die. There is no greater valour than this.

Towards the end of May 1945, the 14th Army decided to make an all-out effort to take Rangoon before the monsoon set in. To achieve this, a two-pronged push was launched, one down the Mandalay/Rangoon railway line and the other to the west down the Irrawaddy River and the road and railway line to Rangoon. As the army liberated various strips *en route* 79 Squadron was detailed to follow the eastern arm moving forward, which promoted a maximum number of sorties per day in close support. The snag was that due to the need for rapid advance to beat the bad weather, the Japs were not completely cleared from surrounding areas but merely pushed back on either side of the advance. Tennets was one of the airfields captured in an uncleared area and handed over to the RAF regiment for security purposes. No. 79 Squadron moved in with a bare minimum of equipment including EPIP tents without side walls. The pilots provided their own camp stretchers which were carried in the spacious cockpit of the Thunderbolts.

On our arrival we were briefed on security arrangements by the CO of the RAF Regiment and much to our chagrin he advised that there were insufficient personnel to guard the aircraft and the squadron sleeping area. Even more sinister was his recommendation that due to the possibility of Jap infiltration, we should bed down with our heads towards the outside of the tents, which as mentioned had no side walls; then, once the hurricane lamps had been doused, we should reverse ourselves so that our feet pointed outwards. I had been unfortunate enough to be allocated the tent closest to the undergrowth and to make matters worse I had the corner bed position due to the fact that I was the last to arrive. A late afternoon rain squall soaked my blanket and since the weather was hot and humid and a blanket wasn't essential, I hung it over the guy ropes to dry. We had also been told to unholster our revolvers and keep them handy and so, a decidedly nervous and unhappy bunch of pilots bedded down for the night.

In the early hours of the morning, something woke me. A fairly strong wind was blowing and nearby trees were rustling. There was no moon; only starlight, and then to my absolute horror I saw the outline of a small person standing at the foot of my bed slightly to the right and he was moving! Without a second thought I grabbed my revolver which was next to my head and pumped three shots in rapid succession through my mosquito net into the 'Jap' infiltrator, but he didn't drop. The whole camp erupted, the RAF Regiment came charging up and chaos reigned until I realised why my 'Jap' hadn't dropped. I'd drilled three holes in the hanging blanket! One doesn't live an episode like that down in a hurry!

Not long after this, the final all-out assault on Rangoon took place, and during one of the many air strikes on the city, one of our pilots noted some writing on the roof of the prison where POWs were housed. It read: JAPS GONE -BRITISH HERE - PULL FINGER. That to all intents and purposes was the end of the war in Burma except of course for mopping up operations which took some time. The little yellow men were certainly tenacious and fanatical.

A total of 93 South African pilots served in Burma of which three did not return. Their aircraft included Blenheims, Beaufighters, Liberators, Hurricanes, Spitfires, Thunderbolts and Dakotas. Two DFCs and one MID were awarded and the pilots flew a total of just under 14 000 operational hours.

Tailpiece

KB operated over Burma for eighteen months; a lengthy period for any pilot under such abominable climatic conditions and in a desolate, disease-ridden country against a fanatical enemy. He also flew on a tour of operations during the Korean War and was the leader of the central aerobatic team before and after his tour.

Ken Whyte

Ace Fighter Pilot Jack Frost

I first met Jack Frost when he formed 5 Squadron SAAF in May 1941. A few months earlier he had been awarded the DFC for his prowess in Abyssinia when he shot down three Italian bombers and one of the two fighters escorting them.

He was a dedicated permanent force SAAF officer, in fact so dedicated that during the early part of the Desert Campaign he held regular early morning parades. These were discontinued when a JU 88 broke cloud over the parade ground.

Jack was a great leader with an enthusiastic, aggressive spirit. He chose me as his No 2, and when available I flew with him on most of his operations. He was completely fearless, the number of opposing enemy aircraft not appearing to concern him and he would dive straight for them usually becoming involved in a dogfight. Under these circumstances it was often difficult to follow him and at the same time watch our tails, so inevitably we became separated.

The Squadron commenced operations in the Desert at the beginning of March 1942, when as part of 233 Wing RAF, it was responsible for the sector of coast from Sollum to Mersa Matruh. Between late May and mid-June, 26 enemy aircraft were destroyed, ten more were claimed as probables and 24 damaged. During this heavy fighting, several of the Squadron's most experienced fighter pilots were lost, including Jack.

On 31 May he had been posted to 233 Wing, but when the new CO Andrew Duncan was shot down and killed on the same day, Jack returned to the Squadron and re-assumed command. Three days later he shot down a JU 87 and another three the following day. By 14 June, the day he was killed, his score had reached 14,5 confirmed victories.

I remember our first combat together in the Western Desert. While on a shipping patrol we were vectored on to an HE 111 which was following a Malta convoy. Jack made his favourite three-quarter head-on attack which had brought him success in Abyssinia. I attacked from the rear and we watched the enemy aircraft going down slowly over the sea with pieces falling off it. We each claimed a half share of its destruction.

176

Ken Whyte.

During April we were operating on bomber escorts and patrols aimed at preventing Stukas attacking our front-line forces. On the latter sorties, Jack always dived straight at the leading Stuka virtually ignoring the fact that a top cover of enemy aircraft existed. Inevitably the mêlée ended as a mixture of Stukas, Tomahawks and Messerschmitts right down on the deck for this was the height which the Stukas favoured as an avenue of escape.

One morning we were returning to base from a Stuka op when Jack was shot down by our own troops. His language over the R/T just before crash-landing, is unprintable, yet normally he was a quiet, modest self-effacing person. There was the celebrated occasion when his aircraft was hit by flak while operating in Abyssinia and he was obliged to crash-land on an enemy airfield, Diredawa. One of his pilots, Bob Kershaw, landed and picked him up, taking off again in the face of Italian gunfire with Jack sitting on his lap. Kershaw was awarded the DSO for this meritorious feat.

Typical of the fighting that took place at low level during Stuka parties was the occasion 5 Squadron, led by Jack Frost, was operating on a sweep over Bir Hacheim. Unfortunately, we spotted the Stukas only after they had dropped their bombs. What a shambles developed with individual mêlées taking place at not more than 100 ft above the ground. An entry in my log book reads:

(Left to right) Jack Frost, Bob Kershaw, S V Theron.

'Major Frost shot down three enemy aircraft. I saw two Stukas and one ME 109 go down in flames. Accurate flak kept us company while flying home on the deck. Most of my aircraft's rudder was shot away and my good friend Basil Thornhill-Cook was shot down. I saw his aircraft hit the ground in flames and explode.' I mention these details as an example of the everyday dramas of that period.

I wasn't flying with Jack on the day he was shot down because I had been downed the day before and was languishing in hospital. Some say that his aircraft fell in flames with no hope of survival. A German Intelligence report claimed that it was one of the two German aces Marseille or Steinhausen who got him. Rod Hojem was on the same operation when Jack was lost. 'There was one hell of a dogfight,' says Rod, and after it was all over I can clearly remember Jack calling up the squadron on the R/T: 'Form up chaps, I'm flying north!' And that was the last we heard of him.

A shocked 5 Squadron couldn't believe that Jack Frost was gone and wouldn't be returning. Everyone believed he was indestructible. He may have gone, but his aggressive spirit lived on and throughout 5 Squadron's exceptional operational record, its COs and pilots were motivated by his image. He had been recommended for a bar to his DFC which only came through after his death.

Tailpiece

Ken Whyte became one of 5 Squadron's most able pilots and COs winning the DSO and the DFC. No doubt his experiences as Jack Frost's wingman encouraged and assisted him in attaining the degree of expertise achieved during his operational career. He lives in Illovo, Johannesburg.

(Left to right) Bob Kershaw being congratulated on his award by Jack Frost.

Ted Strever

Skyjack

My crew and I woke up on 29 July 1942 in well-guarded quarters on the island of Corfu. That night we'd slept more than soundly for the previous day had been packed with drama when our Beaufort had been shot down off the Greek coast while attacking an Italian merchant ship escorted by two destroyers. We were lucky to escape unscathed while ditching the Beaufort with two dead engines, and after climbing into our dinghy we had been rescued by the crew of an Italian Cant float plane who flew us to Corfu.

I had been seconded from the SAAF and was serving with 217 Squadron RAF at Malta. My crew comprised a navigator, P O William Dunsmore RAF and Sergeants John Wilkinson and Raymond Brown RNZAF, who were radio operator and air gunner respectively.

The Italians at Corfu treated us well, providing a first class dinner on the evening of our arrival which included wine and cigarettes and in the morning a substantial breakfast was served. Naturally, escape was a high priority, but our plans were thwarted when advised that we would be flown across the Mediterranean to Taranto in Italy and no doubt a POW camp. This wouldn't leave any scope for escape - or so we thought.

After breakfast we were escorted to the jetty and into a new-looking Cant float plane, a crew of five following us and closing the hatches. Wilkie was brooding about the negative opportunity for escape and asked me: 'Do you think you can fly this thing Ted?' 'Of course,' I replied. 'Any pilot can fly any aircraft once it's airborne.'

'Then maybe we can take on these jokers,' he suggested; a proposal approved by us all.

The first pilot, Tenente Gaetano Mastrodrasa, sat on the left forward seat and behind him was the second pilot Tenente Allesandro Chafari. In front of them the flight engineer was slouched down in the nose while a smallish army corporal with an enormous revolver sticking from the holster on his belt, stood looking suspiciously at us. In between was a wireless operator seated on the right with the wireless on his left. There was no navigator!

Ted Strever.

The Cant taxied into the bay and at 0915 hours, turned into wind and took off setting course for Taranto, some $1\frac{1}{2}$ hours flying time away. As the float plane droned westwards over the Mediterranean sea, Wilkinson smiled gently at the wireless operator next to him pointing to the wireless badge on his RAF uniform. The Italian smiled back acknowledging the existing common bond, but he didn't recognise the falsity of Wilkinson's friendship or the tension which was building up.

'Spitfire' yelled Wilkinson pointing out of one of the starboard windows and the wireless operator's head jerked around, his eyes wide with horror. He was soon put out of his agony as a massive fist smashed into his jaw!

Back home in New Zealand, Wilkinson had driven a six-horse team on a farm. He was a brawny young man with enormous hands growing out of wrists as thick as an average man's forearm. The Italian was slumped on the floor and I yanked him backwards into the arms of Brown and Dunsmore, leaving Wilkinson clear to tackle the guard.

Those two huge hands flashed forward and grabbed the gun and holster on the guard's belt tearing them free with a savage jerk and throwing them to me. I pulled the heavy .45 revolver out of its holster and had it pointing at the dumbfounded guard within seconds. The middle-aged Corsican who was of no great stature, was pulled to the rear of the aircraft by the powerful New Zealander and we had good reason to believe that we had won the day.

Suddenly Wilkinson yelled 'Look out, that other joker has a gun.' The first pilot, Tenente Mastrodrasa, had heard the commotion and dived forward into the aircraft's nose drawing a .32 Beretta automatic and pointing it at me, but I did not fire for behind him was one of the Cant's three engines and a bullet in the wrong place could have caused us more problems. At the same time Mastrodrasa did not want to fire because three of his comrades were behind me, and for what seemed like an age, we looked at each other like two menacing cobras!

Fortunately the flight engineer, sitting on the edge of the nose step facing forward, had been dozing. He suddenly woke up to see his captain alongside him, wild-eyed, pointing a pistol and seemingly having gone beserk. Deciding he was in the wrong place he suddenly jumped up, backed away from the nose coming between Mastrodrasa and me. His backside presented an inviting target so in a flash Wilkie and I streaked forward past the second pilot who was at the controls and two large-sized shoes rammed into the engineer's posterior pitching him forward on to his captain. The two struggling Italians were disentangled by powerful arms and bundled unceremoniously to the rear of the aircraft where Brown and Dunsmore tied them up.

I then turned my attention to the second pilot, Tenente Chafari, who had formed his own idea on how to end the conflict. He had pushed the control column forward and the Cant was diving towards the Med where Chafari no doubt intended to land, until I thrust my revolver under his nose. 'Up, up,' I ordered him, waving the revolver in his face while adopting a hostile attitude. The Italian was no linguist but he got the message pulling back on the stick and opening the throttles.

I left him at the controls and walked back to the other four Italians who were all safely tied up with their own belts! Brown and Dunsmore had found some wrenches and were standing guard over the Italians who were eyeing me with trepidation.

'Africa?' they exclaimed, 'No *benzina!*' I pointed my pistol at the flight engineer motioning towards the petrol cocks and warning him: 'No *benzina*, you're dead.' He realised that I meant business and nodded his head miserably. 'Not Africa - Malta,' I snapped. 'Malta,' howled the Italians, 'Spitfire, Spitfire!' 'Don't worry about Spitfires,' I replied with a grin. 'Wilkie, I'm taking over. Stand next to me facing the rear and cover these monkeys.'

I walked forward, slid into the first pilot's seat, grabbed the controls and began to fly the Cant as if it was a Beaufort, reducing height so that its floats were just skimming the sea. The Italians groaned in protest indicating that the floats would hit the water, but keeping low was imperative to avoid both friendly and hostile radar picking us up.

Dunsmore hunted unsuccessfully for maps and charts but strange to relate, there were none on board. The crew must have been following a radar beam to Taranto. Wilkinson looked at the radio but decided

The New Zealanders in the Skyjack epic. Raymond Brown and John Wilkinson .

it would be safer to leave it alone. Brown paid a visit to the turret and familiarised himself with the free-handling .50 machine-gun, in case the need to fire it arose.

We headed due west intending to pick up the Italian coastline and then to dog-leg towards Cape Passero, the most southerly point of Sicily for we remembered that the course to Malta from this point was 220 degrees.

A tiny dot appeared in the sky away to port which turned out to be an aircraft on an intercept course. I watched it very carefully, not wishing to arouse suspicions by altering direction. The outline of the aircraft soon became clearer as our tracks converged. It was a JU 52 transport aircraft bound for Italy and it was flying at 300 ft. The Jerry passed behind us and I waggled the Cant's wings as a token of friendship, the German returning the compliment - and our courses diverged.

The Italian mountains could be seen above the haze as we flew south and then west again and by a series of dog-legs and guess work, Cape Passero appeared ahead. The Italian flight engineer indicated that he wanted to adjust the petrol cocks so he was released, with Brown and Dunsmore standing threateningly next to him as he turned the knobs and levers. The Corsican guard was looking green in the face so Dunsmore who occasionally suffered from air sickness himself, released the little man and sat him beside the open window hatch.

Mastrodrasa and the wireless operator appeared resentful at the release of their comrades so we untied all the prisoners as they seemed to be suitably subdued and no match for four hefty young men armed with revolvers and wrenches.

When we reached the southern tip of Sicily, I set course on 220 degrees for Malta praying that our memories and guess-work would not let us down. We had been in the air for three hours and petrol was running low. Dunsmore had drawn a rough chart from memory but he was not convinced that it was accurate enough. My mind was in a turmoil when eventually some radio masts appeared ahead. I did not recognise this aspect for we were never allowed to approach Malta from the north as it was the enemy's usual direction of attack. 'Can it be Malta?' I wondered, 'And what if it isn't?'

Suddenly Dunsmore shouted. 'My God look above.' Flying at a thousand feet were four Spitfires in line astern and the leading aircraft had commenced peeling over to the attack. I was so absorbed in trying to locate Malta that the possibility of this situation arising was not on my mind, although I had decided earlier that if it happened we would land and wave a surrender flag.

As the Spitfires screamed down towards us, I grabbed Mastrodrasa and thrust him behind the controls ordering him to land the Cant. In the second pilot's seat, Chafari had already anticipated the order and had eased back the throttles. A burst of fire from the leading Spitfire raised a line of splashes in the sea ahead of us. The aim of the second Spitfire was a little more accurate and the sea boiled with splashes only 15 yards away. Mastrodrasa had turned the Cant into the wind and throttled back its engines when the third Spitfire riddled the port wing with at least 40 shells. However, a safe landing was made and Dunsmore pulled off his white singlet waving it furiously from the open waist hatch. All of us then clambered out on the wings and waved to the Spitfires, and to our relief the pilots got the message and headed towards Malta to organise a rescue launch.

The nine of us stood on the Cant's wings. The Italians seemed resigned to their fate and Chafari even managed to find a bottle of wine which he shared with us all. There was only one air-sea rescue launch on that side of the island and half an hour passed before it arrived. The crew took the Cant in tow but it kept weathercocking into wind and progress was painfully slow. I suggested that if the engines were started we could taxi, but Mastrodrasa shook his head pointing out that when landing, the last drop of petrol had been used!

At last we made it to Malta and were rowed ashore at a small cove in St Paul's Bay. A crowd of excited civilians rushed threateningly towards the Italians for whom they held no respect due to their country's war record and I was obliged to draw my pistol and keep the mob at bay until an army escort arrived. We then saw to it that our Italian prisoners were looked after in the officers' rest camp, not forgetting that we had been well-treated at Corfu. Finally I shook hands with each of them and wished them well. We were debriefed and returned to an enthusiastic reception at our home base at Luqa. It was good to be back.

Tailpiece

This story has been described as one of the most extraordinary events in the RAF's history, an episode with probably no parallel during the entire course of World War II. Ted Strever and William Dunsmore were awarded DFCs and John Wilkinson and Raymond Brown, DFMs.

On 1 November 1944 Ted was involved in a horrific crash at Vavunina in Ceylon when flying as a passenger in a Beaufighter to take command of 211 Squadron in Burma. The aircraft crashed on take off killing three men. Ted was badly burnt but recovered and ended the war as a Lieutenant-Colonel. He lives in Haenertsburg in the Northern Transvaal.

Acknowledgement

Ted Strever's incredible story was included in Roy Nesbit's *Torpedo Airmen* and later reproduced in *The Aeroplane* under 'The Flight of the Heron.' Both parties have kindly authorised the use of a number of extracts from these publications.

Chopper Uplift

I was flying Pumas in 1978 when the South African Defence Force attacked Cassinga in Angola, the SWAPO headquarters which lay 100 nautical miles from the South West Africa/Angola border and thought to be safe from infiltration by our forces.

To the south lay Techamutete, occupied by the Cubans, a river flowed to the west; and to the east there were no roads. An attack could not be made from the north without sacrificing surprise and therefore the only logical alternative was the use of paratroops.

This procedure was adopted on 4 May 1978 when 375 parachute troops were landed on the outskirts of Cassinga, an operation which happened to be the largest of its kind in the SADF's history. C130s and C160s were used to fly in the Parabats and the jets got their first taste of action since the Korean War. Twenty helicopters, mainly Pumas and a few Frelons, were involved in flying the Parabats back to base after the operation had been completed.

The first aerial attack was launched from the north much to Swapo's surprise, as 12 Squadron flying Canberras, emulated their motto in World War II, 'First in Action,' and dropped 1 200 bouncing bombs. Initially 1 000 Swapo troops on the Cassinga parade ground waved at our aircraft believing them to be friendly, but their enthusiasm was soon dampened as the bombs began to fall and another attack followed with Buccaneers dropping 1 000 pounders.

Shortly after the last Buccaneer bomb had fallen, all 375 paratroopers had been landed and it became their task to clean up Cassinga. The first bomb was dropped at 0800 hours and the last of the Parabats were evacuated at 1500 hours.

The choppers assisted the bomber squadrons to navigate accurately to the outskirts of Cassinga. A Puma flown by John Church took off in the dark and flew to a point 15 km ENE of the target area and set up a beacon on which the bombers homed in; at the same time Church located the preselected zone for the main gaggle of choppers where they could assemble ready to uplift the Parabats when the time came.

John Stroh and I led the choppers to the landing zone. Our Puma was fitted with a new navigation system but we didn't trust it, especially

Peter 'Monster' Wilkins.

when indicating our course was 15 km to starboard of track. We decided to adhere to the proven performance of the old system which had not been removed from the chopper and its reading turned out to be correct. Had we relied on the new one our course would have passed directly over Techamutete giving the game away.

On reaching the landing zone, we off-loaded fuel and prepared all choppers for the uplifting of the parabats. The first uplift call came at approximately 1130 hours. I flew our Puma into the centre of Cassinga and landed on the main parade ground. Huge craters scarred the area and buildings were burning fiercely, no doubt the work of Buccaneer bombs. Slit trenches zig-zagging over the area, were filled with bodies of enemy soldiers who had died while taking cover from the bombs and sharp-shooting parabats.

The pick up was routine and 16 parabats climbed into our chopper and were flown to the landing zone to be evacuated in due course back to base. There had been no enemy action against the choppers and we presumed that all was well. However, the Cubans had no doubt heard the bombing and when believing that the operation had been completed they climbed into their T34 tanks and BTRs and came to the rescue of the survivors. On discovering the presence of the parabats, chaos reigned in all directions.

We had previously understood there were about four armoured

vehicles to be dealt with and it was a shock to learn that up to 30 including four tanks, were moving down the road towards our landing ground. At this stage only half the parabats had been uplifted, a situation impressing on us the urgency of picking up the rest who were only armed to deal with half a dozen armoured vehicles and nothing more. The situation was vital and speed was of the essence to complete the evacuation.

Fortunately the Buccaneers and the parabats accounted for the spearhead of the enemy column, its initiative soon grinding to a halt excepting an errant T 34 tank which approached the landing zone and began firing at the choppers. Luckily the tank was on an up-slope and even with its gun elevation, its shells went over us. Enemy troops must also have been close by, for bullets were walking a path between the choppers. Miraculously not one of them was hit.

Some of the parabats were still scattered about the area so a few of the chopper pilots became airborne to search for their missing complement. While landing from this flight, I saw Dries Marais in his Buccaneer, seemingly trying to write himself off. He was diving his large, heavy Buccaneer so low that from time to time it disappeared behind the trees. His quarry was only 200 yards from us but his antics certainly kept the tank off our backs and won him a well earned HC. Apparently he had run out of ammunition and as an alternative was intimidating the tank crew!

Pumas were used to uplift most operational forces during the course of the war in south Angola.

Aerial view of ground fighting during Operation Reindeer at Cassinga, south Angola.

Eventually all 20 choppers collected their full complement of parabats and flew them back to base. Only four parabats had been lost, but over 1 000 of the enemy had been eliminated. The dramatic day was made all the more memorable by the Chief of the Air Force, General Rogers, who met the choppers on the apron after the final landing and congratulated every man who had taken part in that notorious operation deep in the Angolan bush.

Tailpiece

Monster flew on his first operation in the Border War during 1967 and took part in many 'bush ops' covering three years of special duties totalling 1530 flying hours, mostly on Alouette helicopters. He is today a serving SAAF Colonel, OC Air Force Base Durban, and has flown over 5 000 hours on helicopters which is at present the highest total recorded by a SAAF pilot.

Pumas depart from a forward operational base in southern Angola.

Training the Aviators

After the outbreak of war, the Allies desperately needed more pilots and trained aircrews to gain air superiority and carry the war into the heart of Germany. However, before a viciously spurred fighting cock is let loose, the fledgling must be guided to maturity; his natural aggression shaped and honed. Similarly a pilot cannot be let loose with a scarce and valuable aircraft, unless he is adequately trained.

This vital requirement led to the Empire Training Scheme which established pilot, navigator, radio operator and air gunner flying training schools in Canada, Rhodesia and South Africa, where the goal could be pursued in fine weather and far away from enemy interference. South Africa produced 33 347 aircrew during the war from 20 established training schools; an invaluable, unsurpassed contribution to the Allied cause. Without these airmen flowing from the schools, new squadrons could not be manned or operational units kept up to strength.

Achieving and sustaining aircrew production called for exhausting, dedicated work from all concerned. Instructors frequently flew one hour periods four times a day followed by a few hours on night flying instruction. They had to be continually vigilant, for most pupils appeared to be hell-bent on self-destruction every time they went aloft and this phenomenon was accentuated at night.

The Elementary Training Schools used open-cockpit Tiger Moths throughout the war and the Advanced Training Schools operated with open-cockpit Harts, Hinds and Audaxes in the early stages until more modern trainers became available, vastly improving the instructor's lot.

The incessant night flying on the frosted, earthy runways at some auxiliary highveld landing fields with aircraft generating a dustladen, subzero wind, created conditions which were equally as tough as those experienced by operational squadrons. Admittedly the casualty rate was much lower, but then so was the excitement and glory!

World War I veterans came flocking back to arms and performed a variety of useful duties. In addition to our Officer Commanding, Group Captain 'Tanks' Chamberlain, there were six more ex-Royal

The all-purpose Harvard trainer.

Flying Corps veterans at our school, some of them highly decorated, and we young instructors venerated them.

Friday nights were party nights unless you were on night flying. Tanks Chamberlain, aptly named for he was short and round, would lead from the front of the pub with the World War I veterans in close formation!

The veterans included slightly built 'Swazi' Howe, who had flown with Mick Mannock, the highest scoring Allied air ace in World War I. Swazi once related how the squadron had checked into an establishment in Reims for a few days rest from the front. On the very first night the madame was, in their opinion, truculent and unreasonable with her fancy prices, but she developed a more reasonable attitude after some of the pilots had upended her and Mick had poured a bottle of champagne down her pantaloons! Swazi died tragically after the war, when he and another character had a disagreement over a woman. He was shot dead in his ranch house near Big Bend in Swaziland which was then set alight.

Tanks Chamberlain had been presented with a handsome Zulu 'knobkerrie', the kind Chaka's executioners laid across the heads of his condemned subjects when the King was in a particularly uncharitable mood. He cherished this gift and carried it in lieu of a swaggerstick - in which capacity it was a regular visitor to the officers' pub on Friday nights. Captain Lumsden, a tall athletic Scot, was in charge of station security and had that day returned from a course on 'unarmed combat'. Overestimating the efficacy of his course, Lumsden challenged Tanks

The Harvard in modern SAAF livery.

to try to strike him with his 'kerrie'. Fortunately Lumsden, in a party mood, was wearing a heavy plastic industrial type helmet. This saved him from a condemned Zulu's fate when things did not follow textbook rules, and the 'kerrie' crashed through a shattered helmet laying Lumsden cold. If it had not been for the helmet, the ambulance would have been routed to the morgue instead of the hospital!

Scorcher Marshall, the small reserved transport officer, used to become tired and sleepy earlier than the others in the evening and on one occasion when some of the lads retired to the mess for a nightcap after an evening's flying session, Scorcher was found asleep on the carpet. It was winter and cold, so he was straightened out, rolled into the carpet like a cocoon, and propped up against the wall near the fireplace to keep him warm. An African cleaner rushed into the caterer's office early one morning after hearing Scorcher's grunts and groans. 'Boss, boss, come quickly there's a *tokolosh* in the carpet!' The caterer unrolled the carpet and set Scorcher free. He had fortunately been positioned the right way up otherwise a manslaughter charge could have resulted!

Tiger Vigers MC, DFC and bar, phlegmatic and confident, was the OC of the bombing range. Instructor Joe Dunning pulled his pistol one party night and shot out the lounge lights before he could be disarmed.

192

This little trick caused a rapid departure of most customers, but unflappable Tiger rose quietly from his blackjack table and without a word, used a match to find an undamaged wall light which he switched on, and the game proceeded, but only momentarily. Joe pulled a second gun and this light followed the others. I did, however, see Tiger greatly agitated on the day when pupil pilot John Cornish, an RAF trainee, and our first team flyhalf, fell from his aircraft minus a parachute and struck the earth some yards from Tiger's little plotting hut.

During bombing training in those early years, the pupil was secured by a 'monkey chain' attached from his parachute harness to the floor of the aircraft; and the chest-type parachute was ready to be clipped on in an emergency. Cornish had forgotten to secure the monkey chain and an airpocket or a slight stick forward movement, flipped him out of the cockpit. The pilot, a co-pupil who was to be his future brother-in-law, caught hold of him with one hand, but the slipstream tore him out of his grasp.

Another pupil was nervous of the proximity of the deck during a low flying exercise and kept gaining height. An exasperated Tank Odendaal took control and showed him, with an exaggerated demonstration, how to fly low. While the aircraft was approaching a fence, the pupil spoke through the Gosport tube : 'I've got her, sir,' and he lifted the Tiger over the fence with adequate clearance and pushed it down to low flying height on the other side: 'You've got her, sir,' the pupil exclaimed again in a casual tone of voice! Tank was so flabbergasted at this effrontery that he failed to admonish the pupil in the approved manner.

A pupil walked into my office at Waterkloof Advanced Flying Training School in May 1944, saluted and said: 'Sir, I've lost my instructor.' Completely taken aback, I asked him to explain.

'We were practising spinning but when he told me to recover I applied the correct recovery action but nothing happened and the aircraft kept spinning. My instructor took control and tried to recover but again no response. "Bale out" he yelled, but I just froze and he ordered me to bale out a second time. I did not respond so he opened the aircraft's canopy and baled out. As soon as he'd gone, the aircraft came out of the spin and I flew back to base.'

The probable explanation was that the aircraft was in a flat spin and after the instructor's departure, the centre of gravity had moved forward making recovery possible. The instructor arrived a couple of hours later carrying his open parachute and looking rather sheepish!

Pupils received ample practice in forced landings. This developed an overconfidence in instructors who took to the silk only as a last resort, preferring to 'go down with the ship' in the approved nautical fashion. One dark night when the engine of a Hawker Hind quit, the instructor, knowing that he was over flat Free State terrain, decided to stay with the aircraft but advised his pupil to bale out. The pupil replied; 'Sir, I won't leave you,' and sat tight. The instructor glided down and as there was no forward light he used the small bottom identification light to warn him at about 15 ft that he had arrived. Miraculously he levelled out and landed in a mieliefield without damaging the aircraft in the least.

To allow the instructors a break from never-ending circuits and landings, loops, spins etc, they were allowed to practise formation aerobatics on Saturday mornings if the aircraft serviceability state allowed. Early in 1941 during such a practise, instructors Pierrie Retief and Shorty Frier collided and Shortie was killed. Pierrie managed to get out of the damaged cockpit but had to struggle to grab the D ring which, in the battle to scramble clear, had shifted behind his back. From the tarmac at CFS, we saw him disappear behind a nearby koppie with his parachute still unopened, but he made it.

Pierrie was one of those rare *homo sapiens*, a natural pilot. During 1945 he graduated at The Empire Central Flying School and was invited to stay on as a staff instructor ending up as Chief Flying Instructor with an Air Force Cross. The RAF chose him to demonstrate the world record-holding Meteor to visiting dignitaries and potential customers. He contributed greatly towards updating and keeping the standard of SAAF training on a par with the rest of the world. Taking a break from training during the Korean War, he flew Sabres on operations in spite of the fact that at this stage he was 50. Pierrie died when a comparatively young major-general, one of the greatest ever SAAF flying instructors.

During the war years, S V Theron SM, DSO, DFC, AFC and Danie du Toit DFC, had already demonstrated the quality of SAAF instructors when they came first and second on their course in the UK. Tragically four of our senior and most outstanding instructors were killed during their courses at ECFS. They were P J Hayden-Thomas, Eddie Later, Lemmie Le Mesurier DFC and Ken Driver DFC.

Nervous tension and frustration drove instructors to irresponsible actions. One climbed out on the wing of his aircraft, but fortunately had second thoughts about abandoning his fledgling. My old chum Binedell lost his cool one day, took control from the pupil and shot up the Cape - Johannesburg mail train. Not satisfied with the panic of the passengers, he flew under the bridges that span the Vaal at Vereeniging. He should have been court-martialled but Training Command acted wisely and posted him north faster than the Kaiser could have shipped Lenin to Moscow, where it was quite impracticable to court-martial an airman 8 000 km away. Binnie proved himself on operations, winning promotion and a DFC.

A pupil in a Tiger Moth landed on top of Tom Zeederberg, a flying instructor, and the propeller inflicted severe injuries to the tough scion of the famous coachbuilders. It may have been this accident which coaxed Zeedie to dispose of his 'coach', a 1937 Ford, for the considerable sum in 1940, of two hundred pounds. He walked into the Baragwanath airfield's officers' bar, a panelled room with only small high windows, to celebrate his deal. Amongst the clientele was fun-loving, likeable Jack Shone. When Zeedie flashed his role of tenners Jack said: 'Zeedie I've never seen such a wad of notes in my life before. Won't you let me experience the feeling of holding them?' A gullible Zeedie handed the money to Jack who took it, weighed it in his hands a couple of times, and then with a mischievous smile, tossed it out of the window above his head. Amazement, disbelief, and panic flashed across Zeedie's face. His feet hardly touched the ground as he raced out of the bar to collect his loot before anyone thought their lucky day had arrived.

Tailpiece

Training of aircrew was equally as important to the war effort as operations against the enemy. There may not have been flak or hostile aircraft to contend with, but an instructor's task was often dangerous and hair-raising and he could never afford to relax. The AFC awarded to A Q, acknowledged his patience and dedication.

Dean Carman

Was I One of Marseille's 151 Victims?

My mother was superstitious believing that luck plays a vital role in one's life especially when facing danger. On the day I left home to join a fighter squadron in the desert war, she pressed a small woollen cat into my disbelieving hands. It was the family's 'lucky cat' which had hung in our car during times when driving was considered the ultimate in hazards and indeed it still is.

Forty-eight years have passed since those desert days and I clearly remember the pleasure of the congenial company as well as the hidden anxieties while waiting for an operation to materialise. As a member of a small group of fighter pilots, I can recall the exhilaration at the importance of the work assigned to us and the intense pride we all felt as South Africans.

During the months prior to the battle of El Alamein, the air forces were continually engaged, the bomber squadrons by day and often by night. The fighter squadrons flew twice, sometimes three times a day, their main role being to prevent Stukas from attacking our troops and to escort bomber squadrons on sorties against the enemy's lines of communication. These persistent attacks weakened the Axis forces and reduced their fighting capabilities.

A team was always on stand-by. Pilots waited in the mess for the telephone to ring or sat in their cockpits at dispersal, or near take-off point if an emergency was imminent. These were times of tension mingled with anxiety and it was always a relief when the order to scramble was received.

I will never forget the occasion when, on my own in the heart of the desert, nerves jaded after a hectic dog-fight, I knew the terror of being lost in an expanse of nothingness. There were no landmarks in the area and the sun was directly overhead. Instruments were of no use for they had been tumbled after some desperate manoeuvring. Every moment the voids of the desert became more terrifying and when the instruments suddenly stabilised, the relief was indescribable.

The desert was ideally suited for warfare. The countryside could not be desecrated and the sparse population consisted of a few Arabs and their goats or occasionally a camel. One morning I spotted a lone Arab on his camel and decided to have a little fun shaking up their equanimity. Diving towards them there was sufficient time to study their reactions. First the camel knelt on its front knees, then went down on its back legs, totally relaxed with his master alongside. I pulled away in no doubt that they were accustomed to these capers!

Every now and again a much needed break from flying was enjoyed. On one of these occasions Derek White, Dave Murdock, Brian Kearns and I visited Memphis and Saqqara, and near the Step Pyramids were accosted by an ancient Arab soothsayer who insisted on telling our fortunes. He drew mystical signs in the sand, smiled at Dave and Brian and announced that fortune favoured them. Looking at me, he mumbled something about an accident and when confronting Derek, shook his head and remained silent. Thrusting some baksheesh into his hand we dismissed his revelations as nonsense - yet, I've remembered this incident over the years. Was it a coincidence that Dave and Brian lived to return home, whereas Derek was sadly killed in action shortly afterwards? Here is **my** story.

It was an unpleasant dusty morning in September 1942 and after writing a letter to Jean, my fiancée, I can remember walking out of the mess to post the letter, but at that point my memory went blank until opening my eyes in bed in a clean, well-polished room. An extremely beautiful girl clad in white robes was holding my pulse explaining that I was in a British hospital at Tel el Kebir near Kassassin. She added that I had been badly wounded while baling out of my aircraft with a torn parachute which she produced from under the bed as evidence.

A week later Dave and Brian paid me a visit and their account of what happened brought back much of my memory although the true story did not emerge until some years later. Squadrons 2 and 5 had been scrambled to escort six Bostons and six Baltimores of 24 Squadron SAAF and two Mitchell bombers of the USAAF. My position in the formation had been on the extreme right at top cover with John Lindberg, Bill Turnbull and Tom Finlayson to my left, each about 200 metres apart.

The bombers dropped their load over Deir el Shein, approximately 16 kilometres south of El Alamein station, where a battle could be seen raging below, and while turning for home John and I were aware of enemy aircraft approaching from behind out of the sun. According to German records three 109s were escorting a single reconnaissance 109 when the pilots had sighted us and had broken away to the attack. I saw a 109 flying behind John, cannons blazing and he later told the Squadron that he had seen one behind me. He believed that we must

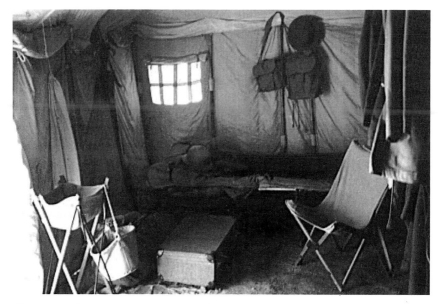

The interior of Dean Carman's tent in the desert.

have warned each other simultaneously over the R/T and therefore could not have received each others' warnings. John was shot down, pursued by his assailant. His aircraft crash-landed but he survived with minor injuries.

I can recall a 109 approaching from behind and estimated that the distance wasn't close enough for the pilot to open fire successfully. A feeling akin to panic gripped me and at that instant, a vivid and curious impression overtook me. I saw someone in a chair about 50 metres away who suddenly pitched forward and dropped sharply. The entire image was momentary but there has never been any doubt in my mind that the person involved was me. This story may sound ridiculous but I have learnt subsequently that others have had similar experiences under conditions of emergency. An example is the story of Frank Jones, related in Laddie Lucas's book *Out of the Blue*, which episode is more extraordinary than mine.

Just what happened to me is far from clear. According to German records, Hans Joachim Marseille, the famous Luftwaffe fighter ace claimed that he shot down two fighters at an identical time and place and these could only have been Lindberg and me. In the light of my memory of events and John's report to the Squadron, it would have appeared impossible for Marseille to have shot us both down simultaneously. Surely if either of his two colleagues had downed an aircraft, one or the other would have recorded a claim? But it did not happen, so an explanation is required.

198

To explain the apparent anomaly, I am inclined to accept the significance of my curious vision. Perhaps I had taken some advice from the experienced fighter pilot Bushy Langerman, that to escape from real trouble when cornered in a dogfight, jerk the stick violently into the top left hand corner of the cockpit and at the same time kick on rudder aggressively. I had conditioned myself to adopt this procedure in an emergency and possibly one of the controls had been damaged causing my aircraft to fall out of control. Over and above this, perhaps Marseille had seen my aircraft falling and when no claim had been made by either of the two pilots, he had done so to boost his score. From all accounts this wouldn't have been out of character.

I can remember a desperate struggle to release the canopy and with the ever increasing speed of the descent not succeeding. I lowered flaps and undercarriage, no doubt throttling back and selecting fine pitch to check the increasing speed. The plane swung to the right and I put both feet on the left rudder and pushed with all my strength. I put one hand over the gunsight to protect my face and total blackness followed. Waking briefly, I found myself lying on my back and could see in the distance what could only have been my aircraft resting on its belly. I was being comforted by someone with an English voice.

Several years later I sat in a Tomahawk and was able to match my scars with a variety of wires and other prominent features which explained how I'd broken my neck and both my legs. I am therefore convinced that I didn't bale out as was first assumed, but that the British soldiers who rescued me had done so in great haste, pulling the ripcord and tearing the parachute in the process. I am eternally grateful for their courage for they would have known that speed was of the essence before fire and an explosion occurred.

Marseille was killed just a month after this incident. At the time of his death he had shot down a staggering 151 enemy aircraft and the truth about whether he had shot me down or not, died with him.

Tailpiece

Dean spent two months at No 27 British Army General Hospital at Tel el Kebir before being evacuated to South Africa and he suffered a further 16 months hospitalisation. The lucky cat had served him well! He lives in Waverley, Johannesburg.

Ralph Aitchison

Yellow Spinners and Hang-ups

No 12 Squadron SAAF had operated Junkers 86s in East Africa and Abyssinia from mid-1940 until May 1941 when it was re-equipped with Marylands which were tough aircraft with a good performance and range. The United States of America had built them for the French Air Force but when France fell, Britain took them over and they were shipped to South Africa.

By the third week of July 1941, the squadron was based at LG 24 near El Daba west of El Alamein, and was ready once more for operations. It was a happy and effective squadron with two first class flight commanders, Bert Rademan and Otto van Ginkel. Bob Preller was appointed CO a month or two later.

Our targets consisted of airfields, stores, ammunition dumps, tank parks, enemy positions around besieged Tobruk and Bardia, and reconnaissance searches for ships and aircraft.

On one occasion, after a fruitless solo search for a submarine in Sollum Bay, our bombs were dropped on Bardia where unfortunately our aircraft met a solid mass of heavy flak and two of the main controls were shot away. I was able to fly the Maryland back to base without elevators or rudder, but a landing was impossible, so my crew and I had to bale out.

I remember Peter Place, my observer, stuffing his equipment including a new special hand-held bomb-sight into his overall before dropping out of his bottom hatch. His last words before unplugging the intercom were a strong expletive. Peter was a *loskop* and while falling through space, he passed one of the gunners whose parachute had already opened and only when he happened to look back and see the 'chute receding, did he realise that he'd better pull his own ripcord! He landed well before the rest of us!

In September, on the way back to base from a solo recce from 18 000 ft to photograph Benghazi, we were chased by ME 109 Es. I spotted them as they were taking off but time was available to complete the photographic runs before diving eastwards. The enemy aircraft could not catch us and fly close enough to open fire. We landed safely

Ralph Aitchison.

after five hours and 30 minutes in the air. This and other incidents made us confident that Marylands had a fair chance of getting away from 109s.

After a successful raid near Gambut on 7 October, the squadron was not so lucky. I was leading the port 'vic' of three aircraft in a formation of three 'vics' led by Bert Rademan when my top gunner, Willem de Villiers, reported enemy fighters. Glancing to the left I saw the big yellow spinner of an ME 109 flying just above my No 3, Jock Smith. Hectic minutes followed.

Bert Rademan brought us down to about a thousand feet flying as fast as 'formation keeping' would permit. Nevertheless, those yellow spinners not only kept up but flew rings around us. They turned out to be 'Fs', very different from 'Es'. We kept in tight formation and our gunners gave the 109s a good 'go', shooting down one and damaging at least one other. Several Marylands were hit, but only Jock's was badly damaged with one engine put out of action. Both gunners were wounded, one fatally. The sudden advent of these 'F' model 109s with the big yellow noses, was to make life difficult for bomber crews and for Hurricane and Tomahawk pilots too.

Jock tells the story of the misfortunes experienced by him and his crew on that fateful morning: 'An enemy shell exploded in the starboard engine's oil sump. The engine continued running for two

Inspecting Ralph Aitchison's Marauder after the raid on the Udine marshalling yards.

minutes before packing up. I tried unsuccessfully to contact my gunners over the intercom and was to discover later that the top gunner had been wounded in the leg and had used the intercom cord as a tourniquet, while the other gunner, Laurie Solomon, had been hit in the chest by an explosive cannon shell and was unconscious.

'Poor Laurie shouldn't have been in the air that day. He was only a volunteer from the squadron's ground radio station and had never flown or handled a machine-gun before. The regular gunner had a badly infected eye and was unable to fly. Since there were no reserve gunners available, volunteers were called for and Laurie came forward without a moment's hesitation. The squadron armaments officer gave him 30 minutes tuition on the range and that was it!

'When the starboard engine seized, we were obliged to drop behind the formation: 'A sitting duck for the yellow-nosed killers,' I thought, but the *coup de grâce* didn't happen. I was to discover that one of the 109s had been shot down by the squadron and the other two had headed back home, no doubt running short of fuel.

'On the way back to base our port engine began to run roughly and was losing oil indicating that an emergency landing would soon be necessary, but as it happened I managed, without hydraulics and with punctured tyres, to land safely on a forward fighter strip just over the Egyptian/Libyan border. We were met by pilots of 4 SAAF (Fighter) Squadron.

'Laurie Solomon's chest and lungs had been severely damaged and he had only been kept alive in the aircraft by the oxygen supply. We

An ammunition dump goes up in smoke.

A Marauder's port wing shot off.

loaded him and the top gunner into an ambulance which took them to a field hospital at Mersah Matruh. Unfortunately the aircraft's oxygen bottles and the ambulance's bottle were soon empty and Laurie died shortly after arrival at the hospital.'

Over the last six months of the war, 3 Wing consisting of 12, 21, 24 and 30 squadrons, now flying Marauders, were based at Iesi near Ancona on the Adriatic coast. Our bombing operations included army support, bridges and railway marshalling yards. Air superiority belonged to the Allies but the Germans made up for this by strengthening their defences and putting up a murderous umbrella of heavy flak over some of our targets.

On 28 December 1944, 3 Wing bombed Udine marshalling yards in northern Italy. As expected, the 88 mm flak was extremely heavy and accurate and several of 30 Squadron's aircraft were badly holed. The next day, the Wing was briefed to attack the same target which was of vital importance to the enemy. I led 30 Squadron on this operation and we were second over the target. As the squadron ahead commenced the bombing run, it was greeted by a thick mass of flak. Several Marauders were hit and a number of parachutes blossomed.

Seconds later it was our turn to weather the sooty 88 mm explosions and a bumpy, noisy run up to the target followed. The bomb doors were opened and I flew straight and level for some seconds allowing Gary Garson to line up his sight. He pressed the bomb-release but four of the eight 500-pounders hung up. It was not practical to make another run over the target so we dived away intending to jettison the hang ups in the Adriatic, but when the bomb doors were opened and the bomb-release pressed once more, nothing happened. Micky

Heyneke, the wireless operator, told me over the intercom that the 'bomb pin' was missing. This I couldn't understand.

My second pilot, John Hockfelden, took over the controls and I went back into the bomb bay to check up. There were two holes, one below and a larger one above. A shell had taken away the gear which operated the starboard bomb door and it had also knocked off the tail-fin of one of the 500-pounders, missing the fuse by a couple of inches and leaving *via* the large top hole. We had no alternative but to take the four bombs back to base.

It is most fortunate that 88 mm shells were time and not impact fused. The Jerry gunner's day would have been made if their luck had been in and our entire bomb load had exploded amongst the 30 Squadron box of aircraft. One 88 mm shell could have destroyed eight or more Marauders!

Tailpiece

Ralph flew Marylands, Bostons, Baltimores and Marauders during his three tours of operations in the Western Desert and Italy when he served with all four SAAF squadrons of 3 Wing. In November 1942, at the time of the Eighth Army's advance after the Battle of El Alamein, his arm was broken by flak while leading 12 Squadron on an operation. He was promoted to Lieutenant-Colonel as OC 30 Squadron and was awarded the DFC. He lives in Claremont, Capetown.

The rains came in Italy.

Unforgettable Encounters

I was introduced to Heinz Migeod at a SAAF Association cocktail party in 1976. He was with the Luftwaffe during the Desert War and we discovered that both of us had flown on the same operation 34 years previously when Heinz was a Stuka pilot and I was flying a Kittyhawk with 2 Squadron SAAF.

In spite of the passing years, I can remember the operation well. The Eighth Army had reached Halfaya hard on the heels of the Afrika Korps and the Luftwaffe was making a last attempt to keep Allied armoured columns at bay. On 11 November 1942, twelve of 2 Squadron's Kittyhawks led by 'Wildy' Wildsmith were patrolling west of Halfaya when 15 Stuka dive bombers were spotted heading towards the front line bent on attacking our forces.

I was flying No 4 to Wildy and initially thought he was going to ignore the enemy aircraft, but he craftily waited until our formation had climbed to a more favourable height and then led us in for the slaughter, an appropriate description because the squadron shot down eight of the 15 Stukas and claimed four probables. Pandemonium broke loose as our Kittys pounced, the Jerry's jettisoning their bombs and breaking up into a loose formation.

Our pilots each singled out an enemy aircraft and individual mêlées commenced all over the skies. I got one and watched it going down until satisfied that it would not fight again.

Heinz was one of the victims of the operation. He was shot down, force-landed in the desert and was taken prisoner. No doubt we were opponents on that memorable occasion and although there is no proof that I delivered the *coup de grâce*, the possibility cannot be ruled out. We may have been enemies at war but today we are good friends.

Another operation which remains in my memory was played out in Tunisia. Towards the end of March 1943 I was briefed to lead a flight of six Kittyhawks to patrol the coastal road between Oudref and Mahres. Intelligence had heard on good authority that Rommel and some of his staff would be travelling along the road at a specified time, so we were to watch out for staff cars.

Hoefie and Heinz.

Crossing the coastline at 9 000 ft, we dived through several layers of cloud to the deck and strafed every vehicle in sight, but no staff cars were seen. This performance was repeated further along the road but still no sight of any staff cars, so we satisfied our aggressive candour by attacking an airfield and setting fire to a number of Macchi 202s.

On the way back to base, heavy flak greeted us. Half my aircraft's rudder was shot away and Vic Martin's Kitty was hit in the radiator. We escorted him out to sea and when his engine packed up 12 miles from Gabes, he made a perfect landing on the water and climbed into his dinghy.

I called 'Commander' control to ask for an air-sea rescue launch, and after returning to base to refuel, four of our aircraft directed the launch to Vic's position. He was successfully rescued but shortly after, while the four Kittys were circling the launch, 112 (Shark) Squadron attacked it with bombs and then fired at 2 Squadron aircraft. After killing a member of the launch's crew, the Shark Squadron pilots no doubt discovered their catastrophic error and hastily withdrew.

In April 1943 I took part in an operation which had my adrenalin pumping overtime. The Axis forces were boxed up at this period in a small area around Tunis and the Cape Bon Peninsula where they were running desperately short of men, arms, ammunition and fuel. Supplies from Sicily had been cut off and so the Huns were making suicidal attempts to fly Rommel's requirements to him by air.

207

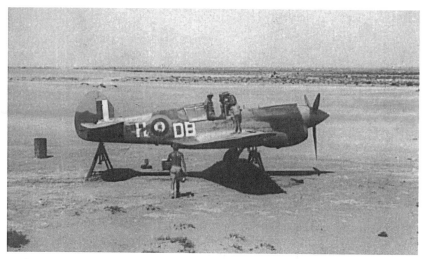

Hoefie's Kittyhawk (with his initials DB-H) being checked.

Being fully aware of the situation, 7 Wing's squadrons took off at dawn every morning and patrolled between Kairoun and Cape Bon, skirting Tunis airfield where ME 109s and FW 190s abounded.

On 19 April Doug Loftus, OC 7 Wing, was leading 5 Squadron, I was leading No 2 as medium cover, and Cecil Golding No 4 as top cover, when a mixed gaggle of about 20 JU 52s and SM 79s were seen flying on the deck towards Tunis. They were escorted by six fighters.

While Cecil and his boys took care of the fighters, Doug and I led our squadrons into the attack and 16 enemy aircraft were shot down,

German bombs in transport cradles, abandoned at Benine.

one of them an Italian RE 2001. The latter aircraft was not claimed as an official kill but three JU 52s were claimed as probables. A large number of the transport aircraft were undoubtedly carrying a full load of petrol for they caught alight from nose to tail and disintegrated as our pilots opened fire. I got one which didn't burn initially but on diving into the ground, it erupted in a huge ball of flame.

On the way home I saw Lieutenant Boyle of 5 Squadron land his Kitty on the sea. He survived and was taken POW. Doug Loftus, who shot down two of the transport aircraft, was awarded an immediate DSO.

Tailpiece

Hoefie spent an appreciable portion of the war as an instructor playing such a valuable part in this essential role that he was awarded the AFC. In 2 Squadron and later as CO of 5 Squadron, he proved himself to be an able, aggressive operational pilot and a first class leader. He lives in Somerset West.

Ray Veitch

The Sea Could Not Claim Me

I was shot down three times during April 1945, evading death or capture on each occasion and packing a lifetime of adventure into one month. I was seconded from the SAAF to the RAF at the time and was serving a tour of operations with 260 Squadron, 239 Wing DAF.

During April when taking part in an attack on enemy transport in the Maribor-Graz area in Yugoslavia, my Mustang was hit by flak. A film of glycol obscured forward vision through the windscreen, an indication that the cooling system had been ruptured and that it was only a matter of time before the engine seized.

A hasty, premature reaction resulting from the fear of being captured when force landing or baling out over enemy territory, urged me to open the throttle to the gate and head for the open sea, but of course common sense should have prevailed with the realisation that there would be a better chance of reaching friendly territory if the overheated engine was nursed. It was west of Orsessa, over the Yugoslav coast, that the Mustang's death throes commenced with ferocious vibrations and vicious knocking until finally the ultimate explosion shrouded the cockpit with smoke and flames and the propeller stopped turning.

Ripping off my helmet and goggles and releasing the Sutton safety harness, I pulled the emergency hood release knob but nothing happened and an acute spasm of fear gripped me when anticipating the distinct possibility that I was trapped in a flaming coffin. Standing on the seat I beat my fists against the hood, but this didn't help and the knot in my guts began to tighten. Panic enveloped me and in desperation I used the normal method of release. Depressing the release catch, I grabbed the handle above my head, gave an almighty tug and the hood took off like a rocket. The normal release system had obviously triggered off the faulty emergency mechanism.

By this time the Mustang was well alight and there was precious little time available to escape, so climbing on the seat I dived into space missing the wing by inches. Seconds later, the erratic plunge abruptly stopped as the silk blossomed out above like the petals of a gigantic daisy. Floating gently down in the crisp morning air I experienced a feeling of calm and relief.

210

Ray Veitch.

The aircraft had been abandoned at 7 000 ft which allowed ample time for meditation during the descent. I watched my beloved Mustang plunge into the sea and disappear leaving a patch of burning oil on the surface and I must admit to a lump in my throat for the loss of an aircraft was like losing a very dear and trusted friend. Little did I know that within the month, two more Mustangs would share the same fate!

It was essential to release the parachute harness just before impact to avoid entanglement with it on surfacing, but judging height so finely under the circumstances didn't appear to be easy until the answer to the problem occurred to me at a height of approximately 200 ft above the sea. I tore off a shoe and threw it below. There was an appreciable time lapse before it landed, but when the other shoe followed, it splashed into the water within seconds. I hit the parachute harness release clasp with the palm of my hand and almost simultaneously, my feet touched the sea.

Although the force of impact carried me well under the surface, I bobbed back quickly due to the buoyancy of the waistcoating Mae West. This life-saving jacket was also responsible for the close proximity of the inflatable dinghy which was floating conveniently alongside. It had been housed in the base of the parachute container attached by a length of cord to the Mae West and had pulled away from the container when the harness was released, becoming automatically inflated.

Half an hour passed before an air-sea Walrus appeared from the south and circled for 40 minutes without attempting to land. I shook my fist at the amphibian's pilot giving vent to my feelings with a tirade of abuse for his failure to land and rescue me. His reason was, however, clarified when a Warwick arrived on the scene a few minutes later from which a lifeboat was dispatched by parachute to within a few yards of the dinghy. On board was a note which read: 'Area heavily mined. Steer a course out to sea where the Walrus will pick you up.'

Starting the lifeboat's engines was simple enough and I set course for the open sea praying that the small craft wouldn't collide with a mine along the route. At midday the Walrus landed and taxied alongside. The crew welcomed me aboard providing every comfort and courtesy.

Back on operations two days later, flak struck another fatal blow while I was strafing a train in the Ljubljana district, also in Yugoslavia. This time the glycol leak was highly conspicuous. The fluid spewed out behind the Mustang in one solid stream and the engine temperature gauge needle disappeared off the clock pointing to the obvious conclusion that a hurried exit would soon be necessary.

Trieste harbour lay beneath when the decision was made to bale out. This time, the hood flew off as soon as the emergency knob was pulled. I should have rolled the Mustang over on its back and ejected myself from the cockpit by thrusting the control column forward, but instead of complying with this recommended method for baling out, I stepped on to the left wing and jumped over the trailing edge. While floating down, it occurred to me that Trieste harbour wasn't the safest area in which to land. Once again a shoe was used to estimate height and this time the first drop did the trick enabling the parachute harness to be timeously released. My eyesight and hearing were temporarily impaired by the short immersion under the sea. The splashes in the water which ringed the dinghy as I climbed into it, appeared initially to be caused by leaping fish, although this perception was swiftly dispelled when the crack of the enemy guns and the impact of the bullets pounding the water around the dinghy, registered on my numbed senses.

I'd landed at the entrance to the harbour where the sea was covered with garbage emitting a potent stench, but there was little time in which to be concerned about odious smells and I began paddling like a madman up the long narrow estuary. It was to be an eventful journey. Thankfully the shooting ceased as the dinghy entered a mist belt which obscured it from the German gun crews but not from Peter Nelson in his Mustang who was intent on thwarting any attempt to end my break for freedom. After spotting two motor torpedo boats dart out of Trieste harbour, he attacked the leading boat with rockets when it was about 100 yards from my dinghy. Fatally holed and listing to port, the crippled

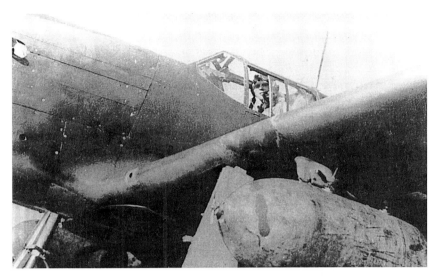
A Mustang prepares for take-off with two 1000lb bombs.

craft turned back towards the harbour followed by the second MTB whose skipper had undoubtedly decided not to chance the inevitable.

The mist began clearing about 0900 hours, but at this stage the German gun crews didn't appear interested in exterminating me while paddling like a mechanical robot up the middle of the estuary. This exercise lasted nine exhausting hours before a lifeboat was dropped in which I was eventually to complete the voyage to safety. During the morning and early afternoon, several attempts were made to pluck me from the water but each attempt was foiled by patrolling Mustangs and Spitfires which sank a total of nine MTBs. At 1530 hours, when 260 Squadron's CO - the affable Peter Blomfield - was patrolling, a ketch in full sail was observed approaching the dinghy. In case it was friendly, Peter fired a warning burst across its bows and when no heed was paid to this gentlemanly gesture, the same procedure was repeated. Sail was lowered and the boat continued on course under oar, but when Blomfield flew directly over it for closer scrutiny, he was astonished to see four crewmen taking pot shots at him with revolvers. British chivalry was thrown to the wind and the brave but foolhardy enemy sailors got what they deserved. Common sense should have warned them that there wasn't a hope of survival when blasted by a fighter air-craft's full complement of guns.

The Warwick arrived at 1615 hours and after a wide circuit, trun-dled across the estuary on its dropping run while coastal guns opened up with a barrage of heavy flak. When the lifeboat had settled in the water some 200 yards from the dinghy, I paddled over to it, clambered aboard and started one of the engines. I didn't bother with the other engine immediately since the coastal guns had been switched in my direction. No doubt it had occurred to the enemy that my chances of escaping were improving. The next two and a half hours required maximum concentration while playing a cat and mouse game with the German gunners who were using the bracketing method which involved dropping shells on either side of the dinghy with a third predicted to fall centrally. I was lucky to survive until getting wise to the enemy's plan, realising that unless bold action was taken, my demise was imminent. Death had linked its arm with mine once more but I seemed to thrive on dangerous situations and I was able to think clearly and constructively.

The remedy for countering this proven method of hitting a target was simple. I waited until the second shell had hit the water and then altered course at full throttle towards the splash down so that the lifeboat would be clear of the third shell when it landed. This manoeuvre was highly successful and kept me alive until nightfall when the guns stopped firing. At 2000 hours I switched off the engines and braced myself for the long, lonely vigil which was to last until dawn. In spite of being awake since 0500 hours, sleep was elusive as I sat huddled up all night listening for the purr of an enemy MTB trying to locate me under the cloak of darkness.

The only sound which disturbed the stillness of the night was the soft lapping of the water against the side of the boat as my mind ran circles around the past and future. I'd achieved a burning ambition when posted to 260 Squadron as an operational pilot and was determined that no German was going to cheat me of my newly-found happiness. I envisaged the cheerful welcome which the air-sea rescue boys would accord me and the 'piss up' which would follow later in the 260 pilots' mess bar. At the first sign of dawn I got the lifeboat under way once more. A low mist hung over the entire area but it was only a thin layer which melted as the sun rose.

A faint drone of aircraft engines was heard from the south-west and the reassuring sight of two Mustangs appeared on the horizon. They flew over the lifeboat waggling their wings in triumphant salute and firing their guns towards the open sea to convey the message that along the path of the bullets rescue would soon be to hand. At 0900 hours, while chugging along 10 miles from the Yugoslav coast with the open expanse of the Adriatic sea immediately ahead, I felt cheerful and relaxed for surely all my trials and tribulations were over and friendly hands would soon be pulling me into the warmth of an air-sea rescue aircraft. I licked my parched lips while thinking about the hot tea, the scrumptious food and the consoling grog which would be pushed into my eager hands, but the smug smile of anticipation was obliterated with dramatic suddenness.

An angry storm had brewed over the Yugoslav mountains and with little warning, it pounced. A howling wind and torrential rain transformed the tranquil sea into a seething cauldron of foaming, white-capped waves. The propellers thrashed the choppy sea as the lifeboat nosed into deep troughs. It hadn't been designed for operation by a one-man crew and I was obliged to dive back and forth between engine and tiller while endeavouring to prevent the craft broadsiding into a wave and capsizing. From time to time the engine was choked to a standstill by a huge wave.

The storm abated almost as quickly as it had arisen and while squeezing the water from my dripping garments I wondered what other unforseen hazards lay ahead. My concern was short lived for within half and hour, a Catalina flying boat landed and taxied to within a few yards of the waterlogged lifeboat bringing to a conclusion my epic voyage to freedom which had commenced at the entrance to Trieste harbour 27 hours earlier. The astonished expressions of disbelief on the faces of skipper and his crew were a sight to behold when they recognised the same wet, bedraggled guy they'd rescued a few days previously when crewing a Walrus. After handshakes and backslaps all round, I was left to towel myself down, change into some dry clothing

A 260 Squadron Mustang carrying 500lb bombs.

and satisfy my aching thirst and hunger before being invited by my hosts to celebrate the rescue. For the second time within two days I was pleasantly surprised to sample the large selection of choice liquor reserved for rescue celebrations. From all accounts such noble operations were frequent and must have involved many memorable drinking hours for the crew!

By the time my air-sea rescue pals had landed me back at Cervia airstrip, 239 Wing's home base during this period, I was already in a party mood and prepared for the thrash which my fellow pilots had lined up in the pub. I can't remember much about this 'booze-up' except that the squadron's lovable washerwoman turned up when she heard of my safe return. Bursting into the bar like a galleon in full sail, with tears streaming down her cheeks, she threw her arms around my neck and smothered me with garlic-flavoured kisses. By the time she pushed off I was very drunk, learning in the morning that while staggering off to bed I had muttered with a sigh, 'Some Italian bints are so sentimental!'

Three telegrams are cherished in the Veitch home. The first reads; 'Congratulations, but why have you forsaken the Air Force for the Navy? Love Mum and Dad.' The second is from Air Vice-Marshal 'Pussy' Foster, AOC the Desert Air Force and it reads: 'From Foster to Veitch. I've appointed you as honorary president of the Desert Air Force Yachting Club... when it is formed!'

The third came from Buckingham Palace. 'Greatly regret that I am unable to present you personally with the Distinguished Flying

A message to Ray from AOC, Desert Air Force.

```
FROM         ADV DAF      021418B

TO           239 WING (FOR 260 SQDN)

GR    ----   BT


AOC/349   2/5

FOLLOWING FOR LT. VITCH FROM A.O.C.  (.)

I HAVE APPOINTED YOU HONORARY COMMODORE OF THE DESERT AIR FORCE

YACHTING CLUB WHEN IT IS FORMED(.)

BT    021418B    THI 021430 B

SENT    V    MMYL    RP   AR K

R     N.,53     021744B    RMP    AR+
```

Cross which you have so well earned. My congratulations and best wishes for your future happiness.' It was signed *George R I.*

The final drama was on 30 April at approximately 1630 hours. I was strafing motor transport near Vittoria Veneto in Italy when an enemy shell hit my Mustang's port wing tearing a gaping hole in the petrol tank. Initially this didn't spell serious trouble since the starboard tank still contained enough fuel to see the aircraft back to base.

While crossing the Adriatic coast at Liguano near Venice, the oil pressure dropped indicating that an oil pipe line had been punctured, and while turning on course for base when approximately 10 miles out over the sea, the familiar sounds of a dying engine urged me to take the plunge once more. Unfortunately this kind of gimmick was such old hat that I became careless.

Throwing off the Sutton harness with great gusto and carefree abandon, I stepped confidently over the side of the cockpit on to the right wing as the Mustang kicked over into a right hand spiral. The launching into space was abruptly arrested when I found myself dangling from the cockpit like a puppet on a string. One glance was enough to establish that the Sutton harness had hooked itself on to a parachute strap. There was only one thing to do. Pull myself back on to the wing alongside the cockpit so that my weight could be taken off the Sutton harness and the parachute strap released. With the aircraft spiralling down in a giant vortex, this was not going to be an easy operation. With momentous effort borne from sheer desperation, success was achieved and I pushed myself off the side of the airframe into space, little realising that clearing a spiralling aircraft was fraught with danger. The tailplane hit my left leg stripping off a large hunk of skin and flesh, but the pain was numbed initially by the blissful knowledge of once again being under the silk.

The sun was close to setting and the chance of rescue before morning seemed slim. I climbed into the inflatable dingy which was bobbing around like a cork on a rough, angry sea, every choppy wave swamping it. Bailing was a pointless activity so I was obliged to spend the entire night sitting up to my waist in ice-cold water which aggravated my open leg wound. At dawn a lifeboat was dropped, but I was so weak from exposure that it took considerable time and effort to climb aboard. The area was heavily mined and before rescue could be attempted, I was instructed to steer further out to sea where an air-sea rescue launch would uplift me. Once on board, the crew ushered me into the main cabin. A prominent sign over the door seemed so very appropriate. It read: 'The Sea Shall Not Claim Them'. Neither the sea nor the air could claim me!

Tailpiece

In March 1945 Ray's brush with some ME 109s caused many a laugh in Desert Air Force messes. He was flying 'arse-end Charlie' when 260 Squadron dive bombed a bridge in northern Italy, and after pulling out of the dive he climbed towards the agreed rendezvous. Seeing a number of aircraft milling around in a defensive circle, he joined them. Suddenly it dawned on him that they weren't Mustangs but ME 109s! 'Help', he shouted over the R/T, 'I'm surrounded by Messerschmitts!' Then suddenly he remembered the golden rule - 'Always look behind'- and sure enough there was a 109 on his tail.

Conveniently, a cumulus cloud was hovering just above, so he whipped into its folds. 'Have you been hacked yet?' enquired the leader who happened to be another South African, Brian Ruiter. 'No' said Veitch, 'I'm hiding in cloud!' Ray died in retirement.

Two Border War Pets

Aircrew have been known to have a way with animals, and pets have long been a familiar scene at operational airfields - Guy Gibson's dog being a case in point. Rundu was in the operational area, a border settlement in Kavango on the Angolan border where many aircrew pets could be found during the Border War. These included dogs, invariably orphans from across the river which found their way to Rundu by Alouette or Cessna; monkeys, snakes, chameleons, bush babies, various buck, birds, insects, spiders, scorpions, domestic cats, a young cow on one occasion, and even Portuguese-speaking goats! This story involves a female ostrich inevitably called 'Straizzh,' and 'Ballas,' a cat.

Straizzh was picked up as an orphaned youngster by an Alouette crew. She grew up in and around the 'chopper happening', a marquee tent which housed all the chopper pilots. She was an exceptionally tame bird with a tremendous character and sense of humour. She would terrorize the other animals and some of the humans by running at them and hissing loudly with her big beak wide open. However, she never hurt or tried to kick anyone and hung around the 'happening' ready to come in and frighten the daylights out of first-timers arriving for a tour of operations! Her favourite 'food' was boxes of matches (sulphur), and a new boy's first sight, sound or feel of her, was often arranged by seating him with his back to the mess tent entrance with a pile of matchboxes on the table. In would trot Straizzh and that long, warm, furry neck would streak by the unsuspecting new guy's neck and peck up the boxes without further ado. The greenhorn would stiffen up and stutter incoherently before regaining his composure!

Straizzh enjoyed pub opening-time, for all aircrew were present and she would receive daily snacks of cheese and chunks of tomato. One day we hid the snacks behind the pub counter and she promptly strutted from man to man, but without luck. Accordingly she did a foot-stomping 360 degree turn, raised herself to her full height and splattered a deposit on the floor before flouncing out indignantly!

As blue-jobs we had to 'educate' her and a conditioning process was inevitable. To teach her the difference between blue and brown,

Monster with Straizzh.

a cunning strategy was adopted. One of the fellows dressed in browns would talk unpleasantly to Straizzh, denying her any food. This was followed by someone in a blue flying overall who coddled and fed her. Did it work? Well, she would chase people who were dressed in brown around the camp but never someone in a flying-overall!

One of her favourite pastimes was a chase. She would arrive on the flight-line and if the Hobart-starter or Clarktor aircraft tractor were manned, she would ask for a chase. This she did by dancing a few 360 degree turns in front of the vehicle. The operator would then, to Straizzh's great delight, switch on and give chase. Such flight-line machines are necessarily slow so when she got too far ahead she would repeat the 360 degrees charge back and set off again with, what one could only imagine, was a secret grin!

Sadly this game led to her demise. One day she mistook two brown-jobs in an open Landrover for her Air Force brethren. These imbeciles didn't know her trick of turning back suddenly, and, driving too fast, ran her over. Her passing was appropriately mourned in the pub, from which the browns were summarily banned for a suitable period. The odd brown tent and bed also collapsed that night and certain browns were queueing for the long drop all night due to some croton-oil mysteriously finding its way into their bully-beef!

The greatest 'character' amongst our pets and remembered most fondly by the fellows, was a cat. But what a cat! He was a smokey grey colour and unusually large. In fact, we put SAAF dark glasses on him for a photo in 1973 and they were not a loose fit! His teeth were 2,5cm long and that's NOT an exaggeration! Apart from his colour he could easily have been some kind of wild cat. He was endowed like a billy goat which was his crowning glory and was responsible for his name, 'Ballas'. Never was there a cat with such a pair! Ballas lived in the 'chopper happening' at Rundu, and woe betide you if you tried to kick him off your bed! Those claws would go through three army blankets, two sheets, your pyjamas and your skin and have plenty left over! He growled like a dog and everyone treated him with respect, even Straizzh who liked terrorizing the cats around the camp. Her first meeting with Ballas was also planned that way. As she got close to him he lashed out and clipped her across the upper beak. Straizzh nearly fell over with shock and from then onwards kept a respectable distance! The dogs were also terrified of him as were the monkeys, for they knew he could climb.

Ballas had one weakness, although he undoubtedly didn't see it that way. The same thing has brought about the downfall of many of the male gender - the fairer sex. The chief wife of this Mormon was a slinky black Persian-like beauty called Cooking Fat. Ballas was not discreet about his affairs. He gave us the impression he liked to show the aircrew how it was done and we were often provided with live entertainment. It was not long before the feline population increased vastly, all sporting grey markings. Many of his offspring found their way back to the Republic. It was inevitable that the day had to come when Ballas would be no more. He was suffering from severe loss of hair and eczema problems and being so loved by the chopper boys they decided to have him put down with dignity. The local vet was consulted and arrangements were made. Came the eve of his exit, and he was given an injection which the vet assured us would increase his lust for life just one more time, and he and 'Cooking Fat' were given the privacy of the tool-shed for the night. The sounds emanating from the tool-shed left no doubt that the vet had provided the right mixture. There was many a disappointed chopper-jock when the vet assured them it didn't work for humans so there would be no issues for taking home!

The next day dawned and an obviously tired but happy Ballas was given his final injection so that he could leave this world a happy cat. The coffin had been made as there had been time to plan, and he lay in state in the pub with his face exposed in a pink-studded satin-lined kiaat coffin. All aircrew and many others, filed past him to pay their last respects and it's no exaggeration to say there was many a lump in the throats of those hardened men. His coffin was carried by no less than four SAAF majors to the gun carriage - a Landrover borrowed from the browns for the occasion, and was transported to the grave site. A 21 gun salute - no less - was a fitting tribute to this magnificent animal before he was laid to rest under a cement slab near his beloved Cooking Fat's hang-out. He may not have been 2 Squadron's Cheetah but he was real magic, and we loved him.

Tailpiece

I've included these delightful stories, so well described by Monster, because they epitomise the human side of life which aircrew experienced at an operations base.

Peter Daphne

Tense Moments at Kufra Oasis

Seven hundred miles north west of Wadi Halfa and 500 miles south of Tobruk, is Kufra Oasis, used for hundreds of years as a stopover for the camel caravans journeying from Lake Chad to Benghazi.

It was here during the Desert Campaign in World War II that three Blenheims of 15 Squadron SAAF came to grief in a pitiless Sahara sandstorm, their fuel exhausted and with little chance of rescue. When they

A 15 Squadron Blenheim at Kufra Oasis.

Peter Daphne.

were eventually found, eight days later, there was only one survivor. The rest of the crew met a gruesome death in the blistering heat.

This unfortunate episode would not have occurred if the new DF (direction finder) station had been operating, providing the crews with a course back to Kufra Oasis. Resulting from this tragic, expensive lesson, further flying was discontinued until the DF station became fully operational. Although primitive by modern standards, the DF was a great comfort to the replacement detachment of three more Blenheims sent to carry on with the patrol duties which assisted the 'Long Range Desert Group' under the legendary Colonel Stirling when operating behind the enemy lines in Libya.

So it was that on 12 August 1942, I was sitting with my crew, navigator Alistair Rodger and wireless operator/air gunner, Karl Ribbink, in a hut of palm leaves built by a local bedouin, when a truck roared up in a cloud of dust, an agitated DF station operator yelling that Major Pidsley from the squadron at Lake Mariut, was flying approximately 50 miles to the south of Kufra heading away from the oasis and calling for a course to steer. They could not make contact so could we perhaps relay a message?

A mad scramble on the back of the truck with our flying gear and out to Blenheim 7610 standing under a camouflage net between the palms. The cowlings were off and Sgts. Schillinger and Baker were busy with a 40-hour inspection. The aircraft was not scheduled to fly that day and no others were available, so the two sergeants broke all time records and maintenance regulations to get us off the ground. We were soon heading south into the haze.

The minutes passed, the aircraft droned on, Kufra radio became less and less distinct, hope faded. Karl Ribbink sat, sweat pouring down his cheeks and around the mask strapped tightly against his mouth, tapping on his morse key and at the same time listening intently for the slightest response. The minutes dragged by and an eerie silence prevailed. Suddenly my ears were deafened by an exultant shout from Ribbink: 'I've got them, they can hear me. They are circling and the DF has a new course for them to steer. I've passed it on and the've got it!' Forty-seven years later I can still feel the electrifying relief and see the look on my navigator's face as we turned and headed for home!

A few weeks later Pip Pidsley and his navigator, Monty Yudelman, led a formation of Bisleys which with heavy losses, helped to sink a fuel tanker near Tobruk harbour, a grievous loss to Field Marshal Erwin Rommel who, it is reported, stamped his feet in fury as he watched the life-blood of his precious Panzers sink beneath the waters of the Mediterranean. So be it.

Pip Pidsley lands at Kufra after his rescue.

Tailpiece

Peter flew on four operational tours during World War II. As the CO of 60 Photo-Reconnaissance Squadron, two of his most spectacular achievements were flights from Italy in a Mosquito to photograph the Focke-Wulf aircraft factory at Poznan in Poland and the Ploesti oil wells in Romania. Alistair 'Fox' Rodger, describes him as a man with a natural charm and an impish sense of humour; a capable leader and squadron commander who was awarded both the British and American DFCs. He lives in Bonza Bay, East London.

Peter Bagshawe

Three Charismatic SAAF Leaders

Lawrie Wilmot, Tank Odendaal and Kalfie Martin will be remembered as three outstanding SAAF personalities, each with his own brand of leadership and totally dedicated to flying.

Lawrie Wilmot

Lawrie knew from childhood that he wanted to be a pilot, and after matriculating, he joined the SAAF, received his first dual flying lesson in an Avion; after three hours' dual instruction he went solo.

He was a natural pilot, a born leader who invariably led from the front. He was totally committed to flying and took anything with wings into the sky. His logbook shows he flew 60 different types of aircraft during his career. On 9 September 1940, 3 Squadron was formed at Waterkloof with Lawrie as commanding officer. He led his Hurricanes to Nairobi on 24 October and they were split up between Mombasa and the frontier districts. He shot down his first enemy aircraft while stationed at Port Sudan.

On 31 December 1940 he took over as OC 1 Squadron at Azaza and on 29 January 1941 he led eight Hurricanes and five Gladiators to attack Gura airfield where ten CR 42s were airborne waiting for them. In the dogfight which followed, No 1 Squadron shot down five Italians without loss to themselves.

The next success was on 21 February when Lawrie led seven Hurricanes to strafe the Italian base at Massawa. Seven enemy aircraft parked on the tarmac were destroyed and all six hangars set alight, the roof of one being blown off by the explosion.

Two days later, Lawrie led a flight of three Hurricanes to attack Makalle airfield and as he was flaming an enemy aircraft on the tarmac, three CR 42s appeared, one of which attacked him from behind. It was shot down by Andrew Duncan but Lawrie's Hurricane had already been hit and he was forced to crash-land near Arbi Addi, where the timely arrival of an Italian soldier saved him from a grisly death at the hands of some incensed tribesmen whose chief had been killed in a recent Allied

Lawrie Wilmot.

bombing raid. He was made a POW but released as soon as the Eritrean campaign was over on 30 June.

Lawrie rejoined the squadron at Amiriya in the desert and continued to command it with skill and aggression. On 2 August, while leading 12 Hurricanes, he became embroiled in a dogfight with 20 ME 109s and Macchi 202s escorting JU 87s. The squadron shot down five JU 87s.

He completed his second tour of ops as Sweep Leader to 258 Wing having been awarded the DSO and the DFC. During this period he led the Wing to strafe an airfield near Magrun, when four aircraft were shot down and three destroyed. He returned for his third tour of ops to command 239 Wing RAF as a full colonel and inspired all the squadrons under his command with his enthusiasm, aggression and leadership from the front.

While his Wing was stationed at Cutella on the Adriatic coast, a flight of USAAF Thunderbolts strafed the airfield damaging several Mustangs and Kittyhawks and killing a Walrus pilot who only two days before had saved the lives of 11 American airmen. Lawrie managed to get airborne quickly enough to follow the Thunderbolts back to their base and acquire all aircraft numbers.

He returned home after the close of his third operational tour but in July 1947 he lost his life while performing an aerobatic manoeuvre in a Mosquito. The wings were fractured, probably due to a combination of their wooden structure and the dry heat of the Transvaal sun. He was one of the SAAF's great pilots who lived for flying and died for it.

Tank Odendaal.

Tank Odendaal

Nicknamed 'Tank' because of his robust physique, he fought with distinction in both World War II and the Korean War. During his first tour of operations with 5 Squadron in Italy in 1943, he chalked up a healthy score of over one hundred enemy vehicles destroyed. Twice he was lucky to escape with his life. On the first occasion while pulling out of a dive bombing operation, flak ignited the ammunition in one of the wings of his Kittyhawk, the explosion flipping the aircraft over on to its back at low altitude. It was only Tank's quick reactions which saved his life. On another occasion, he had just landed from an operation when his No 2, following up behind too close and too fast, crashed into his Kitty chopping it in half just short of the cockpit. He was awarded the DFC during this tour.

Back on his second tour of ops he soon became OC 5 Squadron and on 17 March 1945 he was leading an operation over Yugoslavia when his Mustang was crippled by flak. Leading top cover was A Q de Wet who watched him climb the stricken aircraft towards some mountains. 'Suddenly he shot out of the cockpit without even bidding us *totsiens* and floated down into a thick snow-covered pine forest,' said de Wet.

Fortunately, the territory was held by Partisans who cared for him until the end of the war while he in turn helped them with their clandestine operations against the Germans.

On one occasion, after casting an admiring glance at a beautiful young guerrilla girl, an older leader warned him not to become involved because Tito had forbidden any love affairs for the duration of war. A few days later the validity of Tito's order was horrifically demonstrated when the girl put a pistol to her head and shot herself dead, the penalty for falling pregnant! Tank returned to his squadron at the end of the war to learn that he'd been awarded a bar to his DFC.

In September 1950 he went to Korea with No 2 Squadron as a flight commander. It was a torrid tour of operations during which period seven of the squadron's pilots were lost. The Americans awarded Tank their DFC.

In December he led a flight of Mustangs to search for ground targets along a road near the Ch'ongch'on river. It was during this recce that he saw about 5 000 Chinese crossing the river. He called up 'Control' specifying the target and advising that his flight's aircraft were carrying napalm and he requested permission to attack. Control came back with: 'How do you know they are Chinese?' Tank replied that he could positively identify them, in fact he could even see their big toes sticking through the traditional hoop on their sandals - but Control refused to give clearance for the attack.

Tank recalls another uncomfortable incident: 'While our advance party was fast asleep under canvas, a call came for the OC 2 Squadron, Commandant S V Theron, to report to the base commander who had informed him that a message had been received stating that a powerful Chinese army was massing outside Pyongyang and could attack at any moment. The squadron must withdraw and fly back to Seoul at first light. Owing to complete lack of facilities and the fact that it was raining steadily, we decided to stay in bed and gain some essential sleep. An hour later, exploding bombs jetted us out of bed and in the subsequent charge towards the exit we could not get the tent flap untied. I stepped back a few paces and launched my 100 kilos at the exit, the tent flap tore open and along with a couple of the pilots, we landed outside in the mud. The other chaps dived for the slit trenches but these were more than half full of rain water - so everyone got wet and muddy! We managed to fly out in time next morning, but the enemy, reinforced by thousands of Chinese, pushed the United Nations troops back to 10 miles north of Seoul. I wondered how different the situation might have been had I been allowed to eliminate the Chinks crossing the Yalu.'

There were four flight commanders in Commandant Theron's 2 Squadron. Captain W J J Badenhorst AFC was the first to be killed over the Yalu river on 2 March 1951; followed by Captain J F O Davis DFC and bar on 10 March. Captain Lipawsky DFC and bar and Tank were the third and fourth flight commanders respectively and when Lippy completed his tour and bid farewell to Tank, he chaffed : 'Bad

Kalfie Martin.

luck *ou swaar*. You are now the third flight commander.' He was of course referring to the superstition that fatalities happen in threes. Tank didn't agree and told Lippy that in his opinion the so-called superstition was not transferable. Well, Lippy returned home, joined South African Airways and was killed in the SAA *Rietbok* tragedy in the sea off East London. Before the accident Tank told his wife Joy about a dream in which he had seen Lippy crashing into the sea. Shortly afterwards, the sad news came over a radio news bulletin.

Tank retired as a brigadier with a well earned SM added to his existing decorations. He lives on the mountain slopes near the Great Brak River in the George area.

Kalfie Martin

One of the SAAF's great achievers, he was well-known before the war as one of the mighty Springbok rugby forwards who toured New Zealand in 1937. In June 1940 he was appointed to the responsible task of selecting sites for 30 flying training schools complete with bombing and shooting ranges for the Empire Training scheme.

Because of this task, he only got on to operations in March 1942 when he was appointed OC 12 Squadron, gaining much respect from his men because he flew in a subordinate position until he had mastered operational techniques.

He led many highly successful raids against the enemy. During the advance of Rommel's forces to El Alamein towards the end of June, Kalfie led six Bostons to the Bir Hackiem area. The battle was in such a state of flux that he couldn't find a suitable target to bomb, but his sharp eyes spotted the Germans approaching Sidi Rezegh and he was able to warn the Eighth Army which was not aware of this development. Later in the day he led an attack against a concentration of 200 vehicles in this area.

In mid-June he led four raids in one day against a Panzer Division moving east to attack El Adem. The following day he led 12 Squadron on six raids against 1 000 enemy vehicles, part of a Panzer division massing around El Adem. This outstanding effort won him the DFC.

On 1 August 1943 Kalfie was appointed to command 3 Wing and under his leadership, the El Dobe-Mersah Matruh area was attacked nightly during the following month.

In September the Afrika Korps was bombed every half hour by Bostons, Baltimores and Mitchells despite the consistent umbrella of flak which Kalfie described as 'a grey blanket against the blue skies.'

As a result of these successful operations, he received a personal message from Air Vice-Marshal Coningham: 'The good work carried out by your squadrons is a reflection of the efficient control and direction at your HQ. Your bombers are hitting the enemy hard and your work is being watched by an appreciative army.'

When the Eighth Army entered Tripoli at the end of January 1944, it was ascertained that 3 Wing SAAF had flown 275 out of a total of 375 tactical support sorties flown by all DAF aircraft during January. The Wing had also flown 462 general sorties out of 956 recorded by the entire SAAF during the same month which was one-third of the total sorties flown in the Middle East.

Kalfie was awarded the CBE for his invaluable contribution to operational techniques and the efficiency of 3 Wing. While commanding 12 Squadron, he had spotted the near fatal weakness in the Boston's defence. There were no rear guns in the tail section. He made it possible for two of the Brownings in the Boston's nose to be turned to the rear and fired by remote control by the top gunner. Further essential modifications to improve the Boston's lot were carried out in the workshops at Kalfie's instigation.

In June 1942 Kalfie introduced a new technique for take off which meant that 18 Bostons could take off and form up within 10 minutes. In August 1943, he and his staff carried out tests with Bostons to lay fog screens for infantry. Trials and applications during battle proved to be highly successful.

Back in South Africa after the war, he was awarded the SM, was promoted to Lieutenant-General and became Chief of the South African

Air Force. After retirement, he and Colonel Neil Orpen wrote a series of books on South African Forces in World War II of which *Eagles Victorious* was the sixth volume. This was a factual, detailed account and record of the SAAF at war in Italy and in the Mediterranean theatre of operations from 1943-45. Kalfie lives in Lynwood, Pretoria.

Tailpiece

To write about these three personalities is a pleasing task. Lawrie Wilmot was a legendary, highly respected leader who was OC 239 Wing when I joined it in Italy. My thanks to Jean Wilmot for the loan of her late husband's logbook. Tank Odendaal and I were fellow squadron commanders in 239 Wing so I got to know him reasonably well. This tough, outgoing, friendly personality is typical of the South Africans I knew in those days.

I never had the pleasure of meeting Kalfie Martin, but his name as an achiever who reached the top of his profession, is history. Over and above this, he was a communicator with people; popular and respected by everyone who brushed shoulders with him.

Christmas Stocking

Christmas Eve in Italy 1943. The weather was foul, with heavy mist and rain preventing operations from our airstrip at Trigno on the Adriatic coast. 'Misery, thy name is winter,' under canvas in Italy with mud and slush everywhere. Even the Jeeps got stuck and I couldn't think of a worse prelude to the festive season.

Under low cloud in the later afternoon, Dave Hastie and Tommy van der Veen led two pairs of 1 Squadron Spitfire IXs to escort an air-sea rescue Walrus on a mission to pick up a bomber crew floating in a dinghy near Porto San Giorgio nearly 100 miles up the coast.

The dinghy was spotted with two of its seven occupants waving lethargically. No doubt the poor fellows were cold and seasick after spending some time in miserable conditions. The rough seas and high winds made it tricky for the Walrus pilot to make a landing close enough for the rescue. Nevertheless, he tried but overshot the dinghy and the aircraft was almost swamped with water. It was obvious that further attempts would not be possible until the wind had abated and the sea had calmed down. There was no chance of a change taking place before dark. An attempt would have to be made the next day, so after dropping emergency equipment, the Walrus and Spits returned to base with the pilots frustrated and depressed at having to abandon the operation.

On Christmas morning the weather relented a little so Dave Hastie and I flew off early to Ancona to see if we could locate the dinghy. After an intensive square search, there was no sign of it and we guessed that the Jerries had invited the occupants to be their guests! What a Christmas - to be so close to rescue and then be taken prisoner.

Later on Christmas day, Johnny Ross and I were scrambled, briefed to locate another dinghy. Soon after take-off we flew over an LCI (Landing Craft for Infantry) chugging its way up the coast close to shore, also briefed for the rescue mission. Eventually the dinghy was located near Pescara and reported to 'Commander' control who asked for a fix on our position. When flying low over the dinghy, I ascertained from Hastie and van der Veen's description that it was the same

An air-sea rescue Walrus.

one they had abandoned the previous evening. The wind and current had swept it 60 miles down the coast in the intervening period. I was apprehensive on noticing that the occupants showed little sign of life and had a horrible feeling that some of them may not have made it.

Leaving Johnny to circle over the dinghy and keep in touch with 'Commander', I returned to the LCI and after discreetly identifying myself as friendly, I flew slowly over it several times at about a 100 ft, waggling my Spit's wings and at the same time pointing in the direction of the dinghy. I also flashed an SOS on the aircraft's underbelly light. There were friendly waves at first but then the crew cottoned on to what I was trying to indicate and the LCI headed in the right direction. Later, when Johnnie and I were running short of fuel, 'Commander' sent two aircraft to relieve us.

The LCI reached the dinghy about two hours later to find several of the American crew in a bad way. They had languished in the dinghy for five days and nights after their Fortress had ditched on its way back from an operation over northern Italy. We were relieved to hear that they were all alive and would recover.

Tailpiece

Bomb's diary for that Christmas day opens: 'Twas Christmas in the workhouse - Spent the day as I would have wished it, doing something with 'Goodwill' attached, for a change.

Carel Birkby

A Squadron to Remember

'.. and all those boys
Who shoot a line
Must bear in mind
The One-O-Nine...'

They sing their own ribald parody to the haunting tune of 'Lili Marlene,' the Afrika Korps song that the Eighth Army and the Desert Air Force made so much their own. The pilots of 1 Squadron SAAF are crowded cheerfully around the fireplace built into the wall of their Nissen hut mess, glasses in hand. Beer had come up the line for the first time in weeks. The rain is pouring down outside and I happen to be stranded by the weather at the squadron's landing strip on the Adriatic coast. There's a biting wind coming off the Apennine snows but the mess is cheerful and a young Italian student who has been installed as barman is filling glasses with vermouth. The chaps are wetting Wicky's third pip; Lieutenant W D Wick'ner who shot down one of the most recent of the Squadron's 156 victims, has this day been promoted to captain.

Wicky is vividly popular. He is a lean young South African with a large moustache and a great sense of humour. He always has something amusing to say, in fact he always shoots a good line!

Shooting a line has several connotations in the Air Force, and not all of them are invidious. To boast, the unforgivable service sin, is to shoot a line. To exaggerate in a tale of some experience is also line-shooting and to be deprecated. But the burlesqued overstatement and the hyper-cautious understatement also constitute a recognised line and may be justifiably well received in the mess. Most squadrons that cherish tradition keep a Line Book handy for the recording of remarks that qualify in terms of the laughter with which they are received. Down in it go the naive remarks of the newcomers ('sprogs', as experienced pilots dismiss them), the naive questions, the leg-pulls, the Munchausen tales told with never a smile. Here in a few pages by pencil or fountain-pen you find the spirit of the Commonwealth fighting man who can laugh, thank God, even in war.

236

Hannes Faure.

No 1 Squadron keeps a wizard Line Book, and the cream of it is contributed by Wicky whose third pip we are wetting tonight.

Let's flip over the pages and sample some of the entries: Wicky was stringing along a sprog who had just joined the Squadron and had yet to experience air combat. Said the sprog, obviously buying it: 'Which part of the Jerry kite do you aim at?' Said Wicky, his wits about him: 'I always chip a bit of the wing off first just to give the Jerry a chance to bale out.'

In March last year the Squadron shot down two ME 109s and three Macchi 202s. On their return from slaughtering the enemy's best fighters Wicky exclaimed enthusiastically: 'It's the greatest thing to meet unescorted 109s!'

But Wicky reached his greatest heights in January this year when the Spitfire pilots were hanging about at readiness in the operations tent and yarning to pass the time. He told a tale of a Valentia which was an obsolete British troop-carrier still used for lack of another aircraft in the early stages of the war. It couldn't fly at more than 90 mph in a steep dive and Wicky said that he was a passenger in that snail-like aircraft with nine other guys who panicked when the pilot wrote off the undercart while landing and took off again intent on making a belly-landing. Wicky told his fellow travellers not to worry and while the pilot was making a circuit he kicked holes in the floor and all the guys put their legs through them. When the Valentia levelled off to land we all started running, carrying the Valentia with us. It would have been a perfect landing if one of the blokes hadn't got out of step!

Talk in the mess had turned to operational flying hours. One pilot remarked that during the Nazi advance on Alexandria, RAF pilots had flown as much as eight and ten hours daily. A newcomer, unimpressionable and careless in elementary mathematics, returned: 'That's nothing to shoot a line about. I'm sure that when the Luftwaffe was attacking England, pilots were flying 30 to 40 hours a day!'

The Line Book records that Lieutenant R Chaplin who had expended all his ammunition in a dogfight without achieving a victory, explained afterwards: 'The Macchi I attacked had a self-sealing fuselage!'

Lieutenant E Robinson is credited with the immortal report in the Operations tent: 'When I saw the 190s, I peeled off on to them. Mind you, I was below the telegraph wires myself at the time!' To a sprog who inquired about the intensity of Jerry flak, Lieutenant Tommy van der Veen, of Pretoria, replied airily: 'The sky is often so black with bursts that you have to fly through them on instruments!' It was the same pilot who excused himself for losing his way in the air by saying: 'I've got so much shrapnel in my body that it upsets my compass!' Van der Veen by the way, had the unusual experience of fighting ski-troops with a Spitfire. In the Mailella mountains recently he sighted a patrol of eight German soldiers on skis and while they shot at him with a light machine-gun, he let them have the full blast of his multiple guns.

Two of the squadron's pilots in the old Desert days went out on a shadow-firing practice. One of them had no maps and was over strange country. He grew worried as his companion went deeper and deeper south into the Desert with many changes of course. When they returned he complained: 'Where did you think you were going? I began to think we'd land up in South Africa.' 'Don't be silly,' replied the other vaguely. 'We were nowhere near there!'

Captain Piet Robbertse, a little fellow whom I first knew as a bomber pilot in Abyssinia, transferred to Spitfires and served with the Squadron in North Africa. He was responsible for a bit of terse wit one day when the Squadron was briefed for a shipping patrol and the pilots discussed the prospect of being forced down in the Mediterranean. 'This Squadron,' he said to the CO, 'is going to the dogs. All the pilots have hydrophobia!'

No 1 serves in a South African Spitfire fighter wing led by a brilliant young airman and administrator still in his early twenties, Col D H Loftus, DSO, DFC, who comes from the Rand. Four years ago I remember Doug on a Kenya desert airfield, a boyish second-lieutenant still to take part in his first air combat. His Wing Commander Flying was Lieutenant-Colonel A C Bosman, DFC, once described by Air Marshal

Sir Arthur Coningham as the finest fighter pilot in the Middle East, a man with preternaturally sharp eyes who can recognise and identify ME 109s with the naked eye when they seem mere dots on the horizon.

The Squadron leader is another young fighter ace, Major 'Johnny' Seccombe DFC, who has four enemy fighters to his credit. I remember Johnny as a schoolboy cricketer with ambitions which he would have achieved if the war hadn't intervened, of playing for South Africa. Though a Commanding Officer he still looks like a schoolboy with his

Johnny Seccombe.

crisp, curly fair hair. Small, slight and smiling, he has a sense of fun which sparkles in the Line Book.

The book records that Loftus one day said to Seccombe: 'I want you to save your operational hours. Fly only once a week now, and once a day when the fighting flares up.' To which Seccombe replied with mock anguish: 'I'd rather fly once a day now and once a week when the fighting flares up.'

Johnny Seccombe and a Durban pilot now with him, Dave Hastie,

who had not yet turned 21, both figured in two of the most unbelievable adventures ever recorded in any Line Book. Hastie had the first
experience. He was flying in formation over Italy one morning when
he saw a snake crawling up his instrument panel. He seized it with his
gauntleted hand and pulling back the perspex hood, threw it out of the
cockpit. He got into the Line Book not only because of this startling
experience but because in the mess afterwards he dismissed the whole
business by saying: 'Why do you think I always wear gloves when I'm
flying!'

A couple of days later Seccombe had an even more unnerving
experience with a snake in the air. Here is the simple entry of this
extraordinary episode in the Line Book: When 50 miles north-west of
Naples at 1 500 ft with Jerry ack-ack intense and accurate, Seccombe
was heard plaintively over the R/T: 'I'm not happy in my job. There's
a snake swaying from my reflector sight and he's putting out his tongue
at me.'

He maintained a round-by-round commentary of his struggle with
the snake which he kept beating off with his gloved hand. He could
not get hold of it to throw it out of the aircraft. Eventually when he
landed, it was wrapped round the throttle lever and nearly caused him
to crash. It took air mechanics on the home landing ground three hours
to extricate the snake from the cockpit.

No 1 Squadron as a unit is entitled to shoot a line of no mean
length for it is the senior fighter squadron of the South African Air Force.
It owes its nickname, the 'Warrior Squadron.' to Air Marshal Coningham
who christened it in a congratulatory signal after the famous 'Stuka
Party' over El Alamein on 4 July 1942, when its pilots shot down 13 out
of 15 JU 87s and one ME 109 in a glorious dogfight.

It was the first fighter squadron to leave South Africa for service in
Kenya, and then it went on to serve brilliantly in the Sudan during the
Eritrean and Abyssinian campaigns. It was the first to serve in the
Western Desert and the first into Sicily. Two of its pilots, both lieutenants
from Johannesburg, Robert Peel and Harold Smith, were the first SAAF
officers to serve outside Africa when they were sent to Malta. One of its
pilots, Captain Bryan Boyle, a Selborne College boy, was the first South
African fighter pilot to win the DFC. He heard about it in the Sudan on
Christmas Day, 1940. A one-time leader of the squadron, Gerald Le
Mesurier, an old Bishop's boy who was killed in action, was the first
South African to be decorated at a Buckingham Palace investiture.

No 1 was the first South African fighter squadron to be given
Spitfires. Loftus's successful wing in the Western Desert had used
Kittyhawk fighters throughout and by November 1942, it had certainly
earned the right to these sleek and wasplike machines. The Squadron
had already scored 157 confirmed victories in the air. Of these, only

nine had been claimed during the Sicilian and Italian campaigns for the Allied supremacy in the air had allowed the pilots few opportunities for their favourite game of 'hacking Huns.' Hastie had got the latest, one of the Nazi's new crack fighters, a Focke-Wulf 190. In the Mediterranean campaign so far, Capt J H Gaynor and Lieutenant R E de Jonge had both shot down FW 190s. Seccombe, Wickner and Bomb Finney had each got an ME 109 and Lieutenant S J Richards an ME 410. Capt J van Nus and Lieutenant B T Trotter had shared an ME 210.

The squadron's victories in the Desert numbered exactly 100 plus a half-share in another machine with a sister squadron. The two greatest days in its Desert history were the 'Stuka Parties' in July 1942. I happened to visit them immediately after the first, when they were celebrating the destruction of the 13 Stukas and the ME 109 already mentioned. What made that show particularly outstanding was that it was the squadron's first patrol in the desert after a period back in the Canal Area resting and reorganising; and some of the pilots had not been in action before. On 27 July, that is barely three weeks later, the pilots picked off five more Stukas, damaged another and shot down an ME 109 F. These victories could be expected of a squadron as skilled as No 1. During the Mareth Line battle for instance, six pilots tackled 43 enemy aircraft and later in the same day, eleven took on 31 ME 109 Fs and Macchi 202s, destroying five.

Before the Squadron served in the great Desert advance of 1 500 miles with 11 different landing grounds as its stepping stones, it won glory in the Sudan. Defending Khartoum and Port Sudan and then sporting the advance of Lieutenant-General Sir William Platt, 1 Squadron flying Gladiators or Hurricanes, shot down 48 Italian aircraft besides destroying 53 on the ground and damaging 56 more.

Many of the original members of the Squadron are still remembered with admiration and affection. Major van Schalkwyk, one of the COs, was shot down and killed. At least five of the pilots won DFCs. Andrew Duncan, son of the late Governor-General was also killed in action; Kenneth Driver, who came from Kingswood College Grahamstown, served with great distinction. His elder brother was killed in action with the RFC in the first World War soon after Ken was born; Bryan Boyle who is now commanding another South African Spitfire squadron in Italy; Robin Pare, a Bishop's boy from Constantia, who recovered from temporary blindness and paralysis sustained in a crash in the Desert; and Lawrie Wilmot, one of South Africa's most brilliant pilots who during three tours of operations shot down seven enemy aircraft and destroyed 17 on the ground during the early war years. He was awarded the DSO and DFC for his outstanding bravery and dedication to duty. He is at present a full colonel in command of 239 Wing RAF.

Other squadron members of the early days include Servaas van Breda Theron who shot down nine enemy aircraft and destroyed seven on the ground. He was decorated with the DFC and is at present in command of 250 (Sudan) Squadron RAF; Tommy Ross-Theron AFC was killed in a simple flying accident in Kenya after surviving a narrow squeak in the Western Desert. He baled out after shooting down two G50s, his parachute harness slipping but catching him by one ankle. He floated down to earth suspended upside down like a trapeze artist only damaging his face and shoulder on impact.

The Squadron also has the unusual distinction of having numbered among its pilots three officers who pulled off dramatic feats when landing in enemy territory to rescue comrades who had been shot down. Bob Kershaw, who won the DSO for picking up his squadron commander Major Jack Frost on Diredawa aerodrome under Italian fire, was the first pilot ever to accomplish this feat. (He was not with No 1 then, but joined later.) Kenneth Quirk had a similar experience in the Western Desert somewhere near Gazala if I remember rightly; and H C Liebenberg, then a lieutenant, completed the hat trick when he went down and picked up another subaltern, Mello MacRobert, who had been shot down among aggressively-firing enemy troops south of Halfaya. Liebenberg had to silence the enemy on the ground before he could rescue his comrade. This officer, later promoted captain, demonstrated his courage again when he escaped from captivity. Going down in the enemy lines at El Adem, he was a prisoner for two years and was being taken from Italy to Germany when he leapt from a train in the French Alps and after a long trek which is a saga in itself, reached the Allied lines.

Another officer in the squadron whom I remember with a salute is Charles Martin who led a bomber squadron in Abyssinia as a lieutenant-colonel and then, after a spell back home, he found that there was no appointment available for one of his rank on the Mediterranean front. Though a married man with a family, he sacrificed his rank to return to operations as a captain and ordinary fighter pilot. Sadly he was shot down and killed in action.

Among the memorable characters who have flown and fought with the Squadron is the one-legged South African pilot Douglas Rogan. After losing a leg in action, Rogan like the famous Douglas Bader, returned to operations with an artificial limb. The Line Book records very simply one of his involuntary exploits when he took off in his Spitfire without realising that an air mechanic was still on the tail, acting as ballast. Doug managed to land safely and though a tyre burst, the aircraft didn't tip up on its nose probably because of the weight on the tail.

242

Ever since 1 Squadron helped to cover the initial landings in Italy, its Spitfires have operated from a runway constructed of steel strips laid on the Adriatic coastal plateau from where the enemy's shell flashes can be seen at night. Basuto Pioneers built this landing ground while the Germans were still within artillery range. The Squadron is doing excellent work in conditions not always idyllic. On New Year's Day its camp was almost washed away by an Adriatic storm and the mechanics could scarcely hold their freezing tools in the snow and sleet on that winter day. They remembered then, with some nostalgia, their al fresco camps in the olive groves of Sicily and times when they tired of a surfeit of turkey for dinner night after night.

On many of their missions over Italy 1 Squadron had to face intensive flak which has now become the German's main defence against the irresistible Allied Air Forces. All sorts of tasks are tackled with their graceful Spitfires. They defend airfields and forward troops; they strafe trains north of Rome and German trucks on the Adriatic coast road. The other day they helped destroy a German warship near the port of Zara, Yugoslavia. Led by one of No 1's most illustrious C Os and fighter pilots, Hannes Faure, six Spitfire pilots set the vessel's decks alight with 700 rounds of armour-piercing cannon shells and 2 000 rounds of machine-gun fire which enabled an Australian squadron to sink it. Not long ago they also saved a Walrus of the air-sea rescue service which after landing on the Adriatic to pick up a downed pilot, was attacked by an ME 109. The squadron has been given other unusual tasks such as dropping supplies to units of the Eighth Army immobilised in the mountains by winter snowstorms.

It is a spirited squadron. Only the other day, one of its pilots, Capt Geoffrey Hilton-Barber of Cradock, flew over an enemy landing ground and dropped a challenge to the Nazis to come up and fight!

All these fighter pilots, carefree and courageous, are young men but I thought that the spirit of the squadron was typified not by them, but by their elderly Intelligence Officer. Captain Vivian Voss has been with the squadron for two years and celebrated his 50th birthday with it in the field. He is quiet, baldish, wears silver spectacles and everybody calls him 'Pop'. A fighter pilot in the last war, he flew 700 hours on 'ops' mostly in Bristol fighters. He wrote a book about it called *Flying Minnows*, and a good book it is reckoned too. After the war he studied at Johns Hopkins University in Baltimore and for 20 years before this war he lectured in physics at the University of Pretoria. A man like this goes to war again because he is fighting for principles.

Tailpiece

Carel was a War Correspondent throughout World War II. By chance I unearthed this story from a book he wrote in 1944, *Close to the Sun*, in aid of the RAF Benevolent Fund. He gave me a copy in Johannesburg several years before his death. His wife Karen has kindly allowed me to write an abridged version of the story.

The Big Kill

At early morning briefing at Ondangwa in the late summer of 1982, the Intelligence Officer told two Alouette crews that an unconfirmed Swapo presence had been reported in the Cambino area, approximately 10 kilometres north of Iona situated in a valley, some 30 kilometres north-east of Marienfluss in the north-western Kaokoveld. On the following day the choppers, one of which would be flown by me, were to provide top cover to Pumas while they dropped a reconnaissance patrol to determine the presence of Swapo insurgents, and we were to remain on stand-by for close support during the rest of the operation.

At the briefing I had speculated on whether the mission would be successful. If not, the sea was only minutes away by air and the Cunene River mouth was said to be one of the better fishing spots on the west coast. With this pleasant thought in mind, my wingman Captain Angelo Maranta and I, took off later in the morning for Marienfluss.

I had visited 'Fluss' way back in 1975 when I'd found it to be a

Attack HQ at Marienfluss, with Dakota bringing in extra troops and fuel.

Neall Ellis - Nellis to his friends - shortly after Operation Super. A non-conformist to the end, Captain Ellis was one of the most experienced SAAF gunship commanders.

beautiful valley of approximately 120 x 15 km, covered by an expanse of waist-high yellow grass where large herds of wild game from gemsbok to elephant roamed and grazed, seemingly unexploited by civilisation. I was shocked to observe the change. The area was now a barren stretch of desert with no sign of animal life.

The TAC HQ was situated alongside the runway. Two rows of rusty 44 gallon drums were half-buried in the sand and next to a lifeless windsock surrounded by a ring of whitewashed stones, stood three army issue tents which were to be our home for the next couple of days. There wasn't a tree in sight and therefore no shade, and the heat was intense. On hearing Capt Maranta muttering an expletive about the unpleasant climate, it was obvious that I wasn't the only one who hoped that the contact would be over within a day or two.

There was a full moon that evening and the visibility was exceptionally clear as we enjoyed a braaivleis with those who would be taking part in the operation the next day. The SAAF contribution consisted of a number of Alouette gunships and Puma transport choppers and a Bosbok to act as a communications aircraft.

The operation was scheduled for the late afternoon on the following day at a point north-west of the suspected area where a road followed a river pass through the mountains. The patrol's first priority was to mine the road at the entrance to the pass so that another force entering it would detonate the mine and the patrol would be warned. The mission was carried out without incident and we returned safely to base to await developments. That evening, as we were settling around a fire at approximately 2100 hours, there was a muffled explosion to the north and the Recce sergeant reported over the radio that a truck had passed along the road and had detonated the mine. It was now obvious that the suspected enemy presence in the Cambino area was a reality and excitement rapidly spread throughout the camp.

The next day passed without incident but during the night there was a heavy storm and the mighty Cunene River, only two kilometres away, came down in flood creating a tremendous roar as the water gushed towards the Atlantic Ocean.

Dawn saw us up and trying to make the best of the cool morning air before the heat turned any physical movement into an ordeal. Over a cup of coffee, Major Paula Kruger, the Puma chief, recommended that we carry out a recce along the Cunene River to look for potential insurgent crossing points. It was decided that a Puma would be used so that others could see what the area looked like.

We took off in good spirits and after flying along the river as far as its mouth, the Puma landed on an adjoining beach where a walk and some cool air was enjoyed. On the return flight, when 10 minutes out from 'Fluss', Major Kruger received a message from the Recce sergeant that his men had sighted a Swapo patrol of platoon strength and a contact was imminent. For the first time I began to feel the prickle of excitement; the surge of adrenalin and the tension of pre-battle nerves. This surely must be one of the most stimulating sensations a person can experience.

Parabats board a SAAF Puma during a cross-border operation. Without helicopter support, the war would have ground to a halt.

The immediate problem was to reach the patrol before the contact was initiated and when landing at 'Fluss', we found the Recce leader in a state of agitation for the Recce sergeant had reported that a contact could not be avoided. After a quick briefing on the contact position and deployment of troops, Captain Maranta and I took off in our choppers followed a few minutes later by the Pumas with supporting troops.

Shortly after take-off I made contact with the Recce sergeant who didn't appear to be too happy with the situation. The Swapo patrol of approximately 18 men had commenced monitoring their position. We arrived in the area after a 20 minute flight and could see the contact area, for the burning veld served as a beacon. The only comment from the Recce sergeant on our arrival was rather sarcastic: 'If you'd come yesterday, you may have been of some help.' He and his men had taken up defensive positions on top of a small koppie, some 300 ft high, adjacent to a large rocky ridge with steep cliffs overhanging the contact area.

Both players in the drama could be plainly seen for the bush cover was relatively thin. They were sprawled out on their stomachs facing each other's position resembling toy soldiers, completely inert and harmless. The Swapo insurgents were halfway up the koppie, approximately 40 metres from the Recce patrol's position.

As our troops comprised only one section, they were restricted to a single sweepline with no stopper groups. However, if Swapo could be misled, the sweepline could initially act as a stopper group and once the main punch-up was over, our men could stand up and sweep through the contact area mopping up any remaining resistance. I instructed Captain Maranta and my flight engineer, Sgt Steve Coetzee, to fire at the rear of the Swapo line hoping that this would cause confusion, for the enemy would be caught in a crossfire between the choppers and the Recce patrol. Once confusion is apparent in an enemy, the direction of retreat can be quickly ascertained and stopper groups and sweeplines can be deployed. The effect of both gunships attacking from the rear, and the Recce patrol shooting from the top of the koppie, achieved the desired result and the insurgents made a break in the direction of more open ground with less cover. Before their break became an uncontrolled panic, our troops were deployed in the direction of the expected break-out. Everything went according to plan and the insurgents who were not killed by the initial fire from our choppers, ran headlong into the stopper group which then swept through the area capturing survivors.

At this stage both Captain Maranta and I were low on fuel and we were forced to land above the contact area, from where I controlled the sweepline from the top of the cliffs until the Pumas arrived with fuel for our choppers. The enemy had offered very little opposition during

SAAF Transall dropping paras during Operation Cassinga.

the contact, directing minimal fire at the choppers and ground forces. No doubt our sudden appearance had taken them by surprise and knocked the fight out of them. There were no casualties on our side, but Swapo lost 14 dead and seven captured. We returned to base after making sure that all the Swapo insurgents had been accounted for and the dead bodies searched for weapons and documents.

Immediately after our arrival at the TAC HQ in 'Fluss', the Intelligence Officer began an interrogation of the Swapo prisoners and ascertained some vital information. It transpired that their task had been to build a transit camp and arms cache for a new infiltration route through the Kaokoveld into central SWA. According to the prisoners, there were about 250 insurgents in the camp. They also confirmed that it was defended by shoulder-launched anti-aircraft missiles, presumably SAM 7s, but they were not sure about anti-aircraft guns. The camp's forces were well-armed with the normal, small arms such as RPSs, AKs, RPDs, PKMs and RPKs, and they possessed vast amounts of anti-vehicle mines and rifle grenades.

As soon as the importance of our target to the Swapo effort had been established, wheels were set in motion to fly in extra helicopters, troops, fuel and ammunition. The concern was that if the camp was not hit within the next 24 hours, the remainder of the group might disappear into the bush. Most of the night was spent listening to the interrogation of the prisoners and logistical planning for the extra aircraft and troops. By lunchtime the following day all the required forces had gathered for the attack. By now higher authority had decided that it must take place at 1600 hours the same afternoon. I was not happy with this decision as an entire day would be required if such a large camp was to be eliminated without incurring heavy casualties. Rushing

Captain Jan Hougaard with some of the weapons taken from Swapo insurgents during Operation Super. On his left inspecting the booty is Brigadier 'Witkop' Badenhorst, then OC Sector 10 at Oshakati.

an action usually spelt an increase in the casualty rate. No argument could convince higher authority to wait until the next morning so we duly took off as scheduled. Luckily the mission was aborted because of a rainstorm in the area and I must admit to looking for any excuse to cancel the attack. Our planning was not to my satisfaction and I was sure that the correct location of the camp had not been determined. Later in the afternoon a senior officer arrived at 'Fluss', and he built a sand model of the area on which the prisoners were able to pin-point the exact position of the Swapo camp which was almost 20 miles from the estimated position. The delay was a blessing!

I woke up at first light the next morning feeling excited. The camp

The awesome desert terrain through which the Cunene River flows in the vicinity of where the action took place.

was the largest I had come up against and we were not too strong on the ground or in the air. Our total forces comprised 45 troops, one 81 mm mortar group, our Alouette gunships and the Puma medium transport helicopters for troop deployment. Because of the meagre resources available, the plan had to be simple but at the same time thorough, as any delay in troop deployment or lack of fuel at the HAG (a clearance to be chosen close to the camp where choppers could land), would cause a loss of kills. The new basic plan was to initiate a strike shortly after sunrise for it was known that an early morning parade was held when orders for the day were issued. This also suited us as the sun would lighten the shadows which would help us to see insurgents hiding underneath the bush cover.

Captain Maranta and I were to search for the camp and when successful, I would call in the Pumas which would then transport the

251

sweepline, stopper and mortar groups. After our forces had been deployed, two Alouettes would supply top cover to two small groups situated at the far north of the camp to monitor possible reinforcements and prevent Swapo forces from escaping while the battle was in progress. The HAG would be established about eight miles away from the camp.

Early in the morning we went over the plan once again to make sure the situation had not changed overnight and that the communication plan was understood. The briefing was concluded with a prayer. It is before take-off that I prefer to be alone, to reflect on the beauty of the world and to say a few words to the Lord. It is also a moment to come to terms with the pre-battle butterflies, to create a balance

A member of the press corps handles a Soviet-made SAM 7; several of these were fired at South African helicopters during the course of the battle.

Target reached! Troops deplane inside Angola from Pumas; this was the most vulnerable moment for the aircraft when they were static and subject to accurate groundfire, yet very few were lost this way during the course of the war.

between the feeling of fear and the high from the initial flow of adrenalin. It is also the time when all emotions and any outside influences must be divorced from the mind. All thoughts must be channelled to the task on hand.

Captain Maranta and I took off for the target area at the scheduled time. The skies were clear and blue and we were on our way to kill possibly, hundreds of men. As a child I had imagined that battles were fought in rough, wet weather with thunder and lightning, as if the Gods were also sizing up for the battle.

Once over the river, I got down to the serious business of navigation, staying as low as possible so that the noise of the helicopters did not carry too far and warn the enemy of our approach. Navigation in the mountainous areas when flying on the deck, can be difficult because of the limited horizon and the many ridges and gullies. The Alouette does not carry navigation aids and if a pilot does not concentrate at all times, he could quite easily become lost.

As the target area appeared immediately ahead, I called Major Kruger to check that his Pumas were in the holding area and then we climbed over the ridge bordering the camp area which was situated in a large bowl surrounded by high mountains. By hugging the side of the mountain I hoped that the echo of the engines would confuse the enemy as to our direction of approach and that our chopper's camouflage would prevent visual detection. At this stage I was worried about the anti-aircraft situation at the camp and I had visions of grinning black faces sitting behind anti-aircraft guns, sights lined up on our choppers and itchy fingers waiting for the order to pull the trigger!

Circling the area I expected to see a massive encampment but could only observe scrub. Surely we should be able to pick up a path pattern or the parade ground? All I could see was a large number of

Back row (left to right): Monty Montgomery, Dave Trent, Paula Kruger, Eugene van der Merwe, AN Other; (front row): Neall Ellis, Angelo Maranta, Steve Coetzee.

dew soaked dark-brown rocks, yet I had a strange feeling that somewhere down there, the enemy was watching us! Shortly after sending Captain Maranta to search for the camp in the north of the area, Sergeant Coetzee shouted over the intercom that he could see tents and described them as dark-brown and squarish. I looked in the direction he was pointing and realised that those dark-brown rocks I had seen, were indeed tents. There was also a path pattern resembling a spider's web and I saw clothing hanging out to dry, camp debris scattered around, and then the jackpot!

The ground cover was not too thick and we could see an abundance of bodies hiding under the bushes; one bush resembled a starfish, for at least five insurgents had forgotten about their lower torsos which stuck out in an almost symmetrical star-shaped pattern! I had never seen so many enemy soldiers in such a confined space before. The camp had been built around an old derelict kraal and covered an area of approximately one and a half square kilometres.

The adrenalin was pumping fast and I felt as if someone had punched me in the lower gut. I realised that this was the chance of a lifetime and the game had to be played carefully. The first task was to land the troops as soon as possible for when the insurgents began to break out of the area, the movement would become a flood. My initial task until the Pumas arrived, was to keep the enemy guessing as to whether they had been observed or not. I told Captain Maranta to widen his orbit, to climb higher and to try to act as nonchalantly as possible.

254

I also instructed the Pumas to drop the sweepline to the west of the camp, the stopper groups along the riverlines to the south and south-west, and the mortar team on the conical hill overlooking the target from where they could observe the fall of their bombs and make corrections. The enemy had not yet shown any sign of aggression although some of them were starting to crawl slowly towards the edge of the camp. At the same time we were trying to act in a non-aggressive manner and I felt apprehensive as we flew lazy circles endeavouring to act as though unaware of their presence. I saw the Pumas approaching and the insurgents must have heard the noise of the thumping rotor blades because they started moving more briskly towards the edge of the camp. Both choppers opened fire to slow them down, for as soon as one person moves in a set direction, the rush begins, and to contain large numbers is difficult.

This action halted the rush, and then there was a fierce explosion behind us when every sinew in my body became taut. Captain Maranta shouted over the radio: 'SAM launch six o'clock!' Out of the corner of my eye I saw the distinctive thick whitish-grey smoke trail of a SAM 7 twirling into the sky and I immediately banked to try to locate the site. While turning through 180 degrees I saw a second SAM 7 launch but this time it was directed at Captain Maranta and I shouted over the radio; 'SAM launch nine o'clock.' However, we were so low that by the time I called the launch, the missile was already travelling at Mach 1,5 and it passed just in front of the nose of Captain Maranta's chopper.

We were under heavy automatic weapons fire and the sound of rounds accompanied by a curtain of tracer, resembled the clatter of hundreds of fingers hammering on typewriters in a typing pool!

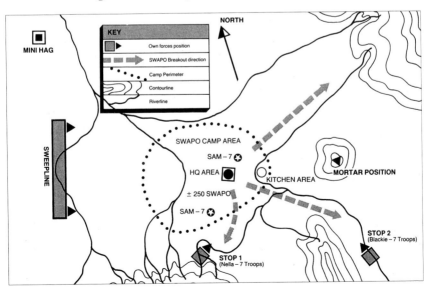

The SAM 7 site was easy to locate because of the smoke rising lazily into the air from the launch. When flying over the site I saw the operators diving for cover beneath the bushes and Sergeant Coetzee quickly killed them with a few well-aimed rounds. The RPGs were starting to make life uncomfortable and although I considered them to be ineffective against choppers, the loud bang accompanied by a large puff of black smoke when they exploded, was disturbing when one was trying to concentrate on directing a battle! I saw another SAM 7 shoot past my chopper's nose but when the site had been identified, Sergeant Coetzee once again eliminated the operators.

By now, the Pumas were approaching the landing zone (LZ), which I marked with smoke, at the same time providing top cover over the LZ which was only two kilometres from the camp. Major Kruger in the lead Puma with three other Pumas, dropped off the sweepline led by Captain Hougaard. The troops formed up quickly and immediately started moving towards their objective. The next task was the dropping of the mortar group and this was accomplished without a problem. The Pumas then returned to 'Fluss' to uplift the stopper groups and the fuel and ammunition for the HAG.

At this stage, the enemy realised that they were contained so they stepped up the volume of hot lead already threatening our choppers. At the same time they directed a mortar barrage at our troops in the sweepline and although not effective, it was an uneasy feeling for us as the bombs were passing through the same orbit as the flak already hammering us. Fortunately, Captain Maranta spotted the mortar sites and took them out.

When our troops began moving through the outskirts of the camp, they came under heavy fire and their progress was slowed down. This was no problem as the break-out had been contained and the whole day was available to wipe out the enemy and with the slower pace, there was less chance of casualties. At one stage, the fighting became so intense that Sergeant Coetzee was eliminating isolated pockets of enemy approximately five metres from our own troops. The lethal radius of a 20 mm cannon shell is five metres and our troops were obliged to keep their heads low during the attack. In fact, some of them picked up slight shrapnel wounds during the engagement. It was like a scene from the movies when Sergeant Coetzee fired at two enemy soldiers who had climbed a tree to get a better view of our advancing troops. There was a mighty explosion and both men were catapulted out of the tree, cartwheeling lifeless to the ground. Sgt Coetzee must have scored a bulls-eye and detonated a grenade which one of the soldiers was carrying!

About 20 minutes after the sweepline was dropped, the Pumas returned with the stopper groups. Captain Maranta was detailed to provide top cover to these drops, call sign 'Blackie', and while this was taking place he engaged a group of approximately 30 enemy insurgents who happened to be at the LZ. There was heavy retaliation and while neutralising the position, Captain Maranta's chopper was hit by small arms fire. I provided top cover to the Puma drop, call sign 'Nella', and while this chopper was on short finals, I saw a group of enemy soldiers running along the gully in which it was about to land. The gully sides were rocky and steep so they couldn't climb out and were an easy kill. All Sergeant Coetzee had to do was to fire above their heads and the ricocheting shrapnel did the rest. However, after the Puma had taken off, a few more enemy soldiers had progressed to within 50 metres of the LZ and 'Nella' experienced contact seconds after being dropped. The position was exposed and we experienced some anxious moments before the opposition was neutralised. Once again Sergeant Coetzee's accurate firing saved the day.

By this time Captain Maranta and I were short of fuel and had run out of ammunition. Major Bent and Lieutenant Schoeman, also flying Alouettes, positioned overhead to carry on with the task of controlling the sweepline and providing close air support. Our forces suffered their first casualty as we were leaving when a sergeant was badly wounded. Captain Maranta casevaced (casualty evacuation) him under fire, just behind the sweepline. After refuelling and re-arming, Captain Maranta and I returned to the scene of the contact and relieved Major Bent and Lieutenant Schoeman. They were positioned to the north and east of

Fuel drop at Marienfluss by C130.

the camp to act as airborne stopper groups as a few of the enemy, after realising the escape routes to the south and west were blocked, used these directions to escape. There were not enough troops to cover all escape routes.

Although most of the opposition had been neutralised, there were still a few pockets of die-hards to be eliminated before a final body count could be taken. During this period two more of our men were lost, a soldier and one of his platoon commanders, Lieutenant Nel who was posthumously awarded the Honoris Crux (silver) for bravery. He was an outstanding leader who accounted for many kills during the action. Some of his contacts were at virtual point-blank range. The clearing up operations took us into the afternoon and it was late before we were satisfied that the enemy were either dead or had escaped.

The final body count was 187 dead and one captured. The total kills for both operations, including the previous contact, was 201 dead and eight captured. The clearing up operations over the following days revealed a number of massive arms caches concealed in the rocky slopes of the surrounding mountains. One arms cache alone comprised 1 000 anti-tank and anti-personnel rifle grenades, 306 x 82 mm mortar shells, 150 land-mines, 10 SAM 7 anti-aircraft missiles and 50 AK 47 rifles. Swapo received a setback to their plans for the western infiltration route through the Kaokoveld, a defeat from which they were not to recover for many years.

Tailpiece

Neall is of the opinion that words cannot do justice to the operations he has described. One has to take part in actions of this nature to appreciate the intense drama involved. He and Steve Coetzee were awarded Honoris Crux medals for their courageous roles in both operations. Today Neall is a serving Commandant in the SAAF and is based in Pretoria.

Spencer Whiting

War was an Invaluable Experience

In retrospect it was a long war. At the time it did not seem so, for I suppose that in our youth we were moving rapidly from one new experience to another and each episode was a whole new scenario with excitement galore, new places, new aircraft, new enemies, new friends and new fears.

I joined the RAF, for I was in England when war was declared. Bill Deas, nephew of Brigadier Kenny van der Spuy, Military Attaché at South Africa House, had worked his way over by boat anticipating the war, and we met on the steps of South Africa House in London. He told me he was determined to join the RAF so what about the two of us going to see his uncle? A couple of telephone calls later and 'presto', two South Africans were in the RAF. I was 18 and Bill I think, was 19. He was killed near the end of the war in Bomber Command. I saw General van der Spuy some three years ago and at the age of 93 he still remembered. Remarkable!

This great adventure kept me in the UK until the end of 1941 when, with the first combined operations unit formed under Mountbatten, I became involved in the invasion of Madagascar. From there to East Africa, then the Western Desert, Cyprus and Italy, a short spell in South Africa and then off once more to Burma and eventually to Java. All at the Government's expense!

I remember those dark foreboding days when England stood alone in Europe. The Battle of Britain promoted for most of us a feeling of 'what the hell can we do to stop the tide from turning against us.' As a fighter pilot it was a time of constant stand-by and frequent alerts, when one was really put to the test. It was a piece of old hat in the air, with something to do. Sitting around waiting wore one down, providing too much time to think. I know of no one who wasn't secretly scared to death - but they tried not to show it and let the side down.

Curiously the memories which remain are not my eight machine-guns belting away at the enemy but the amusing incidents and the horror of seeing London burning night after night. I recall the patrols over Dunkirk; the congestion of troops awaiting evacuation, and the

Spencer Whiting (centre) with ground crew.

seemingly endless flotilla of small boats of every shape and size steaming against all the odds into a seething cauldron of enemy gunfire to uplift troops. I was astounded to see the old Hannibals from Imperial Airways chugging over, landing and bringing back people. What a sight and what a sense of pride to have been there on this historic occasion. I was also involved to a small degree, in the sinking of the *Bismarck* operation when my squadron was detailed to keep away any Luftwaffe intervention. A substantial party was hosted at South Africa House to celebrate the death of the pride of the German Navy.

The invasion force for Madagascar was assembled in Durban so I embarked from Liverpool on the *Cape Town Castle*, a voyage which had me vowing never to sail in a ship again if I survived. One ship in the convoy was sunk behind us and another in front of us, but my vow was to no avail because it was the aircraft carrier *Illustrious* which conveyed us to Madagascar.

This campaign turned out to be an anti-climax for there was little serious opposition, only hazardous terrain and weather to worry us. The Vichy French Air Force lost its enthusiasm after a couple of hours of lukewarm fighting and six months later it packed up altogether.

It was in Madagascar that I first became involved with the SAAF, originally under Steve Melville and then Jimmy Durrant, all great guys. We got very high the night Doug Meaker heard that his wife had produced a daughter. The party ended up on the ridge of the barracks roof where the 'Ish' was passed around until one by one we fell off painlessly! Doug's daughter Moya was to become a Miss South Africa.

In the Desert I was appointed as a flight commander in 94 Squadron flying Hurricanes, our operations consisting of hunting for enemy aircraft and low level sweeps over the islands including Crete. Three months later I took over as CO of 213 Squadron initially flying Hurricanes, then Spitfire IXs followed by Mustang 11s. A squadron detachment was based at Paphos in Cyprus, famous as a place where Venus Aphrodyte was supposed to have emerged from the sea. The only Venus our chaps could find was Katie, the owner of the Olympic Bar - a popular watering hole and well known for the 24-egg omelettes made and served by Katie.

After much persuasion Katie joined the WAAFs and off she went to Haifa. Alas, three months later she was back, for the Chief WAAF thought her behaviour was unbecoming to the service! Apparently she had been too blatant with her charms. Our lads didn't complain, neither did they complain during their visits to Nicosia where all the Balkan cabaret girls had been interned, but with the free run of town. They were said to be tired of the army and preferred the RAF!

It was in Cyprus that the squadron acquired a mascot. One day there was a 'kerfuffle' outside my caravan and I heard a loud voice speaking Afrikaans. A scruffy Cypriot was duly escorted into the caravan carrying a huge cockerel trussed up with string. It transpired that this guy heard that I was a South African and wanted to present me with a gift. He had lived in South Africa for a number of years and it was his favourite country. 'Why did you leave?' I asked. 'Ag, man,' he replied, 'I was a cattle thief and was caught, so they threw me out!'

An interesting problem which the squadron was called upon to solve entailed preventing enemy JU 88s from making reconnaissance

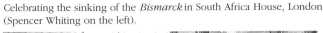

Celebrating the sinking of the *Bismarck* in South Africa House, London (Spencer Whiting on the left).

flights over the island at 40 000 ft which was 10 000 ft above our ceiling height. A Spitfire was stripped down to its bare essentials excepting two guns, and the lighter weight enabled it to reach 40 000 ft and above. The snag was that without a pressurised cockpit, this altitude was too much of a physical strain for some pilots and we lost two who no doubt passed out, their aircraft plunging down in a vertical dive. Eventually the problem was solved and a JU 88 was knocked down. Consequently whenever a Jerry saw a Spitfire threatening him, he turned tail for home.

The only RAF squadron to be fitted with Mustang 11s during that time was 213. It was a superb aircraft, tough and with an incredible range, the main snag being its glycol cooling system which was extremely vulnerable to flak. We moved into Italy and eventually to Biferno becoming part of the newly formed Balkan Air Force. By this time many South Africans were being seconded to the RAF and 213's complement consisted of 33 per cent SAAF pilots.

From now onwards the operational activities on which the squadron was engaged, turned out to be hectic and interesting to say the least. The main German supply line to the southern Russian front was routed through the Danube valley by road, rail, air and river. The Germans were confident that the area was well-protected and in fact they believed it was well outside the Allied fighter aircraft range.

On the first sortie into the area we crossed the Adriatic at about 10 ft above the water, hugged the tops of the Dalmatian mountains and dived down into the fabulous, extensive stretch of the Danube valley. Obviously we had not been detected and around us were an abundance of targets including trains, motor vehicles and river transport.

There was no opposition whatsoever and as many targets as our ammunition allowed were systematically destroyed and then we were sadly obliged to head for home knowing that the Jerries would obviously not be caught napping again and on future operations, strong opposition would welcome our aircraft.

For a few weeks our pilots experienced reasonably flak-free sorties, but before long flak trucks were attached to all trains and machineguns were placed in strategic positions throughout the valley. We were joined by two SAAF Beaufighter squadrons which would have been sitting ducks for the 109s and 190s but with our Mustangs around they kept their distance and we destroyed far more enemy aircraft on the ground than in the air.

Our casualties were high, for at zero feet there was little space for error and very quick action was imperative if a pilot meant to belly-land a disabled aircraft. Surprisingly, several of our pilots got safely down and one or two even escaped and returned to the squadron. Occasionally the squadron was called upon to escort aircraft carrying

Partisans in and out of Yugoslavia which meant landing in enemy territory. Sometimes we flew right through to the Russian front, refuelled and returned to base.

My current operational tour was completed in September 1944 and I was posted for a rest to Waterkloof near Pretoria where Doug Loftus, an old desert buddy, was CO of the Operational Training Unit. I fell foul of Doug on my first flight while making a normal split-arse operational turning approach to land, straightening up just before touching down.

An Erk was waiting for me at dispersal in a Jeep. 'The CO wants to see you immediately.' Doug's back was towards me as I entered the door and without turning around he proceeded to blast the hell out of me. 'Approaches of this nature are not in the book and no pupil at this OTU is permitted to do them and if it happens again, you will be sent back to ground duties.' He then turned around and his expression was quite comical when he saw me, although he did add that there was plenty of time for pupils to learn this type of erratic flying when they went on ops, and would I be good enough to remember this. My reply to Doug is unprintable. I next saw him as liaison officer in London at South Africa House.

Well-rested, I flew back to UK in time for VE Day celebrations and then applied for a posting to the Far East. They wouldn't allow me to fly on operations again and posted me as station commander to Allahabad in India - not my cup of tea. My appendix burst on the way out and I was operated on in Karachi. Luckily my uncle, General

Rocketing a convoy.

Kenneth Ray, was the chief engineer of the 11th Army Group and he organised an introduction to the AOC in Delhi who agreed to transfer me to Group HQ at Comilla in Burma.

Luck was once more on my side and I was posted to 31 Squadron which was busy with supply-dropping from Dakotas. Rangoon was the Squadron's next base where preparation for the invasion of Singapore was a priority, but suddenly the war ended and we pitched up in Singapore with no one to shoot at. It would be appropriate to say that this is where the war ended for me, but it was not to be. Trouble flared up in Java and we moved to Batavia for another six months where casualties were higher than in Burma, but my consolation prize was a wife whom I met in a Jap camp!

All of us who were involved in those five years of war and were lucky enough to survive, acquired an invaluable experience. We had travelled the world for free and learnt a great deal about humanity, about ourselves, about the incalculable benefits of working, living and fighting with other men and women; about how similar we all are and how much we need one another; about how to be fiercely individualistic yet reliant on each other to make a team; about how to conquer fear, and understand it in others; and about God.

Tailpiece

Spencer flew on three tours of operations. He shot down 13 enemy aircraft and his tally of ground targets destroyed by strafing was exceptionally high. A magnificent leader who was awarded the DSO and left the RAF as a Wing Commander. He lives in Lower Houghton, Johannesburg.

Air Chief Marshal Sir Robert Foster
KCB, CB, CBE, DFC.

A Tribute to the SAAF
in World War II

The South African Air Force has, since the earliest days of the North African campaign, maintained a strong contingent with the Desert Air Force. The number of SAAF squadrons with DAF has progressively mounted and at the time of the cease-fire there was in this Force two fighter Wings, one medium bomber Wing, one light bomber night squadron, one long-range fighter squadron and one tactical reconnaissance squadron - a total of thirteen squadrons. Furthermore, in the Desert Air Force, RAF squadrons included many SAAF pilots, and no less than four are commanded by SAAF officers. Some of our maintenance and military units are also manned by SAAF personnel; in addition, a number of senior Headquarters appointments are held by SAAF officers.

The part played by the Desert Air Force in the total defeat of the enemy on the Italian Front has been a notable one, and the SAAF squadrons of this command have played their full share in those successful operations. The number of decorations won by SAAF aircrews testifies to their gallantry and to the excellence of their work. I have been most happy to have these squadrons under my command and I can assert with absolute conviction that there are no finer units within the Allied Air Forces, and that no squadron could have done better than they have done.

The loyalty and competence of the commanding officers and the all-round efficiency of the maintenance personnel have made a great contribution to the first class fighting qualities of the SAAF. Without this we could not have recorded, to the full, the outstanding successes with which the Allied Tactical Air Forces have wound up in this campaign.

I personally have made, as a result of this association, many very good friends in the SAAF; I also know that many such friendships have sprung up during this campaign between the SAAF and the wide variety of British, Dominion and American personnel of which the Desert Air Force has been composed. I hope these will be lasting friendships, and that the very real spirit of comradeship which has developed amongst all of us in the Desert Air Force will be remembered in South Africa for all time.

Tailpiece

The late Air Chief Marshal Sir Robert Foster, 'Pussy' as he was fondly known by those who served under him, wrote this tribute on 11 May 1945 when he was the last AOC of the Desert Air Force.

Lieutenant-General Sir Pierre van Ryneveld
KBE, CB, DSO, MC.

A Tribute to No 2 (Cheetah)
Squadron SAAF
in the Korean War

The Korean War which commenced in 1950 and ended in 1953, has been comparatively neglected by both military historians and the general public. Perhaps this stemmed from the recent cataclysmic upheaval of World War II and the frustrating termination of the Korean War in stalemate, its significance overlooked and underplayed to such an extent that it has often been referred to as a 'police action'.

Statistics however, belie this description. There was nothing limited about a conflict which claimed the lives of 187 000 United Nations and South Korean personnel, resulted in at least 1 429 000 Chinese and North Korean casualties, and left 1 400 000 civilians dead. In this devastating slaughter and destruction, 16 armies from five continents fought against two armies from North Korea and China.

The outstanding record achieved throughout the war by the Cheetah Squadron, was mainly due to the skill and nerve of its pilots supported by exceptionally efficient and hard working ground crews. A course of instruction with the emphasis on Mustangs, was provided at Johnson Air Base in Japan where the Cheetahs were stationed while in transit for Korea, but the Americans soon discovered that the South African pilots were not novices but hand-picked World War II veterans.

After a while the squadron CO, Cmdt S V Theron, became disenchanted with being treated as a novice and put the record straight by climbing into a Mustang and proceeding to carry out a series of aerobatic manoeuvres, the like of which the Americans had never seen before. On landing, SV found himself in the centre of an admiring circle. The Course Commander congratulated him heartily; 'Commandant, we can't teach you anything about flying.' 'That's right,' retorted S V, 'and every pilot in the squadron is as good as I am. Give us some Mustangs and let's get on with the war.'

The Cheetah Squadron received those Mustangs and got on with the war, and when their contribution is reviewed, it is clear that their record was quite exceptional and one is tempted to say that no other similar sized unit matched the same level of achievement.

From November 1950 to July 1953, our pilots flew 12 405 sorties, 10 373 on Mustangs and the rest on Sabres. During the process, they were credited with destroying 18 tanks, 160 field guns, 615 vehicles, four locomotives, 200 railway trucks, 46 road and rail bridges, 49 petrol and oil dumps and 3 021 buildings. They also cut the enemy railway lines in 472 places and killed 2 276 enemy troops. Sadly, the cost was high - 34 pilots and two ground crew killed out of a total of 862 men who served in Korea. The squadron lost 74 out of 94 Mustangs and five Sabres. The reputation the Cheetah pilots gained is clearly reflected in the number of American and Korean decorations they received which included 50 American DFCs.

The Squadron was awarded both the United States and the Republic of Korea's Presidential Unit Citations. The USAF Commanding General of the Far East Air Force paid this tribute to the Squadron before the contingent left Korea: 'I need not dwell on the gallantry, fighting qualities or co-operation of the SAAF - these have been indelibly engraved in our hearts. It has been a privilege and an honour for me to command your forces in the field and I have the same pride in your squadron as any American unit.'

But perhaps the most significant indication of the prestige which 2 Squadron earned within the United Nations Command in Korea, was provided by the USAF 18th Fighter Bomber Wing in which the Cheetah Squadron served throughout the war.

Policy Order No 13 of 28 October 1953, reads as follows: 'In memory of our gallant South African comrades, it is hereby established as a new policy, that at "Retreat" ceremonies held in this Wing, the playing of our national anthem will be preceded by the introductory bars of South Africa's national anthem, *Die Stem van Suid Afrika*. All personnel of the Wing will render the same honour to this anthem as to our own.'

Tailpiece

This tribute was adapted from a speech made by the late Lieutenant-General Sir Pierre van Ryneveld.

Lieutenant-General
J P B van Loggerenberg SSAS, SD.

A Tribute to the SAAF
in the Border War

On 26 August 1966 the South African Police, supported by helicopters of the South African Air Force, attacked a large group of armed Swapo forces at Ongulumbashe in Ovamboland in the north of South West Africa. On 9 April 1989 the joint Commission created by the Protocol of Brazzaville, issued the Mount Etjo Declaration which signalled the end to Swapo's abortive attempt to derail the peace process in South West Africa. In the nearly 23 years which separate these two events, the South African Air Force added another chapter to its long history of service, sacrifice and heroism.

To many observers the undeclared and protracted bush war was a low key event. Although it was interrupted from time to time by a series of actions such as Operation Savannah, Operation Protea and finally Operation Hooper, its significance and scope was underplayed. It was seen as an 'easy' war for the Air Force with no real opposing air threat. Nothing could be further from the truth.

Our airmen faced an air defence system comprising the most modern radars, missiles and anti-aircraft guns to be found anywhere in the world. The fact that we did not sustain much greater casualties than those tragic losses which were suffered, bears testimony to the skill and courage of our aircrews who flew so many sorties over hostile territory. During a visit to an Air Force base recently, I enquired of the Officer Commanding, a former Impala pilot, how many sorties he had flown in the war. 'One hundred and four sorties over the border,' was his casual answer. That makes him and his colleagues who have flown many more sorties than his, veterans in any language.

Veterans like him are to be found throughout the South African Air Force. The early ones were the chopper pilots and their flight engineers who doubled as air gunners. They bore the brunt of the war for many years. Some of them hunted an enemy carrying sophisticated missiles for protection against the ever-present gunships. Others carried troops in assault operations against well concealed and heavily protected swapo bases over the border. They developed almost a sixth sense enabling them to elude the defences and to find their targets. They were the early pioneers of the air war in the bush.

They were soon followed by their colleagues in light reconnaissance aircraft, transport aircraft and fighters. Ever present were those magnificent ground crews, often working under the most difficult circumstances imaginable and never failing to produce serviceable aircraft in spite of an embargo designed to cripple us. Their actions have added further to the long tradition of loyalty and courage that was established by earlier generations in two World Wars and in Korea.

As we in southern Africa are entering into a new and hopefully peaceful era, I salute our airmen of the Border War. The prospects of peace in our region would not have been possible without your dedication to duty.

J P B Van Loggerenberg
Chief of the South African Air Force: Lieutenant-General, 1990.

Postscript

My congratulations to all the contributors to this book on their well told experiences which highlight the calibre of South African airmen at war.

Peter Bagshawe is also to be commended for promoting and editing an exciting record which will remind our countrymen and overseas friends that South African operational aircrew were and still are equal to the best in the world as proved by the Border War.

I knew many of the contributors and was so intrigued by their stories that I couldn't put the book down until the last page had been turned. I was taken back to those dynamic years when each day brought a new adventure and when courage, loyalty and comradeship were a way of life.

During my recent visit to Warsaw, I was saddened when visiting the numerous South African war graves resulting from the calamitous supply drop to the 'Polish Home Army' during 1944. Jack van Eyssen mentioned in his story 'Disaster over Warsaw' that I did my best to persuade Air Vice-Marshal John Slessor and Mr Winston Churchill that the operation would mean a heavy loss of aircrew and aircraft in return for little gain.

It was the heavy casualties on the first operation which persuaded me to express my feelings, but Churchill's reply was brief and to the point. 'From a military point of view you are right,' he said, 'but from a political point of view, you must carry on. Good morning.'

I reminded Slessor that I had only recently received a cable from him congratulating my group on its excellent results when mining the River Danube, operations which in his opinion had reaped greater dividends than any other operation in the entire Italian campaign - yet was I expected to tell my crews that they must sacrifice their aircraft and possibly their lives for political expediency.

Had the Atom bomb not terminated the war with Japan, South African airmen would undoubtedly have continued to excel themselves and enhance our country's name with deeds of valour and expertise similar to those included in this book which I recommend to young and old.

J T Durrant
Johannesburg 1990

P.A.F. Form 96.
S 575 (Naval)

MESSAGE FORM.

Office Serial. No. ....

No. of | Office Date Stamp
Groups
GR

Prefacé OUT

(Above this line is for Signals use only)

TO: ALL STAT.

FROM: A S C   Originator's Number K24   Date 12/5   Your/my

THERE IS NOW No REPEAT
No BOMBLINE IN. AFRICA

| The message must be sent AS WRITTEN and may be sent by W.T. Signature | The message must be sent IN CYPHER and may be sent by W.T. Signature | Originator's Instructions. | Degree of Priority. | Time of Origin **19.10** |

IMM.

(Below this line for Signals use only.)

T.O.R.

T.H.I.

19/5

R.A.F. Form 96.
S 575 (Naval)

MESSAGE FORM.

Office Serial No.

No. of | Office Date Stamp.
Groups
GR

Prefác OUT

TO: ALL STAT.

FROM: ASC   K26   12/5

ITALIAN GERMAN FIRST ARMY HAVE
ACCEPTED TERMS OF UNCONDITIONAL
SURRENDER○ THIS ARMY CONSISTS OF
90 LT DIV. 164 DIV. YOUNG FACISTS. PISTOIA
TRIESTE

| The message must be sent AS WRITTEN and may be sent by W.T. Signature | This message must be sent IN CYPHER and may be sent by W.T. Signature | Originator's Instruction. | Degree of Priority. | Time of Origin **19.55.** |

17/5